The Priesthood of Christ and His Ministers

By André Feuillet

Translated by Matthew J. O'Connell

Doubleday & Company, Inc.
Garden City, New York
1975

Library of Congress Cataloging in Publication Data

Feuillet, André.
    The priesthood of Christ and his ministers.

    Translation of Le sacerdoce du Christ et de ses ministres.
    Bibliography: p. 286
    1. Jesus Christ—Priesthood. 2. Priesthood.
I. Title.
BT260.F4813   232
ISBN 0-385-06009-2
Library of Congress Catalog Card Number 74-9446

Contents

Contents   5

Abbreviations

I. *Scripture*

THE ABBREVIATIONS used for the books of the Old and New Testaments are those of the Jerusalem Bible. Unless some other indication is given in the text or the footnotes, the translation used in this book is also that of the Jerusalem Bible.

Ac.	Acts	Ezr.	Ezra
Am.	Amos	Ga.	Galatians
Ba.	Baruch	Gn.	Genesis
1 Ch.	1 Chronicles	Hab.	Habakkuk
2 Ch.	2 Chronicles	Heb.	Hebrews
1 Co.	1 Corinthians	Hg.	Haggai
2 Co.	2 Corinthians	Ho.	Hosea
Col.	Colossians	Is.	Isaiah
Dn.	Daniel	Jb.	Job
Dt.	Deuteronomy	Jdt.	Judith
Ep.	Ephesians	Jg.	Judges
Est.	Esther	Jl.	Joel
Ex.	Exodus	Jm.	James
Ezk.	Ezekiel	Jn.	John

1 Jn.	1 John	2 P.	2 Peter
2 Jn.	2 John	Ph.	Philippians
3 Jn.	3 John	Phm.	Philemon
Jon.	Jonah	Pr.	Proverbs
Jos.	Joshua	Ps.	Psalms
Jr.	Jeremiah	Qo.	Ecclesiastes
Jude	Jude	Rm.	Romans
1 K.	1 Kings	Rt.	Ruth
2 K.	2 Kings	Rv.	Revelation
Lk.	Luke	1 S.	1 Samuel
Lm.	Lamentations	2 S.	2 Samuel
Lv.	Leviticus	Sg.	Songs of Songs
1 M.	1 Maccabees	Si.	Ecclesiasticus
2 M.	2 Maccabees	Tb.	Tobit
Mi.	Micah	1 Th.	1 Thessalonians
Mk.	Mark	2 Th.	2 Thessalonians
Ml.	Malachi	1 Tm.	1 Timothy
Mt.	Matthew	2 Tm.	2 Timothy
Na.	Nahum	Tt.	Titus
Nb.	Numbers	Ws.	Wisdom
Ne.	Nehemiah	Zc.	Zechariah
Ob.	Obadiah	Zp.	Zephaniah
1 P.	1 Peter		

II. *Periodicals, Dictionaries, Collections*

Ang	Angelicum (Rome)
B	Biblica (Rome)
BO	Bibbia e Oriente (Milan)
BT	The Bible Today (Collegeville)
BVC	Bible et Vie Chrétienne (Maredsous)
BZ	Biblische Zeitschrift (Paderborn)
CBQ	Catholic Biblical Quarterly (Washington, D.C.)
Conc	Concilium (New York)

CQR	Church Quarterly Review (London)
CSEL	Corpus Scriptorum Ecclesiasticorum Latinorum (Vienna)
DBS	Supplément au Dictionnaire de la Bible (Paris)
DTC	Dictionnaire de Théologie Catholique (Paris)
EB	Estudios Biblicos (Madrid)
ET	Evangelische Theologie (Munich)
ETL	Ephemerides Theologicae Lovanienses (Louvain)
EV	Esprit et Vie (Langres). Formerly Ami du Clergé.
Evan	Evangeles (Paris)
ExpT	Expository Times (London)
Greg	Gregorianum (Rome)
Int	Interpretation (Richmond)
Ist	Istina (Boulogne-sur-Seine)
ITQ	Irish Theological Quarterly (Maynooth)
JBL	Journal of Biblical Literature (Philadelphia)
JTS	Journal of Theological Studies (London)
LumV	Lumière et Vie (Lyons)
LV	Lumen Vitae (Brussels)
MTZ	Münchener Theologische Zeitschrift (Munich)
NRT	Nouvelle Revue Théologique (Louvain)
NT	Novum Testamentum (Leiden)
NTS	New Testament Studies (Cambridge)
PG	Migne, Patrologia Graeca (Paris)
PL	Migne, Patrologia Latina (Paris)
PTR	Princeton Theological Review (Princeton)
RBén	Revue Bénédictine (Maredsous)
RHPR	Revue d'Histoire et de Philosophie Religieuse (Strasbourg)
RSR	Recherches de Science Religieuse (Paris)
RB	Revue Biblique (Jerusalem)
RQ	Revue de Qumrân (Paris)
RSPT	Revue des Sciences Philosophiques et Théologiques (Paris)
RT	Revue Thomiste (Paris)

RTL	Revue Théologique de Louvain (Louvain)
RivB	Rivista Biblica (Brescia)
SE	Sciences Ecclésiastiques (Montreal)
SJT	Scottish Journal of Theology (Edinburgh)
SPCIC	Studiorum Paulinorum Congressus Internationalis Catholicus, 1961. Analecta Biblica 17–18. Rome, 1963.
StEv	Studia Evangelica: Papers from the Oxford International Congresses of New Testament Studies. Berlin, 1964.
SvEA	Svensk Exegetisk Arsbok (Uppsala)
TLZ	Theologische Literaturzeitung (Leipzig)
TDNT	Theological Dictionary of the New Testament (Grand Rapids, 1964—)
TP	Theologie und Philosophie (Frankfurt). Formerly Scholastik.
TZ	Theologische Zeitschrift (Basel)
VC	Verbum Caro (Neuchâtel-Taizé)
VD	Verbum Domini (Rome)
ZATW	Zeitschrift für die alttestamentliche Wissenschaft (Giessen)
ZKT	Zeitschrift für Katholische Theologie (Innsbruck)
ZNTW	Zeitschrift für die neutestamentliche Wissenschaft (Giessen)
ZTK	Zeitschrift für Theologie und Kirche (Tübingen)

Introduction

IN HIS CONVERSATION with the Samaritan woman, that "precious jewel" of the fourth gospel,[1] Christ says:

> Believe me, woman, the hour is coming when you will worship the Father neither on this mountain nor in Jerusalem. You worship what you do not know; we worship what we do know; for salvation comes from the Jews. But the hour will come—in fact it is here already—when true worshippers will worship the Father in spirit and truth: that is the kind of worshipper the Father wants. God is spirit, and those who worship must worship in spirit and truth (Jn. 4:21–24).

According to this solemn statement Christ has provided mankind with a new worship, related indeed to that of the Old Testament (since "salvation comes from the Jews") but also immensely superior to it. For the new worship there must be a priesthood, which is also new, and new in the same way; that is, continuous and discontinuous with the priesthood of the old covenant.

Now, in this respect a careful reading of the New Testament will greatly surprise us. For whereas the Christian dispensation, on the whole, is and clearly shows itself to be the fulfillment of the old dispensation, we are tempted to say, are we not, that there is complete discontinuity between the cultic

institutions of the Old Testament and the worship proper to
the New. After all, if we prescind from the Letter to the
Hebrews, the New Testament nowhere expressly calls Christ
a priest or a high priest. Moreover, not even the Letter to the
Hebrews expressly says that in the new covenant other men
are to be set apart from the rest of God's people and invested
with special priestly powers in order to serve as instruments
of the sole Saviour whom the new covenant acknowledges. In
this area, then, there seems indeed to be a complete break
between the Old and New Testaments. What, then, are the
real facts of the case?

It is this basic problem that the present exegetico-theologi-
cal study presents as forcefully as possible and tries to resolve.
We shall mention later on a number of studies that have
helped us in our own work. But we can justifiably say that our
study, taken as a whole, is largely new. Moreover, we want it
to have a permanent value and therefore have looked beyond
current controversies on priesthood.

What we want to do first and foremost is objectively to in-
ventory and meditate on the hidden and relatively unknown
riches of the Scriptures, especially of the Johannine writings,
in this very important area of New Testament priesthood. We
hope that these simply written pages will help many readers
to penetrate the deeper meaning of texts which are among the
most sublime to be found in the Bible: in the Old Testament,
the Servant Songs and especially Isaiah 53; in the New Testament, the prayer in John 17. We hope that with the help of
these texts the readers will come to a better understanding of
those two inseparable realities—the sacrifice and priesthood
of Christ—which are at the heart of the Christian religion.

To avoid all misunderstanding, I must insist on my main
purpose. I have no polemical intentions at all. Nonetheless,
the book does take up questions of great contemporary interest, questions that arouse deep feelings and even divide
men. The book has long been in preparation, yet it probably

would not have appeared in its present form, had I not been asked, as a member of the International Theological Commission, to make a positive exegetical contribution to the study of priestly ministry which the Commission had undertaken.[2]

The problem of priesthood is a very topical one, and for some time now a good deal has been written on it. Much of this writing has amounted to a challenge to the conception of priesthood hitherto maintained in the Catholic Church. The traditional doctrine asserts the existence of a ministerial priesthood that "differ[s] . . . in essence and not only in degree" from the priesthood shared by all the baptized.[3] Today, however, many Christians doubt the validity of this distinction. The result is that priests themselves find it difficult to determine exactly where they belong in the people of God. They even ask what is the use of their being priests.

The causes of this questioning are complex indeed. Some writers claim that Vatican II is itself partly responsible. As they see it, Vatican II, in its desire to act against Roman centralization and an overemphasis on papal primacy, glossed over the problem of priesthood. In any case, it certainly intended to highlight the role of the college of bishops as successors of the Apostles. Moreover, on the basis of Scripture, it proclaimed a truth that had hitherto been too often overlooked: the sharing of all the baptized in the priesthood of Christ. By these two emphases, the Council seems to have spoken as if the bishop and the people of God were the only necessary elements of a priestly Church. In so doing, it somewhat neglected the place of the simple priest (or presbyter).

The Council indeed maintains the special character of presbyteral priesthood as differing in essence from that of the baptized. But whereas it refers to a half dozen Scriptural texts to confirm the reality of the common priesthood, it cannot adduce a single text in favor of the famous essential difference. The contrast between the two successive passages of the Constitution on the Church is striking: the first, and very

welcome one, on the priesthood of the faithful, is based on
Scripture, the second is nothing but a theological development based on some texts of Pius XI and Pius XII.[4] The
bishop, who continues the mission of the Apostles, easily
finds in Scripture the justification for his existence. But the
priest can base his own special character only on papal statements.[5] *Olivier*.

It is not in order to play down the accomplishments of
Vatican II that we quote such a harsh critique. Our intention is rather to bring out the urgency and seriousness of the
doctrinal problem we are here attempting to resolve on the
basis of the New Testament. The problem is this: Were the
Apostles, who are clearly the source and starting point of all
the ministries now exercised in the Church, really constituted
priests by Christ, and is their priesthood distinct from that of
God's people as a whole? Since, however, Christ in sending
the Apostles to men intended them to be prolongations of
and, as it were, substitutes for his own person, there is a more
fundamental question we must answer: Was Christ himself a
priest, and did he think of himself as a priest? If Christ was
indeed a priest, then we must meditate at length on his priesthood, for it must be regarded as the first and perfect model,
and therefore also the primary source, not only of the common priesthood, but of the ministerial priesthood as well.

Most biblical studies of new covenant priesthood have given
a very important place to the Letter to the Hebrews. This is
entirely as it should be, for this Letter is the only New
Testament document to use expressly priestly terminology in
expounding the mystery of Christ's person and work. But it is
precisely here that the present book takes a new tack. We in-
tend to make Chapter 17 of the fourth gospel the primary
basis for our reflection on Christian priesthood. In so doing,
we shall, of course, not fail to make use of parallel data from
the other New Testament writings, and shall be briefly recalling the conceptions of priesthood to be found in the Johan-

nine writings as a whole and in the Letter to the Hebrews. Once again, however, John 17 will be the principal focus of our exegetical meditation.

We have reasons for taking this approach. The first is that the teaching of the Letter to the Hebrews on the priesthood has often been examined and synthesized, and there seems to be no point in a new detailed study of it. The second reason is that in recent studies of the Christian and Catholic priesthood, Chapter 17 of the fourth gospel has, oddly enough, almost always been left out of consideration. Yet this great text has justly been called the "priestly prayer" of Jesus. As such, it deserves our attention, and represents an important lacuna that needs to be filled. The third reason is that, whereas the Letter to the Hebrews never hints that ministers of the Church could also be priests who are subordinate to the sole high priest of the new covenant, the prayer of John 17 shows Christ giving his apostles a share in his own twofold consecration as priest and victim. At least, that is how we interpret the words of Jesus.

In this Introduction we shall not raise all the complex literary and historical problems suggested by the discourses after the Supper, of which John 17 is the climax. It is enough here to recall what is evident enough: The discourses are not stenographic reports; that is, word for word reproductions of what Jesus said. Everyone today acknowledges the considerable part the evangelist played in their composition. In them we find most of the important characteristic themes of Johannine theology. Here, as indeed everywhere else in the gospel, the thought of Jesus comes to us intimately bound up with the official commentaries of the evangelist who, in interpreting what Jesus said, is aided by the Spirit Paraclete and the light deriving from the life of the Church.[6]

It would nonetheless be a serious mistake to see in these discourses nothing but a didactic fiction, a meditation by a late first-century teacher for the use of contemporary Christians.[7]

Nor do we have in them, as is sometimes claimed, an abstract theological dissertation, a more or less esoteric teaching addressed to the "perfect" who are judged capable of being initiated into the secrets of the world above. The discourses are rather an advance explanation by Christ to his apostles of the climactic moment in mankind's religious history, that unique space of time which the fourth gospel calls the "hour of Jesus." It is clear that the discourses after the Supper are primarily concerned with the apostles: they are addressed to men whom Jesus had chosen even though he knew in advance of the defection of "the one who chose to be lost" (Jn. 17:12), men who had lived with him since the beginning of his ministry and to whom he had devoted very special care (Jn. 13:18; 14:7–9; 15:27; 17:12). The discourses are connected with a theme quite familiar to us from the Synoptics: Jesus bestows special revelations on his apostles. Here he is enlightening them on the meaning of his "hour."

What is true of the discourses as a whole is especially true of the prayer in Chapter 17, for it focuses more closely on the hour of Jesus than do various parts of Chapters 13–16.[8] We must, therefore, say a word on the meaning of the "hour of Jesus" and on the special cast it gives to the words of Jesus which this section of the fourth gospel reports.[9]

The hour of Jesus has two antithetical aspects. On the one hand, it is the time of Jesus' apotheosis, the full manifestation of what he is, the definitive revelation of his oneness with the Father in being and action; it is thus the time when light wins its conclusive victory over darkness. But the apotheosis and victory are inseparable from a heart-rending drama: the suffering and crucifixion of Jesus, as well as the blindness of unbelieving men, for it is on account of this blindness that Jesus is condemned to death. Moreover, behind the human agents—Judas, the Jews, the Romans—there stands Satan, the adversary par excellence, the prince of darkness, who secretly directs the action. In appearances, the hour of Jesus is the hour when darkness and the prince of this world win their victory. In reality, it is the hour of Jesus' victory over all the powers of evil.

In the religious history of mankind, the hour of Jesus is a high point that cannot be surpassed. It is the crowning moment in the whole of mankind's religious history up to that point, and it is the first moment of the period proper to the Church and of the final age of history. The farewell discourses in John 13–17 tell us in advance of the life of the Church and the end of history. The eagle eye of John saw accurately the unique greatness of this moment in Christ's life, and he gave it incomparable literary expression.

The two antithetical aspects of the hour of Jesus give the discourses after the Supper a special tonality found nowhere else in the gospel. We find ourselves in a hieratic atmosphere and one marked by the play of contrasting light and darkness. The conversations breathe a supernatural peace, even a joy. As eschatological king and judge of the universe, Jesus rises far above the immense drama of which he is the center and dominates it. The divine confidence that he manifests and wants to communicate to his disciples excludes despair and even any profound agitation. At the same time, however, the tragic shadow of the passion and all its consequences does lie upon the farewell discourses, for a cruel death awaits Jesus, and the disciples will be separated from their Master and subjected to hard tests. The confidence and joy are inevitably tinged with a subdued but poignant sadness.

By reason of its subject matter with its evident importance and topicality, the study we present here is intended for a broad public. For this reason, we have kept scholarly and bibliographical references to a minimum. The notes have been relegated to the end of the Conclusion, and the text is independent of them and completely intelligible without them. Greek or semitic words could not be completely avoided, since the discussion depends on them at times for its meaning; but they are as few as possible and always transliterated.

Countless works, old and new, have been devoted to the fourth gospel. There is, however, no point to our listing them, and we simply indicate in a note at this point the most important recent monographs dealing with John 17 as a whole or with details of it.[10] We must add, however, that we have found two studies to be particularly useful and that we shall often be referring to them, even if we do not always mention them by name: most importantly, the commentary of Raymond E. Brown on the fourth gospel as a whole,[11] and, secondarily, the commentary of Wilhelm Thüsing on John 17.[12]

Our study shall proceed as follows. The first chapter will stress the liturgical character of the prayer in John 17. The second, probably the most surprising in the book, will bring out the hidden relationships between John 17 and the Jewish liturgy for the great day of atonement. In light of this twofold reference to Christian worship (Chapter 1) and the Old Testament (Chapter 2), we shall attempt in a third chapter to define the transcendental nature of Christ's sacrifice and priesthood, which are evidently inseparable from one another. Our fourth and final chapter will deal with the sharing of Christ's ministry in his twofold consecration as priest and victim.

An unusually lengthy General Conclusion will pull together the various stages of the study and point out the biblical sources for an authentically priestly spirituality. The reader who is pressed for time might well begin with this Conclusion in order to get an overview of the book; he could then more easily grasp the detailed analysis.

Chapter 1

The Liturgical Character of the Prayer in John 17 and the Attributions of Priesthood to Christ

IN RECENT YEARS the liturgical character of Chapter 17 of the fourth gospel has frequently been exaggerated and at other times simply misunderstood. Rudolf Bultmann connects this chapter with Chapter 13 and maintains that originally it replaced the account of the institution of the Eucharist. What is now Chapter 17 would have begun as follows: "When Judas had gone [13:31], Jesus knew that the hour had come for him to pass from this world to the Father. He had always loved those who were his in the world, but now he showed how perfect his love was. He got up from table, raised his eyes to heaven, and said . . ."[1] Some scholars conjecture that the prayer was heavily influenced by the Christian liturgy,[2] or even that it had been recited or sung at the Eucharist in the early Church.[3]

Some writers are even more specific. According to Edwyn C. Hoskyns, the discourses after the Supper reflect the very arrangement of early Christian worship: Chapters 14–16 correspond to the didactic part of the liturgical service, while Chapter 17 represents the Eucharistic prayer proper.[4] Catholic liturgists have compared John 17 to the Preface which precedes the sacrificial action of the Roman Mass; just as before entering upon this action the priest in the Preface addresses the Father, so in John 17, Jesus turns to the Father before entering upon his passion.[5]

Imagination plays a large part in such interpretations, for there is no serious argument to support them. Bultmann's observations on the close relations between Chapters 13 and 17 are indeed quite valid. The words "the hour has come" (17:1) do recall the solemn prediction of the coming of the hour in 13:1. So, too, the idea of finishing or fulfillment, which is stressed in 17:4 (*teleioun*), reminds us of the words in 13:1: literally "he loved them to the end [*telos*]." So, again, the glorification of the Son of which 17:2, 4–5 speak is the same as the glorification spoken of in 13:31–32. But if Chapter 17 does undoubtedly refer the reader back to Chapter 13, it is by way of inclusion. The allusions do not justify removing the prayer of Jesus from its present place in the gospel and making it the equivalent of the Eucharistic meal in the synoptics.

A further consideration is in place here. Whatever be its liturgical coloration (of which we shall speak later), the prayer in John 17 is first and foremost the culminating section of the discourses after the Supper, and these evidently belong to the literary genre of farewell discourses. It is a literary genre that is well attested in the Bible and in late Judaism. The Old Testament reports the last words of Jacob to his sons (Gn. 47:29—49:33), the farewell of Joshua to Israel (Jos. 23–24), David's farewell (1 Ch. 28–29), and the instructions of the dying Tobit to his son (Tb. 14:3–11). The New Testament records a farewell discourse of Paul to the elders of Ephesus (Ac. 20:17–38). There are also the Testaments of the Twelve Patriarchs and the Book of Jubilees in which we find the farewells of Noah (10), Abraham (20–22), Rebecca and Isaac (35–36), and others.

Not infrequently the person saying farewell ends with a prayer for his children or the other people whom he is leaving behind. In this regard Deuteronomy provides an especially suggestive parallel when it records Moses' final words to his people, for it ends with two prayers. In the first (32) Moses turns to heaven and speaks to God of the chosen people; in the second (33) he turns to the chosen people and invokes God's blessings upon them. In a similar way, when Jesus reaches the end of his farewell discourses, he turns to the Father in order to speak to him of his present and future disciples and to ask divine protection for them.[6]

Now that these necessary preliminary remarks have been made, we can turn to a problem that is highly important in view of the purpose of our study: To what extent do the context and content of the prayer in John 17 justify us in saying that it has a liturgical character? "Liturgical character" can be approached from two angles. First of all, there are those aspects of the prayer that relate it to Eucharistic worship. Secondly, there are those that suggest that Jesus is acting as a priest, the high priest of the new covenant. We shall connect these latter aspects with the conception of Christ as priest, which the New Testament as a whole suggests, and we shall pay special attention to two points in John 17: the "consecration" of Christ, and his prayer for his disciples.

THE EUCHARISTIC BACKGROUND OF THE PRAYER

IT IS QUITE CLEAR that the prayer of John 17 is not directly concerned with the Eucharistic mystery. Specifically, Eucharistic terminology is completely absent; there is no question of food or drink, bread or wine, the body or the blood of Christ. Yet several observations will show us by their convergence that the atmosphere of the prayer is heavily Eucharistic. We shall deal first with the structure of the discourses after the Supper, then with the basic theme of the prayer in John 17, and finally with its relations to the Didache.

The discourses after the Supper form a literary unit that is clearly set off from the rest of the gospel. But when we begin to analyze the discourses we run into very serious difficulties, the chief of which are as follows. In 14:31 Jesus gives orders to depart, after saying that he shall not be talking to his disciples any longer. If the passion narrative followed immediately, there would be perfect coherence. Instead we find lengthy discourses filling Chapters 15–17.

A further difficulty: The second series of discourses frequently takes up themes from the first; Chapter 16, in particular, is largely a repetition of ideas from Chapter 14. Compare, for example, the mention of the disciples' disturbance of mind in 14:1 and 16:6, the promise of the Paraclete in 14:15–17, 26, and 16:7–11, the defeat of the prince of this world in 14:30 and 16:11, 33, the enigmatic prediction: "in a short time" Jesus will vanish from among them, in 14:19 and 16:19, the assertion that Jesus is going to his Father, in 14:12 and 16:28, and so on.

Those who like to find textual transpositions in the fourth gospel have here a field day for their theories. But the theories have no support in the manuscript tradition or in the witness of the Fathers. The recently published Papyrus Bodmer II, which probably dates from the beginning of the third century, confirms not a single one of the transpositions suggested by the critics.[7] We do better to assume that the gospel was not written at one sitting and that Chapters 15 and 16, in particular, were added to an earlier redaction.

Another solution has been proposed, which is not incompatible with the one I have just suggested. Some exegetes think that a literary procedure was followed in which the same themes were treated twice. Following Heitmüller, E. B. Allo offers this outline of the discourses after the Supper:[8] (1) the precept of love: 13:34–35; (2) Jesus strengthens his own for his departure: 14:1–31; (3) the union of Jesus and believers: 15:1–11. Then: (a) communion of love between the disciples: 15:12–16; (b) the strengthening of the disciples:

16:5–33; (c) prayer for the perfecting of unity: 17. A strong argument in favor of this view is the fact that in the first letter of St. John we find a quite similar literary situation.[9]

Once we accept this kind of structure for the discourses after the Supper, it becomes quite clear that the prayer in John 17 is in continuity with the allegory of the vine. The Eucharistic bearing of this allegory, however, is not in doubt: Christ the true vine and Christ whose blood is the wine or drink of the new covenant are closely connected ideas. This can be shown in some detail.

In 6:56 the mutual immanence of Christ and his disciples as a result of receiving the Eucharist is expressed by the words "live in" (*menein;* literally "remain in"): "He who eats my flesh and drinks my blood lives in me and I live in him." The same idea of mutual immanence, expressed in the same terms of "remaining in" occurs frequently in John 15:1–11 (cf. 4, 5, 6, 7, 9, 10). In Mark 14:25 (=Mt. 26:29) the wine in the Eucharistic cup is called the fruit of the vine. All the accounts of the institution of the Eucharist link it with the sacrificial death of Christ; but the allegory of the vine occurs just before the passion and thus in the same context of Jesus' sacrificial death (15:13 makes explicit reference to it). The branches that must "bear fruit" have a destiny like that of the Master who is the first to "bear fruit" but on condition that, like the grain of wheat cast upon the ground, he die (cf. 15:2, 5, 8, 16, with 12:24).[10]

We may add a point that we have developed elsewhere.[11] In John 15 as in John 6 a sapiential background is readily discernible. By that is meant that Jesus is assimilated to divine Wisdom in the Old Testament, the Wisdom that is a source of life for her disciples whom she feeds with her own substance as it were. The Johannine allegory also recalls, of course, the many passages in the prophets where the chosen nation is compared to a vine, and especially Ezekiel 15:4–5 where the wood of the barren vine is thrown into the fire (cf. Jn. 15:6). But in the Old Testament the vine that is Israel is never called, and understandably, the source of life, whereas when Jesus calls himself the vine he says that he is a life-giving vine, just as he had called himself in John 6 "the bread of life." The symbol of the vine, used in the prophets to designate the chosen people, is applied by Ben Sira to Wisdom, and this in a passage in which divine Wisdom summons her followers to a banquet which foreshadows the Eucharistic banquet: "I am like a vine putting out graceful shoots, my blossoms bear the fruit of glory and wealth. Approach me, you who desire me, and take your fill of my fruits. . . . They who eat me will hunger for more, they who drink me will thirst for more" (Si. 24:17, 19, 21).[12]

From the doctrinal viewpoint there is a notable progression from the end of the discourse on the bread of life (6:51–58), through the allegory of the vine, to the prayer of John 17. The prayer proves to be the climax of a sublime teaching which centers chiefly around the Eucharistic mystery. I would like briefly to show this progression.

The basic idea of Johannine theology is undoubtedly that God, who is in himself Love, invites men to an authentic communion of love with him through his Son and in the Holy Spirit.[13] The Old Testament had already taught us that out of completely unmerited generosity Yahweh deigned to establish a covenant between himself and Israel: "You shall be my people and I will be your God." The fourth gospel and the first letter of St. John show us a personalization and interiorization of the covenant, in fulfillment of the great prophecies of Jeremiah (31:31–34) and Ezekiel (36:25–28) concerning the Messianic times. Johannine theology rises to still greater heights. In the relations between God and men that the new covenant brings, it teaches us to see a reflection, as it were, of the relations within the Trinity: "I am the good shepherd; I know my own and my own know me, just as the Father knows me and I know the Father" (10:14–15). Above all: "May they all be one, Father, may they be one in us, as you are in me and I am in you, so that the world may believe it was you who sent me. I have given them the glory you gave to me, that they may be one as we are one. With me in them and you in me, may they be completely one that the world will realise that it was you who sent me" (17:21–23).

The point we want to make is that in the perspective of the fourth gospel these mutual relations between God and the followers of Jesus are seen primarily as the great fruit of the Eucharist. Chapter 6 teaches us that the reception of the Eucharist guarantees our communion with Christ, and, through him, with the Father: "He who eats my flesh and drinks my blood lives in me and I live in him. As I, who am sent by the living Father, myself draw life from the Father, so whoever eats me will draw life from me" (6:56–57). The allegory of the vine expresses the same idea in a different way: It strongly insists that the disciple must remain in Jesus and Jesus in his disciple as the branches of the vine must remain united to the trunk; without communion with Christ, Christian life would be sterile (15:1–11).

There can be no doubt that the great prayer of John 17 brings this doctrine to its fullest form. We are told there that the followers of Christ must be one with each other as the Father and the Son are one. We are told that the unity of the divine persons in the Trinity is both the source and the model of the mutual union of Christians. This can only mean that the communion of the disciples with one another is preceded and determined by their communion in the divine life, which is itself the fruit of Eucharistic communion. This being so, it is clear that the great prayer of John 17, whose basic theme is the union of believers with one another, has a Eucharistic background and resonances.

Wilhelm Thüsing observes:

At first glance the Johannine texts on the Eucharist do not seem concerned with the unity of the Church in the same measure as 1 Cor. 10:17: "The fact that there is only one loaf means that, though there are many of us, we form a single body because we all have a share in this one loaf." Yet we do find the idea in John, and it is given greater depth by his basic notion of the personal relation with Christ that is enjoyed by the believer who receives the Eucharist: "I am the bread of life . . . Whoever eats me . . ." Unity through the presence of Jesus in the hearts of believers, remaining in the love of Jesus, and glorification of the Son: these are three interconnected realities. The Eucharist is closely linked to the glorification of Jesus and the Father, which is the object of the priestly prayer.[14]

Thüsing finds a still clearer allusion to the Eucharist in the mysterious assertion of John 17:22: "I have given them the glory you gave to me." Lagrange had already shown (against John Chrysostom and Zahn) that this glory could not be the power of working miracles. He noted with good reason: "The 'glory' is rather something of a divine nature which Jesus possesses in its fulness, something which is not a graciously given power but is by itself a source of unity. It is called 'glory' because we think of the divine nature as light."[15] Thüsing reaches the same conclusion: In his view, the glory communicated to the disciples is the divine power that leads them to unity; it is the gift of salvation or eternal life, or the gift of the Holy Spirit, "a gift which includes everything else." But in the discourse on the bread of life, all that is the fruit of Eucharistic communion. When he wrote 17:22, John must have been thinking of the Eucharistic bread, which, according to the other evangelists and St. Paul, had been given to the disciples that same evening.[16]

The Eucharistic background of John 17 is confirmed by the themes this chapter has in common with the Didache, that collection of teachings and practical regulations for the use of the early Christian communities, which is probably of Antiochene origin[17] and must date from the second half of the first century.[18] The manifest likenesses, which we shall point out, between the Eucharistic prayers of Didache 9–10 and the prayer of John 17 have provided some scholars with an argument of the strictly liturgical and Eucharistic character of John 17. In answer, we need only point to one major difference: the Didache explicitly mentions bread and wine, but John does not. But the likenesses do prove at least that the themes developed in the prayer of John 17 were readily associated in the early Church with the Eucharistic liturgy; the prayer is thus basically oriented toward Christian worship and the Eucharist.

In Didache 10:2 the liturgical prayer begins thus: "We thank (*eucharistein*) you, Father"; in John 17:1 we have the same invocation, "Father," which is repeated in Verse 11 as "Holy Father" and in Verse 25 as "Father, Righteous One." The theme of the glory that Jesus gives the Father appears frequently in the Didache (9:2, 3, 4; 10:2; 4, 5); it is basic in John 17. The Didache asserts in 9:5 that no one may receive the Eucharist without having first been baptized "in the name of the Lord"; in 10:2 it thanks the Father for "your holy name which you have made to dwell in our hearts"; in 10:3 we read that "the Lord created the universe for the honor of his name"; so too, in mysterious formulas which we shall be discussing later on, John 17 speaks of the divine name given Jesus by the Father, and Jesus says that he in turn manifests the Father's name to the disciples (17:11–12). In 9:3 and 10:2 the Didache thanks God for "knowledge," all that he has made known to us through "Jesus, his servant"; in John 17 there is a notable stress put upon knowledge of the divine mystery (17:3, 6–8, 23, 25–26). In 10:5 the Didache prays, as does John 17:15, that God would deliver the Church from evil (or the evil one). In the same passage the Didache also asks that God would bestow upon the Church the perfection or completion of love and that, having consecrated or sanctified her, he would gather her into the kingdom he has prepared for her; evidently these are themes that play a key role in John 17.

THE CONCEPTION OF CHRIST AS PRIEST IN THE NEW TESTAMENT AND THE PRIESTLY BACKGROUND OF JOHN 17

A PROPERLY PRIESTLY TERMINOLOGY is apparently just as lacking in John as is a Eucharistic terminology. And yet, especially since the sixteenth century,[19] Chapter 17 has consistently been given the title of "the priestly prayer of Jesus." Before we show that the title is fully justified, we must first give an answer to the following question: To what extent does the New Testament as a whole justify us in attributing priestly dignity to Christ? It is only after giving at least a summary answer to this question that we can take up what directly concerns us: the priestly significance of John 17.

According to a notion that is becoming ever more widespread today, almost none of the New Testament writings adopt a strictly priestly perspective in presenting to us the person and work of Christ. Even when they show us Christ fulfilling the prophecies concerning the suffering Servant, they are linking Christ with the prophetic tradition. The New Testament writings have no intention (we are told) of connecting Christ with the priestly tradition of the Old Testament.

In this interpretation only the Letter to the Hebrews is an exception to the general New Testament outlook; we cannot but admit that the Letter does make use of properly priestly terminology. And yet even this exception is more apparent than real, for the writer of the Letter claims that there is a radical discontinuity between Old Testament priesthood and liturgy, on the one hand, and Christian worship, on the other.

Now, it would be antecedently surprising that such an interpretation of the New Testament should be completely justified. After all, the New Testament does maintain that, generally speaking, the Christian dispensation is the fulfillment of the older dispensation. The earlier state of affairs was a divinely willed preparation for the later; consequently there cannot be total discontinuity between the two. Rather there is simultaneously a continuity and a discontinuity.[20] This rule should hold for cultic institutions and for priesthood as well as for anything else. One purpose of the present study is precisely to show that in this area too there is continuity as well as discontinuity between the two dispensations.

It is unquestionably true that in the New Testament only the Letter to the Hebrews calls Christ a priest (*hiereus:* six times) and, even more, a high priest (*archiereus:* ten times). But modern scholars (most of them non-Catholic) have more or less successfully endeavored to show that the teaching of Hebrews on priesthood is different in expression rather than substance and that the rest of the New Testament, including both gospels and letters, contains the same teaching in outline or in equivalent form.[21] Arguments of varying value have been put forward to prove this very important point. It is worth our while to recall the chief of these arguments, although we cannot here undertake a detailed critical examination of them.[22]

It is a fact that in late Judaism there was widespread expectation of a priestly Messiah, a Messiah from the house of Levi to whom the kingly Messiah from the house of Judah would be subordinated, an ideal priest who would be quite different from the traditional priesthood in which men were so disappointed. The evidence for the hope of a priestly Messiah can be found in the Qumran texts (1 Qs. 9:11; 1 QS.ᵃ 12f.), the Damascus Document (12:23; 14:19; 19:10; 20:1), the Testaments of the Twelve Patriarchs (Reuben 6:7f.; Simeon 7:8f.; and *passim*). Even though Jesus criticized the priests of his day, he may well have applied to himself, if not the name, at least the concept of a new high priest. The reluctance of the New Testament to call Jesus a high priest has been explained by the prescriptions of Judaism: every high priest must come from the tribe of Levi, specifically from the family of Aaron, and must be descended from Zadok; any non-Aaronite claiming the priestly dignity was to be put to death (Nb. 3:10; 2 Ch. 26:16–21).

Let us look first at the synoptic gospels. A number of Jesus' actions, such as would not be regarded as Messianic according to contemporary ideas, have been interpreted by some modern authors as priestly actions: the blessing of the little children, the exorcisms and expulsions of demons, and especially the forgiveness of sins whereby Christ reconciled men to God. The name "the Holy One of God" (Mk. 1:24; cf. Jn. 6:69), which is given Christ by a possessed person, is sometimes said to be a priestly title, since priests were said to be "consecrated to their God" (Lv. 21:6; 2 Ch. 23:6; 35:3) and the high priest was to wear on his turban a plate with the inscribed words: "Consecrated to Yahweh" (Ex. 28:36). Jesus liked to apply to himself Psalm 110 in which the Messiah is a king and a priest according to the order of Melchizedek (Mk. 12:35–36 and parallels; 14:62 and par.). In the account of the transfiguration, the white color of Christ's garments has sometimes been connected with the white color of the high priest's robe, and the radiance which surrounds Christ has been likened to the radiance which late Jewish tradition attributed to the priestly ornaments and function. In Luke 24:51 Jesus blesses his disciples as he leaves them and ascends to heaven; this solemn blessing seems to recall the blessing given either by the high priest (cf. Si. 50:22) or by Melchizedek, in whom the Letter to the Hebrews sees a prefiguration of Christ the priest (cf. Heb. 7:1, 6, 7). Even the most demanding of the critics usually admit that, once the sacrificial character of the rite performed by Jesus at the Last Supper is assured, Jesus' priestly attitude on this occasion is automatically demonstrated.

A few words are in place concerning the letters of the New Testament, although we shall leave aside the first letter of St. John, since we shall be discussing it later on. In Ephesians 5:2 we see Christ offering himself in sacrifice. According to Romans 8:34 the glorified Christ "at God's right hand . . . stands and pleads for us"—which is a priestly function. Whereas Christ's answer to the Sanhedrin shows us "the Son of Man seated at the right hand of the Power" (Mk. 14:62 par.), in the account of Stephen's death this same Son of Man is *"standing* at the right hand of God" (Ac. 7:56), probably in the act of intercession. The explanation given by some Fathers of the Church, that Christ is standing to greet and welcome his first martyr, is agreeable but improbable. The theme of access to God, as expressed in the characteristic term *prosagōge,* occurs three times in the New Testament: "Through our Lord Jesus Christ, by faith we are judged righteous and at peace with God, since it is by faith and through Jesus that we have entered this state of grace" (Rm. 5:1–2); "For he [Jesus] is the peace between us, and has made the two [Jews and pagans] into one . . . Through him, both of us have in the one Spirit our way to come to the Father" (Ep. 2:14–18); "Christ himself, innocent though he was, had died once for sins, died for the guilty, to lead us to God" (1 P. 3:18). The idea of approaching a superior is also to be found, of course, in the juridical sphere and in the style of a royal court. But the problem of approaching God is a problem of worship: How can sinful men draw near to the thrice holy God?

It is significant that two of the three texts just quoted allude clearly to the sacrificial death of the Servant of Yahweh who brings peace to sinful men by reconciling them to God (Is. 53:5, 10). The verses quoted from Romans follow directly upon the reference to "Jesus who was put to death for us and raised to life to justify us" (Rm. 4:25), a text which itself alludes to Isaiah 53:4–6, 12. 1 Peter 3:18 is only a paraphrase of Isaiah 53.

In our opinion, the numerous reminiscences of the last

Servant song (Is. 53, in which the Servant's martyrdom is described) offer the clearest proof that the idea of Christ as priest is present in the New Testament as a whole.[23] The first three Servant songs (Is. 42:1–7; 49:1–6; 50:4–7) show the Servant as resembling the prophets, the masters of wisdom, and Moses the mediator of the covenant, while also containing a few scattered allusions to his kingly status. But the last of the songs (Is. 52:13—53:12) suggests very strongly that the Servant is a priest, since he offers his life as an expiatory sacrifice for the sins of his brethren.

We must give special attention here to the word *'asham* in 53:10; it is a technical term for sacrifices of reparation in the priestly stratum of the Old Testament. The authenticity of the term has indeed at times been called in doubt, but the term can be shown to harmonize quite well with the context in which it is found.[24] Moreover, the idea expressed by the term is equivalently, and emphatically, to be found in the prophecy as a whole. This is why we are in entire agreement with J. S. van der Ploeg's conclusion:

> The suffering and death of the Servant can be described as *a true sacrifice in the strict sense of this last term. To* have a genuine sacrifice there must be a priest, a victim and the immolation of the victim. If the sacrifice is to be effective, God must accept it. Now the Servant offers himself freely; he does not kill himself but he does offer his life to Yahweh. He offers it in the name of other men, not as if he had been appointed their representative but as if he were taking their place. This point is mentioned five times in the fourth song, in order to show the importance of the idea. The Servant is also a victim and is immolated. Finally, Yahweh accepts the sacrifice, for he willed it. *We can conclude, therefore, that the Servant is a priest.*[25]

Other commentators express pretty much the same idea. Thus, Pierre Grelot says with good reason: "The use of cultic language makes it clear what the prophet is thinking: what the expiatory victims offered in the temple by the Israelite clergy cannot accomplish, the Servant wins from God, because 'he was bearing the faults of many and praying all the time for sinners'" (Is. 53:12).[26] It has been observed that the great prophecy in Isaiah 53 begins with a kind of penitential liturgy (1–6) and that the Servant is both the celebrant and victim of this liturgy.[27] Edmond Jacob asserts that in the mysterious person depicted in Isaiah 53 "the prophetic current and the priestly current come together in a higher synthesis."[28] We shall show further on how very justified this last statement is.

We believe, then, that we have here the most decisive reason for thinking that Jesus was a priest and that he regarded himself as a priest. For it is beyond doubt that he recognized himself in the mysterious figure of the Servant beyond all others; that in a paradoxical fashion he combined in his own person and mission the humble figure of the Servant and the transcendent Son of Man of Daniel; that he was the first to connect his suffering with Isaiah 53; and, finally, that, following Jesus' lead, the New Testament writers developed their teaching about the Cross as the source of salvation for mankind by making use mainly of that same prophecy.[29] We think, then, that we are justified in making a statement whose implications are far-reaching: *every time the New Testament speaks of Christ's role by alluding to the self-offering of the Servant of Yahweh, it is implicitly presenting Jesus to us as the priest of the new covenant.* The accounts of the institution of the Eucharist, in which Jesus refers to Isaiah 53 (he gives as food and drink his own body and blood that are offered for mankind in his passion), are usually considered to be an implicit testimony to his priestly status (cf. above). If what we have been saying is correct, similar *implicit* testimonies are frequent in the rest of the New Testament as well.

After these somewhat lengthy but necessary preliminaries, we are now in a position to show the priestly character of the

prayer in John 17. The clearest indication of this priestly character is the reference to Isaiah 53. It is, in fact, easy to show
that John 17 displays the current evangelical conception of the
transcendent Son of Man who becomes a servant and offers his
life as a sacrifice for the salvation of men, in keeping with the
prophecy of Isaiah 53:10: "If he offers his life in atonement,
he shall see his heirs, he shall have a long life and through him
what Yahweh wishes will be done."[30]

We must insist, first of all, that such is the most likely
deeper meaning of the symbolic scene of the washing of feet
in Chapter 13 (with which Chapter 17 is closely connected
as we indicated above, following the lead of Bultmann). We
are going to show in a moment that the usual Johannine expression, "Jesus lays down his life," has practically the same
meaning as the words in Isaiah 53:10: "If he offers his life
in atonement." Now, according to some commentators, John
alludes to this important equivalence by the language he uses
in the account of the washing of feet. The unusual expression,
"Jesus lays [aside or down]" his garments (with *tithēsin* instead of the *hypotithēsin* we would expect) would, in their
view, be intended to recall the formula in which the redemptive suffering of Jesus is regularly predicted: Jesus "will lay
[down] his life," that is, like the Servant, he will give his life
for men. And when Jesus "takes" his garments again, the
evangelist uses the same verb as in 10:17–18 and would be
suggesting to us that Christ "will take [back] his life again"
in his resurrection.[31]

Even if we consider such allusions to be problematic, we
must at least admit that there is a strong connection between
Isaiah 53 and the mysterious episode of the washing of the
feet. In this episode, upon which we shall comment at length
in our final chapter, Jesus adopts the position of a slave and
performs an action reserved to slaves. As we see it, there
can be no doubt about the basic significance of this strange
behavior: The washing of the feet is an action parable, a sym-

bol of the passion in its two dimensions of astounding humiliation and saving, purifying action, which had been foretold in Isaiah 53.[32] Because such is the meaning of Jesus' action here, in refusing to let Jesus wash him Peter risks being excluded from the privileged group of Twelve (we shall show in our final chapter that this is indeed the meaning of Jesus' threat). To become part of that group, Peter must humbly accept the mystery of the Cross; he must accept to be loved by Jesus in precisely that way! In short, we have here the same situation and the same attitudes on the part of Peter and Jesus, as we have in the synoptic gospels at the first prediction of the passion which likewise echoes Isaiah 53 (Mk. 8:31–33 par.).

For the moment our concern is with the reference to the Servant's expiatory sacrifice. The reference is clear in John 17 and is our main reason for thinking that Christ is here acting as both priest and victim, a priest who, like the Servant of Yahweh, is himself the victim of his sacrifice. The reference is to be found in 17:19: "For their sake I consecrate myself" (*hyper autōn* [*egō*] *hagiazō emauton*).

We may leave aside for the time being the verb *hagiazein*, which we shall be studying at length later on. Here we should like to call attention to something that is often overlooked: The statement "for their sake I consecrate myself" is cut from the same cloth as the Johannine formula according to which Jesus "lays down his life for" men (*tithenai tēn psychēn hyper*), that is, in effect, sacrifices his life for them. The latter formula occurs seven times in the fourth gospel, with four of the occurrences being in the parable of the good shepherd, where the good shepherd lays down his life for his sheep (10:11, 15, 17, 18); the other occurrences are in 13:37–38 and 15:13. The formula is also to be found in 1 John (twice in 3:16). In the last section of the discourse on the bread of life, the thought takes a slightly different form: "The bread that I shall give is my flesh for the life of the world" (6:51).

The implication, however, is the same, and the words here recall the institution of the Eucharist with its clear allusion to Isaiah 53: "my body which is [given] for you; my blood shed for the multitude" (cf. 1 Co. 11:24–25; Mk. 14:22–23 par.).

Like St. John, St. Paul makes repeated use of the theme of the Servant who gives his life for men, but he uses a more Greek turn of phrase: Christ "sacrifices himself for our sins" (Ga. 1:5); "I live in faith: faith in the Son of God who loved me and who sacrificed himself for my sake" (Ga. 2:20); "What proves that God loves us is that Christ died for us while we were still sinners" (Rm. 5:8); "Since God did not spare his own Son, but gave him up to benefit us all, we can be certain, after such a gift, that he will not refuse anything he can give" (Rm. 8:32); etc.

Paul and John agree, therefore, in insisting that the mystery of redemption is the great manifestation of divine *agapē*, the love not only of Christ but of the Father as well: "a conception we find expressed in this way only in these two writers."[33] (Compare especially Rm. 5:8 and 1 Jn. 3:16; Rm. 8:32 and 1 Jn. 4:9, Jn. 3:16). Some exegetes have concluded that John depends on Paul.[34] But the Johannine formula "lay [down] one's life" is not derived from the Pauline letters; it comes directly from the phrase, *sīm naphshō*, in Isaiah 53:10.[35] This leads us to conclude that the Johannine formula is quite parallel to a passage in the synoptics which also echoes Isaiah 53:10, and is not to be explained, as is sometimes said, by any influence from the Pauline teaching on redemption. The synoptic verse in question is the well-known logion on ransom: "The Son of Man himself did not come to be served but to serve, and to give his life as a ransom for many" (Mk. 10:45; Mt. 20:28).[36] Both formulas are strongly Semitic in flavor, but John's is more so. A further element the two have in common is that they refer directly to the Massoretic text of Isaiah 53:10 and leave no room for any influence from the Septuagint; this direct dependence, we are told by Zimmerli and Jeremias, is characteristic of such references to the Servant as originate in Jesus himself and are not the work of the community.[37]

The Johannine formula, "lay [down] one's life," then, along with the related declaration, "For their sake I consecrate myself" (Jn. 17:19), are to be connected with Isaiah 53:10 and put us in the presence, implicitly, of Christ as a priest who offers himself as victim. But the verb "consecrate" (*hagiazein*) as well as Jesus' prayer for mankind in John 17 put us even more clearly into a specifically priestly context.

THE TWOFOLD "CONSECRATION" OF CHRIST (JN. 10:36 AND 17:19)•PRIESTLY CONSECRATION, BAPTISM IN THE JORDAN, AND PASSION•JESUS' INTERCESSORY PRAYER FOR MANKIND (JN. 17:9, 15, 20).

IF THE PRAYER OF JOHN 17 is eminently a priestly prayer, it is because it portrays, in close connection, the two essential aspects of a priest's role: sacrificial offering and intercession. Let us turn first to the sacrificial offering and an analysis of the verb *hagiazein*.

This Greek verb, which we translate as "consecrate," is simply a biblical variant of the classical word *hagnizein*, which is used in John 11:55 and 1 John 3:3. Neither Liddell and Scott's *Greek-English Lexicon* nor Moulton and Milligan's *The Vocabulary of the Greek Testament* show the form *hagiazein* as occurring outside the Scriptures or authors who depend on the Scriptures. The Bauer-Arndt-Gingrich *Greek-English Lexicon of the New Testament* cites some magical or gnostic texts, but these may be influenced by the Bible.

In order to understand the meaning of *hagiazein* in John 17, we must therefore turn to the Septuagint where the verb is a frequent translation of *qiddesh*, the latter expressing the idea of separation and of setting aside for God. All studies of *hagiazein/qiddesh* stress the various meanings of the Hebrew word: to set aside, to consecrate, to sanctify, and sometimes to sacrifice. The importance of *hagiazein* in John 17 is all the greater in that the verb occurs only four times in the fourth gospel, three times in this prayer, and once in 10:36 (a passage that has a certain relation to Chapter 17, as we shall see). In the other gospels the word rarely occurs: Mark does not use it at all; Luke uses it only in the Our Father (11:2); Matthew uses it in the Our Father (6:9) and twice in a cultic context (23:17–19).

In the Septuagint the verb *hagiazein* may express God's setting apart of a person or group of persons for a mission he intends them to carry out (Jr. 1:5; Si. 45:4; 49:7; 2 M. 1:25–26). The divine action imposes on those chosen the duty of moral holiness, but it does not imply that moral holiness is an antecedent condition. Jeremiah, for example, was "consecrated" while in the womb.[38]

The Bible knows cases in which the consecration is more directly related to moral sanctity. The concept of sanctity was originally connected with that of ritual purity but was spiritualized under the influence of the moral character of Israel's God. Thus, when Isaiah comes into the presence of the thrice holy God, he becomes aware of his sinfullness (Is. 6:5). It is possible, then, for a man to "sanctify himself" by observing God's commandments. Amid a list of sins against monotheism and domestic morality, Leviticus issues the following admonition: "You must make yourselves holy, for I am Yahweh your God. You must keep my laws and put them into practice, for it is I, Yahweh, who make you holy" (20:7–8). Along with the verb *hagnizein,* this same conception of moral holiness is found in 1 John 3:3: "Surely everyone who entertains this hope must purify himself, must try to be as pure as Christ."

The verb "consecrate" (*hagiazein*) can also mean the setting apart of persons or objects for the sacrificial liturgy. Thus, we find the Sabbath set apart (Gn. 2:3; Ex. 31:14; Ne.

13:22), the first-born (Ex. 13:2, 12), places and objects for cult (Ex. 29:44; 30:29; Lv. 8:11; Nb. 7:1; 2 S. 8:11), the priests (Ex. 28:41; 29:1–9; Lv. 8:12, 30; 21:6–7), the offerings (Ex. 29:33–34; 1 S. 21:5), the victims (Ex. 29:27; Lv. 16:8).[39]

In some passages we see a parallelism between "consecrate" and "offer in sacrifice." For example, Deuteronomy 15:19: "You must consecrate every first-born male from your herd and flock to Yahweh your God," and, in Verse 21: "If it has a blemish, if it is lame or blind, or has any serious defect at all, you must not sacrifice it to Yahweh your God." This passage suggests another point. We observed above that being set apart by God for a mission does not imply the holiness of the one set apart. But being set apart for liturgical purposes does presuppose a "holiness" of a ritual kind; that is, a freedom from defects. What is defective cannot be offered to Yahweh. Men, too, are excluded from liturgical functions if they have certain physical defects (cf. Lv. 21:16–24). We shall have occasion more than once to point out how these conceptions are transposed to a different order by the prophets and even more by the religion of Christ.

We must now explain the two passages in the fourth gospel which speak of the "consecration" of Christ: 10:36 and 17:19. The two passages shed light on each other.

In a debate with the Jews who have accused him of blasphemy, Jesus says: "You say to someone the Father has *consecrated* and sent into the world, 'You are blaspheming,' because he says, 'I am the Son of God'" (10:36). It is clear that the "consecration" of Christ here, linked as it is with his being sent into the world, can only refer to his being set apart by God for a mission. This consecration, then, is of the same kind as the consecration of Jeremiah to be a "prophet to the nations" (Jr. 1:5). We are also reminded of Moses' consecration (Si. 45:4). But a careful examination of the context in

John 10 suggests a deeper meaning than is to be found in the parallel passages just cited.

According to F.-M. Braun,[40] it is not accidental that Jesus should be speaking of his consecration by the Father just on the Feast of Dedication, which the Hebrews called Hanukkah, and the Greeks Enkainia or "renewal." In the Septuagint, *hagiazein* is used in Numbers 7:1 for the consecration of the tabernacle, but a little further on, in Numbers 7:10–11, *enkainizein* is used for the consecration of the altar; the two words, then, are almost synonymous. The Feast of Dedication, which commemorated the rededication of the altar that had been desecrated by Antiochus Epiphanes (cf. 1 M. 4:59), by that very fact also recalled the consecration of Solomon's temple (1 K. 8:64) and the consecration of the tabernacle by Moses (Numbers 7:1). In Braun's view, then, the consecration of Jesus, placed as it is here in the context of the Feast of Dedication, designates him as the new temple of God, far superior to the old.

The suggestion is an interesting one, for it relates to an important theme of the fourth gospel. Jesus implicitly says that he will be, as it were, the new Bethel above which the angels will ascend and descend (1:51); that he will replace the material temple at Jerusalem (2:18–22); and that he will be the temple foretold by Ezekiel (47:1–11), from which fructifying waters will flow (7:37–39).[41] There is, however, an objection to Braun's explanation. While the prologue of the fourth gospel does suggest that a new temple will be the result of the incarnation (1:14), the Johannine perspective links the gift of the Holy Spirit (making Christ the sanctuary of the new covenant) with the "glorification" of Christ. This is clearly suggested in 2:18–22 and 7:37–39, and probably, though more obscurely, in 1:51.

W. Thüsing points the way, we think, to a better interpretation of 10:36,[42] and we shall adopt his viewpoint and carry it further. The following facts serve as our guidelines. The fourth gospel speaks only twice of a consecration of Jesus: The first consecration is that which the Father bestows when he sends his Son into the world (10:36); the second is the consecration Jesus effects in himself at the end of his earthly life (17:19). The two are closely connected. More exactly, the first is ordered to the second. The first, in turn, sends us back to the great text in John 3:16, which reveals the meaning of the consecration. This basic text, then, must be our starting point.

The evangelist describes the mystery of the redemptive incarnation in this way in 3:16: "God loved the world so much that *he gave his only Son,* so that everyone who believes in him may not be lost but may have eternal life." Since the next verse speaks of the Son being sent into the world ("For God sent his Son into the world not to condemn the world, but so that through him the world might be saved"), the verb "gave" in 3:16 is to be related first and foremost to the incarnation. But the world must also be related to the crucifixion which has been mentioned in a symbolic way in the immediately preceding verses: "the Son of Man must be lifted up as Moses lifted up the serpent in the desert, so that everyone who believes may have eternal life in him" (3:13–15). In similar fashion, to express the gift God gave to us of his Son on Calvary or the gift Christ made of himself there, St. Paul uses the verb "give" (*didonai*) in Galatians 1:4 and the verb "hand over" (*paradidonai*) in Romans 8:32 and Galatians 2:20. The Old Testament backdrop for these statements can only be Isaiah 53 where the Servant is handed over by Yahweh or gives himself, as priest and victim, in expiatory sacrifice for the sinful multitude.[43]

Since the consecration of Christ in 10:36 and 17:19 is connected with his mission in the world (as understood in 3:16), the consecration cannot be simply in the line of Moses or Jeremiah, for these men did not have to give their lives in expiatory sacrifice as Christ the Servant did. The consecration must be as both priest and victim, and be in the line of the consecration of priest and sacrificial victims in the Old Testament (as Thüsing has seen[44]). With Thüsing we may refer, for example, to Exodus 28:36, 41, where "consecrate" is short for "consecrate as priest."

Consecration as priest logically and chronologically precedes consecration as victim. The priestly consecration is what is meant in 10:36 ("someone the Father has consecrated and sent into the world"). It coincides with the very moment of the incarnation, although this does not mean that hypostatic union and priestly consecration are necessarily identical.[45] When the Father sends his Son into the world, he bestows upon him a human nature that is completely set apart by its holiness from the sinful race the Son is to bring back to God. Much more than the Old Testament high priest, whose turban bore the inscription "Consecrated to Yahweh" (Exodus 28:36), Christ will truly be "the Holy One of God," as Peter proclaims him to be in 6:69. Thüsing puts it very well: "To say that the Father has consecrated his Son means not only that he has sent him into the world but also that he has made him a being wholly set apart from the world. He has destined him to live in the world and to testify there, even to the point of dying, to the holiness of God, that is, his total apartness from the world."[46]

Max Thurian connects the ordination of Christ with his baptism and supports this view by the testimony of some of the Eastern Fathers.[47] Theodore of Studios sees John the Baptist as "the priest of Christ the high priest, who is to transmit to Jesus the messianic priesthood."[48] St. Ephraem likewise says: "Christ received from John the Baptist the dignity of prophet and priest. The royal dignity proper to the family of David he received at birth, because he was of David's family, but he received priesthood, proper to the family of Levi, at his second birth, that is, at his baptism which was administered by a descendant of Aaron."[49]

These statements are open to criticism. Baptism in the Jordan certainly did not effect in Jesus a new reality, namely, his status as prophet and suffering Servant, to the latter of which his status as priest is linked. When the Father speaks in the baptismal theophany, he refers to Isaiah 52:1 and to Psalms 2:7, and simply authenticates and proclaims qualities which Jesus already has: "You are my Son, the Beloved; my favour rests on you" (Mk. 1:11 par.). With this text we must compare the precursor's testimony in the fourth gospel, for it too refers to the Servant of Isaiah 52:1: "Yes, I have seen and I am the witness that he is the Chosen One of God" (1:34).[50]

At the baptism of Jesus the Holy Spirit intervenes at the very beginning of his public ministry and causes him to commit himself to the very humble kind of Messiahship that marks the Servant songs, to a voluntary solidarity with sinners that will bring him to the sacrifice of Calvary. In an enigmatic declaration to the sons of Zebedee, Jesus will later, with good reason, call his passion a baptism (Mk. 10:35–40; cf. Lk. 12:50), thus connecting it with the baptism in the Jordan, a rite intended for sinners which Jesus had been able to receive only as a sign of his solidarity with the sinful world.

Here we meet the interesting theory elaborated by Oscar Cullmann and a number of other contemporary exegetes.[51] They say that by receiving baptism from the Precursor, Jesus showed his intention of offering his life in sacrifice for guilty mankind. We accept this interpretation, but only with reservations, inasmuch as it seems unduly to restrict the significance of Jesus' baptism. The baptism of Jesus, we believe, is a prelude to the whole of his Messianic activity and not only to his passion.[52] But there is indeed no doubt that the baptism, when understood in sufficient depth, is closely connected with his vicarious expiatory suffering. Jesus could indeed become humanly aware of this connection only in a progressive way; he was much better able to grasp it at the period of the sons of Zebedee episode than at the beginning of his public minis-

try. The marvelous unity that marks the earthly life of Jesus
from the baptism in the Jordan to the final drama of Calvary
by no means excludes a real progress which we think inseparable from his authentically human existence.[53] In any
event, it is quite certain that during his passion Jesus definitively identified himself with the cause of sinful mankind and
thus brought to full realization what the event at the Jordan
could only forecast in a general way. Due to this continuity
the name "baptism" which Jesus gave to his atoning death
was quite justified.

The second consecration of Jesus of which the fourth
gospel speaks—"For their sake I consecrate myself" (17:19)
—corresponds to this atoning death. We pointed out above
the connection between this statement and Isaiah 53:10: "if
he offers his life in atonement." We must also be aware, however, of the connection between the statement in 17:19 and
the earlier consecration by the Father of 10:36 and the gift
which the Father makes of his Son to the world according to
3:16. In consecrating himself as a victim, Jesus expresses his
full acceptance of the Father's plan of salvation; he brings to
fulfillment the intention behind the consecration effected by
the Father in the incarnation. The sacrificial interpretation of
John 17:19 is proposed by a large number of the Fathers,[54]
and we can make our own the comment of St. John Chrysostom which Bultmann quotes approvingly: "What does he
mean, 'I consecrate myself'? He means, 'I offer sacrifice.' "[55]

The statement *"For their sake* I consecrate myself" might
suggest that Jesus' sacrificial offering is intended to benefit
only the apostles. In the next chapter we will see that the limitation of perspective to the close disciples here is due simply
to the structure of the prayer in John 17. In point of fact,
Jesus sacrifices himself for all of sinful mankind. So much is
explicitly said in other Johannine passages: "I shall give . . .
my flesh for the life of the world" (6:51); "Jesus Christ . . .
is the sacrifice that takes our sins away, and not only ours, but

the whole world's" (1 Jn. 2:2). The same truth emerges from the account of the institution of the Eucharist: "my blood, the blood of the covenant, which is to be poured out for many" (Mk. 14:24), where "many" is to be understood in the light of Isaiah 53. Here the "many" (*rabbim*) of 53:11–12 is effectively equivalent to the "all" of 53:6. We may note that in the Damascus Document (14:6; 15:8) the "numerous ones" are the people, the whole community.[56]

Two important and closely interconnected characteristics of the Servant's sacrifices are brought out at the end of Isaiah 53. First of all, the sacrifice has been voluntary: "he shall divide the spoil . . . for *surrendering himself* to death" (53:12); secondly, the sacrifice has been accompanied by and will be prolonged in a prayer of intercession: "he was bearing the faults of many and praying all the time for sinners" (ibid.).

Earlier in the prophecy the Servant's free acceptance of his painful fate is expressed in a touching way, especiallly in Verse 7: "Harshly dealt with, he bore it humbly, he never opened his mouth, like a lamb that is led to the slaughter-house, like a sheep that is dumb before its shearers, never opening its mouth." What a contrast with Jeremiah who, when persecuted, calls down the avenging wrath of God on his enemies! The contrast seems deliberately intended, since at several points the Servant's lot is described in terms that recall the lot of the prophet from Anathoth. Compare Isaiah 35:7 with Jeremiah 11:19, and note how in Isaiah 53:8 the words "he was torn away from the land of the living" remind us of Jeremiah 11:19. There is, however, this difference: The image of lamb led to slaughter in Jeremiah 11:19 only points up the innocent ignorance of the victim in face of the danger of death, while the same image in Isaiah 53:7 expresses the immovable meekness and patience of the Servant in the very hour of sacrifice.

In Isaiah 53:12 a prayer of intercession is closely connected with the immolation of the Servant. Sacrificial offering and intercession are not simply coextensive, since the former is an event which occurs at a specific moment and will, strictly speaking, not be repeated, while the intercession that begins in the very act of sacrifice is the permanent mediatorial role which the Servant took on himself in agreeing to be an expiatory victim: literally "he intercedes for sinners." But this distinction does not mean that the two aspects—gift of his own life and intercession—can be separated. The prayer for sinners shows that the Servant has not submitted in a purely passive way to his painful fate but has entered with all his heart into the intentions of Yahweh who wills the suffering and death of the Servant for the salvation of a sinful world. On the other hand, the Servant's sacrifice of his own life proves beyond doubt that his prayer for sinners is far more than the ritual recitation of ready-made formulas.

In full conformity with Isaiah 53, the fourth gospel stresses the fact that Jesus gives his life voluntarily; no one takes it from him (10:18; 14:30; cf. 7:30, 44; 8:20; 10:39; 19:11); when they come to arrest him he knows in advance "everything that was going to happen to him" and he surrenders himself to enemies whom he could fell to the ground with a word (18:4–11).

As in Isaiah 53, sacrificial offering and intercessory prayer for men are closely linked in John 17, as a single comprehensive act of Christ in his role as priest. The verb "pray" (*erōtān*) is repeated three times (17:9, 15, 20). Nor may we challenge the title "priestly" for this prayer on the fallacious grounds that the thought of sacrifice has little place in it, for, if sacrificial offering and intercession are as closely connected with one another as they are, then the prayer in John 17 is priestly throughout.

One important difference here should be noted between Isaiah and John. The Servant's prayer is intercession with a view to restoring the covenant between God and sinful mankind. The prayer of Christ seeks unity among Jesus' disciples; in other words, its object is to bring the covenant between God and men to the peak of its perfection. The union among believers is to be so complete that it will be a reflection of the union between Father and Son.[57]

That Chapter 17, the theme of which is the unity of the disciples, also refers to the priesthood of Christ, seems to be confirmed by the scene in which Christ's garments are divided (19:23–24). John tells that Jesus' tunic was seamless and that the soldiers were careful to avoid tearing it. We may suspect that in recording this minor event the evangelist meant it to have a symbolic meaning. But what meaning? The exegetes are not in agreement. For some, Jesus' seamless tunic recalls the likewise seamless robe of the high priest[58] and means that the crucified Christ is a priest and his death a sacrifice he offers to God. For others,[59] the seamless tunic that is not divided means that in the Church of Christ there are to be no "tearings," that is, schisms; had not the prophet Ahijah of Shiloh foretold the schism among the twelve tribes by tearing his new cloak into strips (1 K. 11:29–31)?[60]

The fourth gospel is the fruit of long meditation, and the various parts of it shed light on one another. If it be true, then, that the prayer in John 17 is both a priestly prayer and a prayer for unity, these two symbolic explanations of the seamless tunic are not only not mutually exclusive; they demand to be taken together.

In ending this chapter, which is only an initial outline, we would like to call attention to one fact. The conception of Christian priesthood that emerges from the New Testament as a whole, and which we shall be trying to make explicit throughout this book, is a rich and complex one. It includes the preaching of the word of God, to which so much importance is being rightly attributed today. It also includes the reconciliation of men to God through the forgiveness of sins.

But we cannot forget that both the prayer of Jesus in John 17 and the great prophetic passage on the priesthood of the new covenant (Is. 53) consider as fundamental to this priesthood both sacrificial offering and intercession, as we have just shown.

Chapter 2

The Prayer of John 17
and the Jewish Liturgy
for the Day of Atonement

WE HAVE SEEN that the prayer in John 17 is implicitly both eucharistic and, above all, priestly, even though in it Christ is not formally called priest and high priest, as he is in the Letter to the Hebrews. The priestly aspect will emerge much more clearly once we show the hidden but substantial relations between John 17 and the Jewish liturgy for the Day of Atonement: *yom hakkippurim* (more usually in the singular, *yom kippur,* reflected in the *hēmera exilasmou* of the LXX).[1]

The festival of atonement was an especially solemn one. Even Passover, despite the magnitude of the events it commemorated, did not possess the efficacy inherent in the Day of Atonement, for the latter purged Israel of all its sins and made it once again a holy people. As A. Gelin puts it, Israel was on that day "restored to covenant relationship."[2] It was, therefore, the greatest of festivals, or simply the *Yoma* (the title of the treatise in the Mishnah concerning the Day of Atonement). Oddly enough, the historical and prophetic books of the Old Testament (including Ezekiel) do not mention this festival. Some have therefore concluded that it is of recent origin, but the conclusion does not follow. Neither does Ezekiel speak of Pentecost, but there is no doubt that this festival existed in his day.

The high priest to whom 1 Chronicles (23:13) attributes a holiness that turns him, like the sanctuary, into "the holy of holies," played an important role in the liturgical service of atonement. In fact, this service was the most important act in his whole ministry. He prepared for it by seven days of retreat in the temple and by numerous ablutions to keep himself in a state of purity. He was indeed the instrument of atonement (*keli kapparah*) that had been given to Israel.

The festival of atonement seems clearly to have influenced the Christian liturgy of the early centuries. Louis Ligier has uncovered a striking parallelism between an essential element in the liturgy of atonement, the *Seder Abodah* (or "order of service"), and several Eastern eucharistic liturgies. Especially in the lengthy eucharistic prayer in Book 8 of the Apostolic Constitutions (dating probably from the end of the fourth century), we find two sections separated by the Sanctus. The first section commemorates the events recorded in the Old Testament (creation, earthly paradise, Adam's sin, the parallel succession of early just men and early human sins), while the second section concerns the dispensation inaugurated by Christ. The *Seder Abodah* has an analogous structure. The first part is a commemoration, that is, an evocation of the past that is intended to relate the liturgy of atonement to the history of sin from creation on. The commemoration leads up the recall of the institution of the Day of Atonement, and only then does the sacrificial part begin; that is, the account of the sacrifices and confessions of the high priest. Without being as clear and fully developed as in the liturgy of the Apostolic Constitutions, the same structure is discernible in other eucharistic prayers of the fourth and fifth centuries. It is not probable, however, that the *Seder Abodah* depends on the Christian liturgy, for it is certainly very old and may even date from the period of Ben Sira. The influence, then, runs from the Jewish liturgy to the Christian.[8]

This fact leads quite naturally to a further question. If the liturgy of atonement has exercised such a great influence on Christian texts, may not the same influence have been exercised on other texts at a much earlier date? The answer would seem to be "Yes."

According to E. J. Kissane and A. Gelin, when Yahweh, in Isaiah 53:6, makes the suffering servant carry the sins of the multitude, or when the servant offers himself as an atoning victim (53:10), allusion is probably being made to the liturgy of atonement, including the scapegoat over whom the high priest confessed the sins of the people so that the animal might carry them away with him.[4] In any case, when the author of Ecclesiasticus sets out to praise the high priest Simon, son of Onias, he depicts him at the most solemn moment in the liturgy of expiation, when he emerges from the holy of holies where he has offered the great atonement, and shows himself to the people again. This took place but once a year: "How splendid he was with the people thronging round him, when he emerged from the curtained shrine, like the morning star among the clouds, like the moon at the full, like the sun shining on the Temple of the Most High" (Si. 50:5–7).[5]

The work of Christ, understood as "the forgiveness of sins" for mankind (Mt. 26:28; Lk. 24:47; Ac. 2:38; 5:31; 10:43; Ep. 1:7; Col. 1:14), must readily have reminded a Jew of Yom Kippur, which was "the day of forgiveness" beyond all other days. In Romans 3:25 St. Paul calls Christ an instrument of atonement (*hilastērion*); many commentators see in this passage a reference to the mercy seat which the high priest sprinkled on the Day of Atonement.[6] To these various texts we think John 17 must be added.

As we see it, John 17 refers to the liturgy of atonement in two ways: by its very structure and by its content. This means that we cannot discuss the hidden relationships between this prayer of Jesus and the liturgy of atonement without first taking up the problem of the structure of the prayer and highlighting some of its doctrinal characteristics: the large place

given to the manifestation of the Father's name, and the fact
that in this prayer Jesus speaks as if he had already ceased to
belong to the earthly world. In the third gospel we may find
confirmation for the relations we see between John XVII and
the liturgy of atonement; in any event there are very significant
parallel passages in the first letter of John and in the Letter to
the Hebrews.

THE STRUCTURAL PROBLEM OF JOHN 17

PARALLELISMS ARE FREQUENT in the prayer of John 17. The
most striking of them is found in Verses 20–23, where there
is a perfect correspondence between 20–21 and 22–23.
Specifically: Verse 21 contains four statements introduced
respectively by "in order that" (*hina*), "as" (*kathōs*), "in
order that" (*hina*), and "in order that" (*hina*); Verses 22–
23 also contain four statements introduced respectively by the
same conjunctions.[7]

A quick reading of the whole of John 17 shows that the
prayer contains three parallel petitions by Jesus. St. Thomas
Aquinas describes them thus: Jesus prays first for himself
(*primo pro seipso*), then for the group of apostles (*secundo
pro discipulorum collegio*), and finally for the whole Christian
people (*tertio pro universo fideli populo*).[8] Despite this division, however, the whole passage is highly unified. F. Godet
succeeds very well in bringing out this unity:

> Commentators usually divide Jesus' prayer into three parts:
> prayer for himself: 1–5; prayer for his apostles: 6–19;
> prayer for the Church: 20–26. And the division does match
> the progress of the prayer as a whole. But the thought ex-
> pressed in the prayer is one: when Jesus prays for himself,
> he is not thinking of his own person but the work of God (cf.
> Verses 1 and 2); when he prays for his apostles, he is recom-
> mending them to God as the agents and continuers of the

work; and when he looks out to all believers present and future, he sees them as the objects of the work. He prays for all believers because it is in them that the glory of his Father is to shine forth; his own work and the Father's glory are, in Jesus' eyes, one and the same thing. The structure of the prayer is therefore indeed brought out in the generally accepted division, but *the pervading thought is of the work of Christ or the Father's glory*. The prayer as a whole, then, springs from the filial heart of Jesus.[9]

Nonetheless, the overall structure of the prayer has given rise in modern times to numerous controversies which we cannot leave unmentioned. J. Becker[10] and R. E. Brown[11] provide good résumés of them, and our own summary will depend on these authors. We shall then present at greater length the results of an especially close analysis made by E. Malatesta.

A. Loisy distinguishes seven sections: 1b–2, 4–5; 6–8; 9–11; 11c–12b, 13, 14; 15–19; 20–23; 24–26. Verses 3 and 12 would be prose additions to what is a poetic text.[12] The division is open to many objections, as is the distinction between the original poem and the prose additions. The style in this passage is not strictly poetic, certainly much less so than the prologue of the gospel, which shows some striking affinities to John 17 both in form and in substance.[13]

M.-J. Lagrange sees Jesus uttering four successive prayers: for himself (1–5), for his present disciples (6–19), for his future disciples (20–23), and ending with a supreme prayer that embraces present and future and has eternal life for its main object (24–26). Lagrange is not very sure that this fourfold division into very unequal parts has a really solid basis in the text; he admits that the final section (24–26) could be put with the preceding one.[14]

C. H. Dodd proposes another fourfold division: 1–5, 6–8, 9–19, and 20–26. This has the same drawback as Lagrange's division: The units are very unequal in length. But such an object is not decisive, since John 17 is not strictly speaking a poem.[15]

A. Laurentin adopts an original position which he thinks is based on quite objective criteria. Verses 1–4 form a first part that begins and ends with the theme of glory. The invocation of the Father (1) and the words "I have glorified you" (4) set up an inclusion with Verses 25 and 26. Verses 5–6 which begin with "and now" (*kai nun*) are a transition and form an inclusion with Verse 24. Verses 7–12 are the first part of the prayer, which begins with a "now" (*nun*) and includes in its development a declaration (7–8), a petition (9), and a reference to glory (10) and unity (11). Verses 13–23 are the second part of the prayer; this, too, begins with a "now" (*nun*) and includes the same elements in its development: a declaration (13–14), a petition (15), and a reference to glory (22) and unity (21–23). Verse 24 is a transition that corresponds to the transition of Verses 5–6. Verses 25 and 26 are the conclusion of the prayer.[16]

Laurentin has correctly noted certain parallelisms that are too clear to be accidental. But his division is too exclusively a literary one and hardly takes into account at all the development of the thought.

The same must be said of the structure which J. Becker proposes. He is of the opinion that we have a general prayer (1–2) that is then developed in four specific prayers: 4–5, 6–13, 14–19, and 22–26. These four prayers all follow the same pattern: a statement of what Jesus has done, a petition, and the motives for expecting the petition to be granted.[17]

We find R. E. Brown's analysis a very attractive one that deserves to be presented in some detail.[18] The key to the structure of John 17, in Brown's view, is to be found in the three indications Jesus himself gives us concerning the object of his prayer: He prays for himself (1), for the disciples the Father has given him (9), and for all those who will believe because of the disciples' preaching (20). These indications introduce three literary units of almost equal length: 1–8, 9–19, and 20–26.

The three units have numerous points in common, a good indication of the care with which the chapter was constructed. Each section begins with a reference to the object of the petition: Verses 1, 9, and 20. Each includes an address to the Father in whom unity has its source: Verses 5, 11, and 21. Each takes up the theme of glory: Verses 1–5, 10, and 22. Each mentions the men whom the Father has given to Jesus: Verses 2, 9, 24. Finally, each speaks of Jesus communicating the Father's revelation to men: Verses 6, 14, and 26.

The great objection to this division is that the dividing line between the first two units is not very sharply drawn. In fact, Verses 6–8 are already concerned with the disciples and seem to belong to the second section rather than the first in which Jesus is praying for himself. Several authors, among them R. Bultmann, therefore make these verses part of the second unit. W. Thüsing likewise distinguishes three parts but makes the second part include Verses 6–19.[19]

Brown sees the objection and answers that if in Verses 1–5 Jesus is asking for his own glorification, he is doing so in order that he may bestow eternal life upon his disciples; consequently, his cause and that of the disciples become one, at least to some extent. Brown's point is a valid one. E. Malatesta's essay, of which we shall now be speaking, reaches the same conclusion by another path. Later on, reference to the Jewish liturgy of atonement will enable us better to understand why the dividing line between Jesus' prayer for himself and his prayer for his disciples remains blurred, with the result that the two prayers seem closely bound up with each other.

Malatesta's study is marked by an attention to minute detail and a wealth of literary observations which are very helpful in grasping the overall movement of thought. We cannot list here all the details of his analysis and of the strophic division of the text; to do that we would have to reproduce almost the entire article. Only the general results of his study concern us here; we agree with them almost without exception.[20]

According to Malatesta John 17 has five parts, but the first two—and the last two in their turn—are so closely united with each other that we end up with the tripartite division which most exegetes accept. Malatesta therefore rightly speaks of a *triptych*. With him we may characterize as follows the various themes that are developed in each panel of the triptych. We shall begin with the first and third panel, since it is in the light of them that we can better grasp the meaning of the central and most important panel.

The first part (1–5) of the first panel, in which Jesus asks the Father for his own glorification and defines eternal life, is made up of three statements. The last of these ("I have glorified you; glorify me") repeats the theme of the first but in reverse order ("glorify your Son that he may glorify you"). The second part of the first panel (6–8) also contains three statements, the first and last of which have to do with knowledge of the Father and the Son, while the second (7 and 8, down to "they have truly accepted this") concerns the mediation of the Son. The general sense of the first panel, taken as a whole, is: *Jesus asks the Father to glorify him so that he may continue the glorification of the Father which he has already begun in his disciples.*

The first part of the third panel contains three long, majestic proclamations (20–21, 22–23, 24). Here the "I want" of the final proclamation corresponds to the "I pray" of the first, and there is an evident parallelism between the theme of unity as found in 21 and the same theme as found in 22–23. The second part of the third panel (25–26) concludes the entire prayer by picking up, in an inclusion, the knowledge theme that had been so heavily stressed at the beginning of the chapter. In fact, if we view the third panel as a whole, it turns out to be a development of the first panel. It stresses the idea that *eternal life, along with the knowledge of Jesus and the Father that will ensue from the glorification of Jesus, are to be given the world through the very unity of future believers, which will reflect the unity of Father and Son.* If the love of the Father and of Jesus himself are to remain in the disciples in this world, it is because Jesus has in view the eternal contemplation of his own glory by believers and, consequently, the glory of his Father as well. Heavy emphasis is here put on the theocentric nature of Christian life.

In the central panel (9–19) Jesus prays for his apostles. The whole is clearly divided into three parts, each set off by an inclusion. The introduction to the petition begins with "I pray for them" (9) and ends with "and I am coming to you" (11a). This is followed by a prayer for the protection of the disciples (11b–16), beginning with "Holy Father, keep those you have given me" (11b) and ending with "protect them from the evil one" (16); and by a prayer for the consecration of the disciples (17–19) that begins with "Consecrate them in truth" (17) and ends with "so that they too may be consecrated in truth" (19). We may note the presence also of two negative themes: the "son of perdition" or "the one who chose to be lost" (12) and the world's hatred for the disciples (14). This central panel is the largest of the three and, even if considered only from this quantitative viewpoint, may already be seen to be the one that gives the whole prayer its main direction. These verses are highly important for us in this book, and as we move on we shall be frequently explaining them in greater detail. Their general meaning, however, is clear: *Through the mediation of his favored disciples, that is, his apostles, who are closely united to one another, Jesus will communicate to others (the whole Church) eternal life and the knowledge of Father and Son and will form them into a community that is truly one.*

Our study of the structure of John 17 requires some further

observations on the use of the formulas "those whom you have given me" and "that which you have given me." It is important to determine the meaning of these at each stage in the prayer; otherwise the reader may receive an impression of disorder from the prayer, whereas, in fact, Chapter 17 is a fine example of literary composition.

To begin with, we must eliminate Verses 11 and 12, since, as we shall see further on, the reading "those whom you have given me" is to be rejected. This leaves Verses 2, 6, and 24. In Verse 2 the formula "that you have given him" follows upon the phrase "the power over all mankind," "evidently for the purpose of saving all, since all fall under his dominion."[21] Although the words "that you have given me" imply some kind of being set apart from the rest of mankind, we ought not speak here of predestination in the strict sense of the term, but simply recall what was said in 6:37, 44, 65: Men must be drawn by the Father if they are to attach themselves to Christ and be faithful to his word.[22]

Verse 6 replaces the neuter "that" with the masculine, and this with reference to a very limited group of disciples: the apostles, who alone hear the discourses after the Supper. Jesus speaks of them as "the men you took from the world to give me. They were yours and you gave them to me." Lagrange comments: "They were good Israelites who wanted to please God and yearned for the coming of his kindgom."[23] At a given moment the Father had separated them from the rest of mankind and given them to Jesus. In 15:19 this leaving of the world is said to be caused by the action of Jesus: "my choice withdrew you from the world," that is, in Lagrange's translation: "I caused you to go out from the world by my choice."

Because the Twelve are envisaged from 17:6 on, some authors (P. Schanz, F. Godet, R. Bultmann, C. K. Barrett, W. Thüsing) want to make the second part of the prayer begin at this point. They would seem to be correct. Yet the purpose of Verses 6–8 is to explain Verse 4, that is, the work done by the Son while on earth. Which position shall we adopt? That there are more reasons for connecting 6–8 to what goes before than to what follows. It is true enough that at this point only the apostles are envisaged and that the passage, therefore, quite naturally leads into the special prayer that Jesus will offer for them. On the other hand, they are not here being considered precisely as apostles, for although they form a privileged group that the Father has drawn apart from the world, they are here representative of that entire mankind which the Father has given to Jesus (Verse 2); that is, of all the men to whom Christ brings the full revelation of God and eternal life.

From one end to the other of the discourses after the Supper the apostles are considered under these two aspects: sometimes as a group clearly distinct from the rest of the disciples and beneficiaries of special revelations, sometimes as the nucleus or starting point of the whole community of believers. As far as this second role of the apostles is concerned, we do not have, on one side, the community, and on the other, the apostles, as though they were set over the community in splendid isolation. Rather, the Church began with the choice by Christ of twelve privileged disciples, and if Christ willed that the latter be charged with the government of the Church, they are not therefore outside the community. The unity of the Church for which Jesus prays in John 17 could not exist without the apostles whom he has given to the Church. This means that the institution of the apostolic group is from above and does not originate in the community. On the other hand, however, their ministry is carried out within the community and exists only for the service of the community.

Verse 24 returns to the neuter form of Verse 2, since the Greek text says literally, "what you have given me." The neuter is vaguer than the masculine. Lagrange thinks the choice of gender is probably deliberate "in order to include all the future faithful."[24] Concretely, the "what you have given me," with its verb in the past tense, means, according to Verse 20, all those who in time to come will believe in Jesus because of the words of the apostles or their successors; these future believers are already present to the divine gaze.

A careful examination of the structure of John 17 is indispensable if we want to grasp the connection of ideas in this sublime prayer. The beauty of the composition, which may be called poetic in the broad sense and in which the use of various techniques (parallelism, chiasmus, inclusion) does not lessen the evangelist's freedom, is great enough here, more than any place else in the gospel (except the Prologue), to rival even the richness and depth of the thought. And we must add that this same beauty is in sharp contrast to the poverty of the vocabulary.[25]

Now, we are convinced that the Jewish liturgy of the Day of Atonement casts a good deal of light on this carefully worked out structure of John 17 (a tripartite structure, as the great majority of commentators acknowledge even when they suggest variations that are of secondary importance).

In the Bible the festival of atonement is described for us in Leviticus 16 and 23:26–32 and in Numbers 29:7–11. The high priest makes atonement first for himself, then for his house; that is, the Israelite priesthood and finally for all the chosen people. Twice we are told that Aaron will perform "the rite of atonement for himself and his family" (Lv. 16:6, 11). But in Verse 17 of the same chapter we have the complete formulation: "When he has made atonement for himself, for his family, and for the whole community of Israel. . . ." This threefold atonement corresponds to the threefold division of John 17, where Jesus prays in turn for himself, for his apostles, and for the faithful.

However, an examination of the ritual of atonement as described in Leviticus 16 gives a rather different view of things. We are speaking of the chapter as we now have it and do not take into account the fact that the critics see in it an amalgamation. It is not surprising that the text should reflect varying situations since the Old Testament liturgy could not have remained changeless through time but must certainly have been adapted to the circumstances of each successive period.

According to what we are told in Leviticus 16, the high priest was to act as follows. He is to begin by taking the blood of a bull whose throat he has cut; he enters the holy of holies and, dipping his finger in the blood, sprinkles the eastern side of the mercy seat and sprinkles in front of the mercy seat seven times (Lv. 16:14). The Mishnah understands this to mean one sprinkling in an upward direction and seven sprinklings downward (Yoma 5:3). In this way the sanctuary is purified of the uncleanness of the high priest and the priests. Next comes the atonement for the people (Lv. 16:15–16). After slaughtering a goat (the one intended for Yahweh, as distinct from the scapegoat intended for Azazel and driven out into the wilderness, as we read in 16:20–22), the high priest once passes through the veil into the holy of holies, and uses the goat's blood in the same fashion as he had the bull's blood. In this way the sanctuary is purified of "the uncleanness of the sons of Israel" (16:16). From all this we can see that the threefold atonement mentioned in 16:17 takes the form, in reality, of two ceremonies, since there is a single rite of purification for the high priest and his family; that is, the other priests.

Now, what we have already seen in John 17 matches quite well with the description in Leviticus 16. At first sight, we seem to have a threefold petition in John. But the division turns out to be only bipartite, since Jesus' prayer for himself and his prayer for his apostles are intimately connected. Then, in Verse 20, "I pray not only for these, but for those also who through their words will believe in me," we clearly pass over to a new prayer that embraces the universal Church of all

ages. Whereas the commentators are uncertain about where
to divide the first petition from the second, most of them
(Loisy, Lagrange, Dodd, Thüsing, Brown, etc.; cf. above)
have no difficulty in accepting Verse 20 as the beginning of a
new prayer.

Some further literary observations confirm our point;
namely, that while there seem to be three successive petitions,
there are, in fact, only two, just as on Yom Kippur the triple
atonement is reduced to a twofold rite of purification. Some
important formulas or themes of John 17 occur only twice:
once in the section 1–19, and again in the section 20–26.
Thus, "Holy Father" (11) corresponds to "Father, Righteous
One" (26); the Father's gift of men to Jesus so that he may
win eternal life for them is expressed in 2 and 24; the manifestation of the Father's name by Jesus in 6 and 26; the life
of Jesus with his Father before the creation of the world in 5
and 24; and the major theme of unity in 11 and 21–23.

THE REVELATION AND GIFT OF THE FATHER'S NAME TO
JESUS (JN. 17:6, 11–12, 26)

IF THE RELATIONSHIP BETWEEN JOHN 17 and the liturgy of
the Day of Atonement were limited to the points made in the
preceding section of this chapter, the reader might well consider the whole connection purely accidental. But there are
two further similarities that go deeper and concern teaching.
One is the stress put in John 17 on the revelation of the
Father's name; the other is Christ's entrance into the heavenly
dwelling, with which entrance his prayer for the moral protection of the disciples and for their action in the world is
closely connected. Elaborating the affinity of John 17 with
the atonement liturgy on these two points is a good way for
us to penetrate more deeply into the meaning of Jesus' prayer.
Let us begin with the first of the two similarities mentioned.

All Jewish sources tell us that in late Judaism it was forbidden to pronounce the sacred tetragrammaton, Yahweh: "Whoever speaks that name distinctly will have no share in the world to come" (Mishnah, Sanhedrin 11:1). Yet on the Day of Atonement the high priest spoke the name several times.[26]

The invocation of Yahweh's name by the high priest on this occasion is not mentioned in either Leviticus or Numbers, but it plays a very important role in the Mishnah (Yoma 3:8; 4:2) and the two Talmuds. It is also attested in Ecclesiasticus (Si. 50:20) when the writer is describing the majesty of Simon, son of Onias, during the liturgy of Yom Kippur: Once the liturgy was ended, "he would come down and raise his hands over the whole concourse of the sons of Israel, to give them the Lord's blessing from his lips, being privileged to pronounce his name."

According to the Mishnah, on the Day of Atonement the high priest confesses his sins and those of his family (the other priests) in these words: "O Name, I and my family have gone astray, we have transgressed, we have sinned in your sight. O Name, pardon the sins, transgressions, and faults which I and my family have committed through our sinfulness and faithlessness in your sight. For it is written in the Law of Moses, your servant: 'For on that day he will be forgiven'" (Lv. 16:30). And the others present respond: "Praise be to the Name for the glory of his kingdom, now and forever" (Yoma 3:8). A second confession followed in almost the same words (Yoma 4:2). A third confession is pronounced, not over the bull sacrificed for sins, as the first two confessions had been, but over the scapegoat (Yoma 6:2). The Gemara of the Palestinian Talmud tells us that the high priest spoke the name of Yahweh ten times during the liturgy of atonement: six times over the bull, three over the scapegoat, and once while drawing lots. The Gemara also describes the prostration performed by the assembly each time the holy was uttered (Jerusalem Talmud 3:8, 40d).[27]

To this invocation of the name of Yahweh there corresponds the fourfold mention of the Father's "name" in John 17 (Verses 6, 11–12, 26). This repeated reference is characteristic of this chapter, since elsewhere in the gospel there are only three references to the "name of my Father" (5:43; 10:25; 12:28). In his commentary on John 17:6, C. K. Barrett recalls, as we have, the annual utterance of the name of Yahweh, but he draws no conclusion from the parallel.[28] Yet, mentioned as it is at the beginning (6), middle (11–12), and end (26) of this chapter, the Father's name obviously plays an important role in it. The first and last of the three passages correspond to each other and seem at first sight easy enough to understand; Verses 11 and 12 are more mysterious. In fact, however, as we shall see, the four texts are all connected and shed light each upon the others.

Verse 6: "I have made your name known to the men you took from the world to give me," is to be understood as referring to Christ's whole life, including his passion which he looks upon as an accomplished fact (he has just said, speaking of the passion: "I have . . . finished the work that you gave me to do": Verse 4). Revealing the Father's name to men means communicating new knowledge to them. If we look at it as the Bible does, this "knowledge" is not of a theoretical kind but calls upon all of man's powers and is intended to bring him into communion with the very life of God. The revelation of the Father's name concerns two points: It teaches men that God is the Father of Jesus Christ in a totally unique way, and it teaches them that God wants to become their Father in a wholly new manner.[29]

In the fourth gospel Jesus is constantly stressing the fact that he is "sent from the Father" (more than fifty times, with the verbs *pempō* and *apostellō*). But, unlike what happens when one man sends another, the one sent is not at any moment separated from the one who sends him: The Father who has sent his Son into the world never leaves him to himself there (8:29; 16:32); Jesus and the Father are always one (10:30), always in each other (10:38; 14:11; 17:21). Therefore, when Jesus loves men and gives his life for them, the Father's love is embracing them through him: "To have seen me is to have seen the Father" (14:9).[30] In this way, then, men have come to know the Father's name and have also learned that God is Love, just as the name of Yahweh reminded the chosen people that the God who had saved them is the only true God, "He who is," unlike the idols which are nothing.

At the end of his prayer (26), Jesus says: "I have made your name known to them and will continue to make it known, so that the love with which you loved me may be in them, and so that I may be in them." Here Jesus is implicitly referring to the future sending of the Spirit Paraclete who will internalize the great revelation that Jesus had communicated of the Father's name and of the God of love (cf. 14:16–17, 25–26; 16:12–15). W. Thüsing is even more specific: If the glory Jesus says he has given to his disciples (22) can only be the salvation or eternal life which is identical with the gift of the Spirit (cf. our Chapter 1) then the love of the Father for the Son, which Jesus communicates to the disciples, also intends ultimately the gift of the Spirit.[31]

We come now to the more difficult verses, 11 and 12. Following a well-attested reading, many exegetes translate the passage in this way: "Holy Father, keep them in your name which you have given me. . . . I have kept them in your name which you gave me." They explain that to keep the apostles in the name which the Father had given to Christ means to keep them faithful to the name of the Father; that is, faithful to that knowledge of God as Father which Christ, in fulfillment of his mission, had brought to men. W. Thüsing offers this comment on Verse 11:

> The name of the Father, that is, the revelation, through Jesus, of his love, means here a place, as it were, which God sets aside for those who belong to him. The latter do not enter it by their own power, but have been drawn into it after having been chosen; consequently, neither can they remain in that place by their own power. The Father keeps them there by the power of his revelation, and by that alone. Therefore the expression "keep them in your name" does not mean simply: "keep them in the place which revelation creates"; it also means "keep them there by the power with which revelation lays hold of them," that is, in the last analysis, by the power of the Holy Spirit. This petition, then, corresponds to the promise of another Paraclete, who will remain in and with the disciples forever. (cf. 14:16–17).[32]

Other commentators, J. Huby for example,[33] reject this explanation, maintaining that the expression "name of the Father" seems to designate the person of the Father and all that is personal to him; consequently, the "name" cannot be given to the Son. They think, therefore, that the expression "keep in, or by, the Father's name" can only mean to keep by virtue of the Father's protecting power. As a result, they propose to read the Greek text as many Greek manuscripts and the Vulgate do: "Holy Father, keep in your name *those whom* you have given me" (with the relative pronoun in the masculine form) or even, "keep in your name *that which* you have given me" (with the vaguer neuter relative pronoun); and, "When I was with them, I kept in your name *those whom* (or *that which*) you have given me." The translators (French and English) of the Jerusalem Bible have followed this interpretation.

We have tried to present these two divergent explanations of Verses 11 and 12 as objectively as we can and to let the reader choose between them. We ourselves, however, think the first explanation much the better one, since the reading on which it rests has the older witnesses in its favor and, in addition, is the more difficult reading ("the more difficult reading is to be preferred"). The readings which show the relative pronoun (masculine or neuter) seem to be awkward corrections of an obscure text and efforts to make 11–12 harmonize with 2, 6, and 9, where Jesus speaks of men given him by the Father.

Having chosen the first exegesis, we would like to carry it a bit further; in so doing we are following the line suggested in the excellent commentaries of M.-J. Lagrange and R. E. Brown on these difficult texts and in an interesting essay of J. Bonsirven.[34] In this way we shall find ourselves considerably closer to the proclamation of the divine name that marks the liturgy of Yom Kippur.

Despite claims to the contrary, the Father's name, which it is Jesus' mission to manifest to men, does not mean primarily his fatherhood in relation to men or his loving plan for mankind (truths, both of them, which had already been taught to some extent in the Old Testament). The revelation of the name means, above all else, the revelation of the fact that from all eternity the Father has a Son to whom he communicates all that he has and is. That is the view of Lagrange, who appeals for support to a splendid text of St. Cyril of Alexandria as well as to St. Thomas Aquinas' observation that "under this aspect the Father had not been known to anyone; his eternal fatherhood became known through the Son when the apostles came to believe that he was the son of God."[35]

Apropos of Verse 11, Lagrange rightly observes that to keep the disciples in the Father's name that had been given to Jesus means to keep them in the knowledge of what Jesus is as Son of God. It is to keep them "in a Name which fuses worship of the Father with worship of the Son. This Name, then, is the bond which will unite the disciples. . . . It is because [the Father] will keep them in the unity of this Name that the disciples will be able to be one with each other, a single community in spirit and soul," and a reflection, as it were, of the unity of Father and Son.[36]

In late Judaism there was a close connection between the sacred tetragrammaton "Yahweh" and "the Name," an expression readily used as a substitute for the tetragrammaton. This fact invites us once again to penetrate more deeply into the Johannine formulas, along the lines of what R. E. Brown has written about them.[37]

Like the glory that the Father eternally gives the Son and of which the Son communicates a share to men (17:22), the name that the Father gives the Son is nothing else than the divine nature. It is that which makes God be God, absolutely transcendent over the whole created universe. Moses had received the revelation of this transcendence: "I Am who I Am" (Ex. 3:13–15). Christ manifests this name of the Father to men and tells them that he too is "I am" by the same title as the Father. The various "I am" formulations of the fourth gospel spring to mind here. In some of them the "I am" stands without qualification or predicate: "If you do not believe that I am [He], you will die in your sins" (8:24); "When you have lifted up the Son of Man, then you will know that I am [He]" (8:28); "I tell you most solemnly, before Abraham ever was, I Am" (8:58); "I tell you this now, before it happens, so that when it does happen, you may believe that I am [He]" (13:19; cf. also, perhaps, 18:5, 6, 8). In other formulations the "I am" is accompanied by a predicate; in these there is heavy emphasis on the "I" of Jesus as the sole source of life, light, and salvation. Thus: I am the bread of life which comes down from heaven (6:35, 41, 48, 51), the light of the world (8:12; 9:5), the door for the sheep (10:7, 9), the good shepherd (10:11, 14), the resurrection and the life (11:25), the way, the truth, and the life (14:6), and the true vine (15:1, 5).[38]

Seen against this extensive backdrop, the manifestation of

the Father's name to which 17:4 and 26 refer proves also to be a revelation of the Son. And keeping the disciples in the Father's name which had been given to Jesus comes down to keeping them in their belief in the divinity of Jesus as one who is in the fullest sense equal to and consubstantial with the Father. Thus, the manifestation of the name, to which John 17 refers, is the fulfillment of the Old Testament promises, such as the one in Isaiah: "My people will therefore know my name; that day they will understand that it is I who say, 'I am [here]' (*egō eimi*)" (52:6).[39] But the manifestation of the name in John 17 also corresponds to the proclamation of the sacred tetragrammaton on the Day of Atonement: Yahweh="I am who I am." The difference between the two manifestations is the essential difference between the Jewish and Christian religions: in the former, Yahweh is presented simply as the one God; in the latter, this one God has a Son who is one with him and, like him, says "I am."

THE ENTRANCE OF CHRIST INTO THE HEAVENLY SANCTUARY •HIS PRAYER FOR THE MORAL PRESERVATION OF THE DISCIPLES AND FOR THEIR ACTION IN THE WORLD•COMPARISON WITH THE FIRST LETTER OF ST. JOHN, THE LETTER TO THE HEBREWS, AND THE THIRD GOSPEL

WE READ IN LEVITICUS, at the beginning of the description of the liturgy for the Day of Atonement: "Yahweh spoke to Moses. He said: 'Tell Aaron your brother that he must not enter the sanctuary beyond the veil, in front of the throne of mercy that is over the ark, whenever he chooses. He may die; for I appear in a cloud on the throne of mercy. This is how he is to enter the sanctuary: with a young bull for a sacrifice for sin and a ram for a holocaust'" (16:2–3). As Hebrews 9:7 reminds the reader, the high priest entered the holy of holies only once a year, on the Day of Atonement. He did so only while carrying the blood of a sacrificial victim, which was, as it were, his protection.[40]

Having entered the holy of holies, the high priest sprinkled the mercy seat, or throne of mercy, with the blood of the sacrificed victims, as we noted earlier. This was the decisive act that restored to Israel its condition as the holy people of God, for to this rite God had attached the purification of his people from their sins. The rite in the holy of holies was completed by sending out into the desert a scapegoat to which the priest had transferred the sins of the people (cf. Lv. 16:10, 20–22). The sins were thus thought of as having been carried far away. What we have here is undoubtedly the remnant of an ancient popular practice, which Yahwism exorcised and preserved.[41]

Corresponding to the central ritual act of the Day of Atonement there is in John 17 Jesus' statement that he is going to the Father, to the heavenly dwelling place of which the temple at Jerusalem was only a distant symbol, and also the fact that his entrance into the heavenly sanctuary is accompanied by an insistent plea that the Father would preserve the disciples from evil, protect them against the evil one, and make them morally holy. Jesus' statement and his prayer must now be examined in somewhat greater detail.

The prayer of Jesus in John 17 is introduced by the words: "Jesus raised his eyes to heaven and said" (1). The synoptics also report that Jesus raised his eyes to heaven before the first multiplication of loaves (Mk. 6:41 par.), and the fourth gospel tells us that Jesus raised his eyes to heaven when he thanked God just before the raising of Lazarus from the dead (11:41). The action was a usual one at the beginning of any prayer. By contrast, the tax collector was so humbled by the memory of his sins that he did not dare raise his eyes to heaven (Lk. 18:13).

In John 17:1, however, the action has a special significance in view of the fact that the words Jesus goes on to speak show him already on the threshold, as it were, of eternity, halfway between this world and his Father.[42] (We may remark in passing that the synoptic gospels, too, in their accounts of the Last Supper, show Christ in the same condition, though in a less-marked degree.[43] (We recall that according to the fourth gospel both Jesus himself (3:13–21) and the bread of heaven which he identifies with himself (6:32, 33, 38, 41, 42, 50, 51, 58) have alike descended from heaven. Moreover, heaven is Jesus' permanent dwelling place (3:13). As Lagrange notes, it seems that from the beginning of his prayer, in 17:1, Jesus intends "to situate himself in the heavenly realm."[44] Thüsing points out that Jesus' earthly life was one long gaze directed to the Father, one ceaseless desire to return to him.[45] This is brought home to us by the repeated statements "I am going to the Father," which mark the public ministry of Christ in the fourth gospel: "I shall go back to the one who sent me" (7:33); "I know where I came from and where I am going" (8:14); "Where I am going, you cannot come" (8:21); "Jesus knew . . . that he had come from God and was returning to God" (13:3); "Where I am going you cannot follow me now" (13:36); "You know the way to the place where I am going" (14:4); "I am going away, and shall return" (14:28); "If you loved me you would have been glad to know that I am going to the Father" (14:28); "Now I am going to the one who sent me" (16:5); ". . . proved by my going to the Father and your seeing me no more" (16:10). In John 17 the long desire is on the point of fulfillment. Jesus no longer says, as he had earlier, "I am going to the Father" (with the verb *hypagein*), but "I am coming to you" (with *erchesthai*).

We must remind ourselves at this point that, in the Johannine vision of things, what saves men is neither the passion of Jesus by itself nor his resurrection by itself but the sequence of events that the evangelist calls the return of Jesus to his Father or the passage of Jesus from this world to his Father. This explains the paradoxical "I am going away, and shall return" of 14:28, and a number of other sayings that are at first hearing just as surprising. "Does this upset you? What if you should see the Son of Man ascend to where he was before? It is the spirit that gives life, the flesh has nothing to offer. The words I have spoken to you are spirit and life" (6:62–63). "Do not cling to me, because I have not yet ascended to the Father" (20:17).[46]

A careful examination of earlier sections of the fourth gospel already shows a certain parallelism between the return of Jesus to his Father and his journeys up to the temple at Jerusalem, especially his appearance in the temple in Chapters 7 and 8.[47] The parallelism corresponds to that which is implicit in Luke's scene of the child Jesus being discovered in the temple: "Did you not know that I must be busy with my Father's affairs?" (Lk. 2:49).[48] We are now in a position to determine more exactly the significance of the parallelism. Jesus' return to his Father, which will definitively guarantee the effectiveness of his redemptive activity, corresponds to the entrance of the high priest into the holy of holies on the Day of Atonement. As the entrance of the high priest into the holy of holies was the climactic moment in the rite of atonement, so the entrance of Christ into heaven will make possible the perfect glorification of the Father by the Son ("glorify your Son so that your Son may glorify you," 17:1), as well as the complete revelation of the Father's name to Jesus' disciples: "I have made your name known to them and will continue to make it known" (17:26). At his appearance in the temple Jesus had said to those listening: *"Where I am you cannot come"* (7:34). Speaking now as one who has already returned to his Father's house, Jesus declares in his prayer: "I want those you have given me to be with me *where I am,* so that they may always see the glory you have given me" (17:24). On both occasions we are confronted with a divine "I am" that is timeless (for in reality Jesus has never left his Father's house), yet, paradoxically, linked each time to a distinct stage in a history of salvation which unfolds in time.[49]

Jesus' return to his Father's house establishes him in a definitive and unqualified way as the priestly mediator whose duty it is to pray for those who have become his disciples. It is the function mentioned in Isaiah 53, where, by agreeing to be the expiatory victim for the sins of men, the Servant of Yahweh becomes their official mediator with God (52:12). In the discourses after the Supper, the same function has already been connected with the return of Jesus to the Father: "I tell you most solemnly, whoever believes in me will perform the same works as I do myself, he will perform even greater works, because I am going to the Father. Whatever you ask for in my name I will do, so that the Father may be glorified in the Son" (14:12–13). Jesus then adds, as if to show that he is infinitely greater than any ordinary intercessor: "If you ask [*me*] for anything *in my name*, I will do it" (14:14).[50] Lagrange adds an important qualification: "The issue here is not the effectiveness of any prayer whatsoever, but only that of the prayer of the faithful for the good of the Church; *that* prayer is always heard."[51]

In his great intercessory prayer in John 17, Jesus tells his disciples that he is going to leave and will no longer be visibly present as their protector. In fact, his departure is the reason for his prayer for them now. Since, moreover, the section of Chapter 17 in which he prays for his disciples is the central and most important panel in the triptych, it follows that the departure of Jesus is the principal reason for the prayer as a whole. Because he is returning to his Father's house, Jesus now asks the Father to protect his disciples from all evil and to give them a share in his own "consecration." The thought of Christ moves from his apostles to the Church whose duty it will be to mirror the divine holiness. This is why he addresses the Father as "Holy Father" (17:11). As R. E. Brown notes, we are reminded of the prescriptions in Leviticus: "Be

holy, for I, Yahweh your God, am holy" (19:2); "Be consecrated to me, because I, Yahweh, am holy, and I will set
you apart from all these peoples so that you may be mine"
(20:26; cf. 11:44).[52]

Each year, during the festival of atonement, the high priest
entered the holy of holies and restored to Israel its condition
as a holy people that was consecrated to Yahweh amid a
pagan world. So too, in John 17, Jesus the high priest enters
the dwelling of the Father and intercedes with him to keep
from sin the new people of God whom Jesus has won by his
redemptive sacrifice, to preserve it from the attacks of the
evil one, and to consecrate it by maintaining it in unity and
thus turning it, as it were, into a mirror of the unity between
Father and Son. The petition for "protection from the evil
one" (17:15) evidently recalls the Our Father (Mt. 6:13),
the prayer which Christ had given to his disciples.[53]

Here we have the reason why Jesus says he does not pray
for the world (17:9). The text in no way justifies speaking
of a Johannine particularism that is opposed to the universalism of the synoptics and St. Paul. In the fourth gospel the
Father gives his Son for the salvation of all men (3:16),
and the Son comes into the world not to condemn it but to
save it (3:17). So too it was in order to save the world that
the Father consecrated his Son a priest at his incarnation and
sent him into the world (10:36).

In John 17, however, the world for which Jesus does not
pray is a hostile mankind that rejects Christ. The glorified
Christ is not directly the priestly mediator for that group of
men, since it has no interest in him and even rejects him.
He is mediator with the Father for the believing community
of the Church. For this community he asks from the Father
the graces of holiness and unity that will make of it, in the
eyes of men who look on from outside, an abiding reason for
believing in Christ. This idea finds expression twice in John 17
(which is enough to prove that the salvation of the world in

its entirety has an important place in the prayer): "May they all be one. Father, may they be one in us, as you are in me and I am in you, so *that the world may believe it was you who sent me*. I have given them the glory you gave to me, that they may be one as we are one. With me in them and you in me, may they be so completely one, *that the world will realize that it was you who sent me*" (17:21–22). In order, then, to accomplish the salvation of the world, Christ the priest counts on the influence of his Church's oneness and holiness, and it is for this reason that in John 17 the Church is the sole *immediate* beneficiary of his prayer, even though he looks, through the Church's action, to the good of all mankind. As Barrett puts it, the hostile world must cease to be the world in this sense and enter, via the Church, upon the way of salvation. We should recall here that in the Old Testament the setting apart of Israel was, in God's plan, for the benefit of all mankind (cf. the promise to Abraham in Gn. 12:3).

The various ideas we have been proposing are briefly and powerfully synthesized in 1 John 2:1–2: "I am writing this, my children, to stop you sinning; but if anyone should sin, we have our advocate with the Father, Jesus Christ, who is just; he is the sacrifice that takes our sins away, and not only ours, but the whole world's."

Before the Father the glorified Christ is the advocate or intercessor—the paraclete—for the members of the Church who are still exposed to sinning. The word paraclete does not have precisely the same meaning here that it has in the discourses after the Supper where it is applied to the Holy Spirit (Jn. 14:15, 26; 15:26; 16:7). In both cases it suggests the idea of someone who is called upon for help.[54] But the Spirit receives the title of paraclete chiefly because, as the divine teacher, he gives the disciples an interior understanding of the revelation brought by Jesus and, in the last analysis, of Jesus himself who is the way, the truth, and the life.[55] Christ, on the other hand, is called a paraclete (the term is not really a title as applied to him) because he helps his disciples by being their priestly mediator and intercessor with the Father, along the lines foretold in Isaiah 53. It is no accident that Jesus is called "just" in 1 John 2:1, as the Servant had been in Isaiah 53:11: "the just one, my servant" ("the just one" is omitted in JB; cf. note on the passage); the reminiscence is deliberate.

There is more to be said. Christ, who thus intercedes for his disciples does not limit his intercession to believers alone, as some of the language in John 17 might lead us to think. In fact, on the cross he became "the sacrifice that takes our sins away, and not only ours, but the whole world's" (1 Jn. 2:2). Here we have a new reminiscence of Isaiah 53 (cf. *'asham— hilasmos* in 53:10). As in Isaiah 53, the atoning sacrifice which Christ offered in surrendering his life is the basis for his role as priestly mediator.

The world *hilasmos* is a highly significant one. It is often translated as "propitiation," and this is indeed in keeping with the use of the verb *hilaskesthai* in classical Greek where it meant "to appease, render favorable." But, as A. Richardson points out, whereas in pagan religions man sets out to appease the angered gods, such an idea has no place in the Bible and especially in the New Testament; for in the latter there is no question of exercising some influence, properly so called, on God to make him change his attitude, but only of removing the stains of sin through means prescribed by God.[56]

Moreover, in the Septuagint *hilaskesthai* and *hilasmos* usually correspond to a Hebrew root (*kpr*) which means to obliterate or expiate. It is better, therefore, to translate the *hilasmos* of 1 John 2:2 as "expiatory victim," just as it is better to translate the *hilaskesthai* of Hebrews 2:17 as "to make expiation for sins." It was in order to carry out this task, says the author of Hebrews, that the Son of God became a compassionate and trustworthy high priest.[57] It is possible that the *hilasmos* of 1 John 2:2 is intended as an allusion to the expiatory sacrifice (*'asham*) of Isaiah 53:10.

In any event, the same noun *hilasmos* that is used in the New Testament only in 1 John 2:2 and 4:10, both times with reference to Christ, is also used in the Greek Bible for the Day of Atonement (*hēmera exilasmou*). This, we think, strikingly confirms the validity of the connection we see between the prayer in John 17 and the liturgy of atonement. The texts of 1 John 2:2 and 4:10 show that John had this connection in mind.

The texts would have the same force if we were to suppose, with some writers,[58] that, like the word *hilastērion* which St. Paul applies to Christ in Romans 3:25, the word *hilasmos* alludes to the mercy seat or throne of mercy, that is, the cover of the ark on which the cherubims stood. For this greatest symbol of Yahweh's special presence, this focal point of worship according to the Mosaic law, was also the spot at which the climactic rite in the liturgy of atonement took place.

The Letter to the Hebrews offers a further confirmation. But since we shall be presenting in the next chapter a synthesis of the teaching of this Letter on priesthood, we shall say only a few words on the point here.

Exegetes have often noted the doctrinal similarities between the fourth gospel and the Letter to the Hebrews. The similarities are especially striking in the prayer of Jesus in John 17.[59] The following common traits may be noted. In both, Christ is seen chiefly as a priest who is also the sacrificial victim; Christ is the sanctifier and others are "sanctified" by him (cf. the use of *hagiazein* in Jn. 17:17, 19 and in Heb. 2:11; 10:10; 13:12); Christ receives his glory from the Father (Jn. 17:1–5 and Heb. 5:4–5); believers have been given to Jesus by his Father (Jn. 17:2, 6, 9; cf. Heb. 2:13: "Here I am with the children whom God has given me"); Christ rescues his disciples from the devil's power (Jn. 17:15 and Heb.

2:14); the task of Jesus is to lead men to perfection (with the verb *teleioun:* Jn. 17:4 and Heb. 10:1, 14; 11:40); finally the two functions of sacrificial offering and intercession which are specific to the priest and show that the prayer of Jesus in John 17 has an authentically priestly character, are attributed to Christ by the author of the Letter to the Hebrews who lays great stress on them.

Once we admit that John 17 is to be read in the light of the Day of Atonement, we have a further likeness between John 17 and the Letter to the Hebrews. For in the latter the parallelism between the redemption wrought by Christ and the Jewish festival of atonement plays a large role; in it, too, the redemptive activity of Christ is completed only when he enters the heavenly sanctuary, just as the climactic point in the liturgy of atonement was reached when the high priest entered the holy of holies in the temple.

We may draw attention, finally, to one more parallelism, though a much more hypothetical one. A. Pelletier would have us see in Luke 23:43–45 an authentic parallel with the Letter to the Hebrews and thus also with the fourth gospel.[60] If such a point of contact were confirmed, it would be added to an existing twofold set of similarities. On the one hand, there are the similarities between the third gospel and the Letter to the Hebrews, similarities so impressive that some have made St. Luke the author of this Letter.[61] On the other hand, there are the numerous affinities between the third and fourth gospels; these may be found almost everywhere in Luke's writing, but especially in the infancy narratives and the narratives of the passion and resurrection.[62]

Pelletier notes, to begin with, that the veil that is torn at the death of Jesus was the outer curtain that was hung before the opening into the sacred antechamber and was intended to hide from profane eyes the site of Yahweh's Dwelling and the rites that went on there. Ever since the ark and its accessories had been lost in the sixth century, the outer curtain had acquired a greater importance than the inner curtain which hung directly before the holy of holies. According to Pelletier, the sign of the torn veil is to be connected with the entrance of Christ through the veil into the heavenly holy of holies, of which Hebrews 10:19–22 speaks: "In other words, brothers, through the blood of Jesus we have the right to enter the sanctuary, by a new way which he has opened for us, a living opening through the curtain, that is to say, his body. And we have the supreme high priest over all the house of God. So as we go in, let us be sincere in heart."

Admittedly (as Pelletier himself observes), the torn veil has certainly a different significance in the first and second gospels.[63] It is only in the gospel of St. Luke that the sign of the torn veil would refer to the entrance of Jesus into the heavenly sanctuary. The words of Jesus to the Good Thief, "Indeed, I promise you, today you will be with me in paradise" (Lk. 23:43), would have reference to the opening to all men of the eternal sanctuary into which Christ has entered before us.[64]

Chapter 3

The Greatness of Christ's Sacrifice and Priesthood

IN THIS CHAPTER we want to determine what it is that makes
the sacrifice and priesthood of Christ uniquely great. We shall
work toward the answer along two lines. First of all, we
shall show how the Old Testament concepts of sacrifice and
priesthood are transposed and spiritualized in the New Testament. Indeed, the beginnings of this process are to be found
well advanced in Isaiah 53. The completion of the process is
reached, however, only in the New Testament, and notably
in the Johannine writings. Secondly, we shall seek support
in the parallel teaching of the Letter to the Hebrews on the
priesthood and sacrifice of Christ. A brief exposition of this
teaching will enable us to make a fruitful comparison with
the data given in John.

It will be more evident in this chapter than in the first two
that we must not limit ourselves to the narrow bounds of
John 17. The inquiry must extend from the unusual anticipations to be found in the Old Testament to the whole Johannine
corpus (fourth gospel, first letter of John, and Apocalypse)
as well as to the Letter to the Hebrews whose theological
perspectives are very close to those of John on the subject with
which we are dealing. At the same time we must always bear
in mind our chief objective, which is a deeper understanding

of the important teaching on the priesthood that is implicit in John 17. As we shall show, the main theme of John 17— the unity of believers, modeled on the unity of Father and Son—which is continued in the first letter of John, is connected under the surface with the liturgical and priestly texts of the Old Testament.

We are concerned here simultaneously with sacrifice and priesthood. It could not be otherwise, since the two realities are closely linked and it is impossible to speak of the one without reference to the other. It is primarily because of the definitive and abiding effectiveness of Christ's sacrifice that his priesthood is unique in kind. But, conversely, the exceptional effectiveness of the sacrifice depends on the transcendence of the offerer.

THE SPIRITUALIZATION OF OLD TESTAMENT CONCEPTIONS OF SACRIFICE AND PRIESTHOOD IN ISAIAH 53

THE RELIGIOUS SENSE is based on the twofold conviction that man is separated from God, the Wholly Other, by an impassable gulf and that, nonetheless, man must, if he is to live, receive support and protection from this Wholly Other.[1] In Israel, belief in a God who was one and incorporeal led to a considerable development of these two convictions.

In the history of mankind priestly functions have not always been handed over to specialists. Even in Israel these functions were, in early times, exercised by the heads of families and tribal chieftains. This accounts for the expression "be a father and a priest" for an individual or group (Jg. 17:10; 18:19). Priesthood as exercised by kings (David and Solomon are important examples) is simply a continuation of this non-professional priesthood. But the history of Israel shows this natural priesthood of leaders and kings disappearing before the functional priesthood of the levitic order.[2]

The pagan priesthood in the peoples with whom Israel came in contact was occupied with various forms of nature worship; the aim was to bend the divine power to man's purposes by means of suitable rites. The functional priesthood of the chosen people, on the contrary, was intended to relate the people to a God who was one, transcendent, holy in the extreme, and essentially moral, and who in sheer mercy had condescended to enter into a covenant with Israel.

The history of Old Testament priesthood is very complicated. It can be said, however, that Wellhausen's theory, which assigned a postexilic origin to all the priestly traditions, is today discredited, at least in part, in the eyes of many critics. The origin of the priestly tradition is rather in a real tribe of Levi. It was from this tribe that Moses recruited the priests in charge of the ark; it was from it that the priests of the various sanctuaries were chosen after the settlement in Canaan. The reigns of David and Solomon saw the pre-eminence of the Jerusalem priesthood. The Deuteronomic reform under Josiah attempted to restore the levitic priesthood to its early purity and to rid it of any compromises with the local Canaanite sanctuaries. In the Torah of Ezekiel, which was composed in exile, it is decreed that only the sons of Zadok, who had remained faithful to the national sanctuary "when Israel strayed far from me," are to retain the privileges of priesthood (Ezk. 44:15–16). This is how the distinction between priests and levites arose.

Later on the high priest assumed increasing importance, and the priesthood even became linked to Messianism. We can see this tendency already making its appearance in Jeremiah 33:14–22, a postexilic oracle which shows royal and priestly powers linked together in the period of Messianic salvation. The author of Ecclesiasticus seems to make descent from Aaron more important than descent from David (Si. 45:24–26). We have already noted that in the New Testament period people expected an Aaronic Messiah as well as a Davidic Messiah.

The levitic priest had three functions. First of all, he could give oracles. In early times people went to consult the man of God who gave answer by means of the divinatory ephod (the Urim and Thummim): cf. Numbers 27:21; Deuteronomy 33:8; 1 Samuel 14:41 (LXX); etc. From David's time on, this oracular function was left to the prophets. A second important function of the priest was to watch over the Law and to instruct the people of God in it: cf. Deuteronomy 33:10; Jeremiah 18:18; Ezekiel 7:26; Ecclesiasticus 45:26–27 (Hebrew). Whereas the prophets aimed at making God's viewpoint understood in the face of changing historical situations, the priest's role was to preserve and teach what was laid up in tradition. In late Judaism the scribes and teachers of the Law increasingly take over the priest's teaching role. Finally, the priest had to carry out the liturgical services (cf. Dt. 33:10; 2 K. 23:9; etc.); as R. de Vaux says, "The priest was, then, in a very real sense, the 'minister of the altar' and this Christian expression can trace its ancestry far back into the Old Testament."[3]

Priests were set apart from the rest of the people for functions which the layman was forbidden to perform under penalty of death (Nb. 18:7). This explains the strict demands laid on them and the stern reproaches addressed to them by the prophets for their moral failings: Hosea 4:10–11; Malachi 2:8–9; etc. In the verses immediately preceding those just referred to, Malachi gives clear expression to the traditional conception of a priest: he shows us Levi, first with his attention directed to God and filled with a sense of God's transcendence, then adding to this sense of God a virtuous life and a profound knowledge of the Law. This was why he converted many: "He respected me and stood in awe of my name. The teaching of truth was in the mouth, falsehood was not to be found on his lips; he walked with me in integrity and virtue; he converted many from sinning" (Ml. 2:5–6).

All priestly functions were summed up in that of mediation: in the name of men they approached God, and in the name of God they returned to men (cf. Ex. 18:18–20, the words of Jethro, priest of Midian, to Moses). Consequently, when the levites were to be consecrated to the service of Yahweh "the sons of Israel" had to "lay their hands on them" (Nb. 8:10). Therefore, too, the pectoral of the high priest had twelve stones set in it, bearing the names of the twelve tribes of Israel (Ex. 28:17–21), and the shoulder straps of the ephod likewise had two precious stones set in them, each of them engraved with the names of six of the tribes (Ex. 28:9–11).

It can be said that, broadly speaking, the priests acted as a barrier between the Israelites and the fearsome majesty of Yahweh. On the one hand, they "carried" the sins of the people, and on the other, they won pardon for the people by means of the sacrifices which it was their duty to be constantly offering: cf. Exodus 28:38; 29:36; 9:15; 18:1, 5. (In fulfilling this duty, they transformed the temple into "a huge slaughterhouse," as one writer aptly put it.[4])

Too often the theologians are satisfied with saying that the sacrifices of the Old Testament were a distant preparation and prefiguration of the sacrifice of Christ. In fact, however, there is an abyssal difference between the animal sacrifices of the old covenant and Christ's sacrifice. How could such a shift have taken place? With G. von Rad we think that this extraordinary transformation is unintelligible if we do not advert to the biblical tradition on the prophets who act as intercessors.[5] The example of Jeremiah, Ezekiel, and especially Moses are particularly enlightening. Against this background we will be better able to understand what we are being told in Isaiah 53. For, despite all that is radically new in the passage, there had been a preparation for this oracle in the experience of the prophets, their sanctity, and their commitment to the service of God.

In a remarkable study on mediation in the Old Testament, A. Robert makes some remarks that are highly important.[6] It is true enough that the prophets were primarily mediators of revelation and instruments God used in order to speak to men. But the Bible also shows them as intercessors. It would indeed be going too far to say that the priests who represented the people in acts of worship remained mute and simply performed rites. At the same time, however, although the Scriptures give us so many details on the liturgical ceremonies the priests were to perform, they say nothing about the prayers the priests spoke, except for the blessing of which we learn in Numbers 6:22–26. On the other hand, the Scriptures dwell on the mediatorial prayer of prophets. Such prayer did not consist of predetermined formulas like the just-mentioned blessing of the sons of Israel, but of entreaties that sprang spontaneously from the often dramatic lives of the men of God and from their burning love for God and the men for whom they regarded themselves as spiritually responsible. Because the prophets were holy men and intimates of the Lord, the people relied on their prayerful intervention with him and gladly had recourse to it.

In varying degrees and various forms, all the great prophets acted as intercessors: Samuel (1 S. 7:8–10; 12:19–23; 15:11), Elijah (1 K. 17:20–22), Elisha (2 K. 4:33; 6:17), Amos (7:1–6), Hosea (14:2–4), Isaiah (37:4), etc. The same was true of the patriarchs, who were likened to prophets; cf. Genesis 20:7: "He [Abraham] is a prophet and can intercede on your behalf for your life." We cannot but recall the moving prayer of Abraham for Sodom and Gomorrah (Gn. 18:22–23). Or the intercession of Job (Jb. 42:8); his friends offer a sacrifice to win pardon for themselves, but it is due to the prayer of Job, "my servant," that God does not punish their folly as it deserves. In point of fact, material sacrifice is not enough to recover the favor of Yahweh (1 S. 3:14; 7:9; 15:22).

Jeremiah represents a turning point in the prophetic tradition; G. von Rad defines it as the irruption of the prophetic task into the personal life of the man of God.[7] We cannot indeed say that there is a radical difference between him and the earlier prophets, since Elijah, Amos, and Hosea, too, had suffered greatly from the heavy mission imposed on them. Nonetheless, in Jeremiah we find a much more poignant experience, in which the prophet is, as it were, torn asunder. As P. Volz has very perceptively noted,[8] we see in the soul of Jeremiah a kind of dissociation between the herald of Yahweh, who pitilessly foretells the condemnation of the guilty people, and the compassionate man who seeks to fend off the divine judgment from his compatriots and suffers greatly at the thought of the disasters threatening his country: Jeremiah 4:19–21; 8:18–23; 14:7–9, 19–22; 16:16–18; 32:16–25; 42:2–4. While the prophet takes God's side, the man pleads and prays for the people. May we not see in Jeremiah an anticipation of the idea of mediation which emerges so strongly in Isaiah 53?

In quite a different way, Ezekiel bears witness to the same personalization of the prophetic task. The son of Buzi is appointed as a sentry for the house of Israel and must devote his whole life to his ministry (Ezk. 33:1–9). His reproach to the false prophets is that "you have never ventured into the breach; you have never bothered to fortify the House of Israel, to hold fast in battle on the day of Yahweh" (Ezk. 13:5)—images which doubtless signify intercessory prayer. In addition, Yahweh requires Ezekiel to sleep for many days, first on his left side, then on his right, in order to bear successively the sins of the House of Israel and the sins of the House of Judah (4:4–8). These men of God, of course, had often had to perform symbolic actions. What is new here is that the prophet must bear the sins of the people. As

W. Zimmerli observes,[9] the sins of the chosen people awakens profound echoes in the personal life of the son of Buzi; he suffers from them as though he himself were the guilty one, whereas in fact he is innocent. Once again, we have here a conception that leads toward the "vicarious" suffering as developed throughout Isaiah 53. We shall come back to this point a little further on.

We have deliberately left Moses to the last, for several reasons: he is the greatest personage of the Old Testament, a kind of superprophet; even as regards intercession he represents a high point never surpassed in Judaism; finally, the way in which the writers speak of his intercession shows the influence at several points of the language of the prophets who came after Moses.

Like the latter, but much more than they, Moses was first and foremost a mediator of revelation. But he was also a mediator through intercession. The part of the Pentateuch that critics call the Yahwist document often mentions Moses' intervention through prayer with a view to obtaining the salvation of the people: Exodus 8:4, 8, 9, 24–27; 9:28–29, 33; 33:12–17; Numbers 11:2. But the Elohist too provides us with a striking example of the power of Moses' intercession: in Exodus 17:11–13 the Israelites are victorious over the Amalekites as long as Moses keeps his arms raised, and they weaken when Moses lets his arms fall. In a reminiscence of Ezekiel 13:5 (quoted above), Psalms 106:23 says: "He [Yahweh] talked of putting an end to them and would have done, if Moses his chosen had not stood in the breach, confronting him, and deflecting his destructive anger." The Psalmist is evidently alluding to the incident of the golden calf and to Moses' plea for pardon (Ex. 32:11–14). A little further on (Ex. 32:32), with reference to the same incident, Moses makes Yahweh this noble offer: "And yet, if it pleased you to forgive this sin of theirs . . . ! But if not, then blot me out from the book that you have written." Deuteronomy, in turn, paints a picture of Moses as a suffering intercessor, which is a considerable step in the direction of Isaiah 53: "Then I fell prostrate before Yahweh; as before, I passed forty days and forty nights eating no bread and drinking no water, for all the sin you had committed in doing what was displeasing to Yahweh, thus arousing his anger. . . . And once more Yahweh heard my prayer" (Dt. 9:18–19).

We must now return to the Servant of Isaiah 53. In the light of what we have seen he now appears to be a living synthesis of priestly and prophetic mediation.

In Chapter 1 of this book we showed that even if he does not have the name, the Servant of Yahweh does have the function of a priest, since he offers his life in expiatory sacrifice (Is. 53:10). What we have been saying in this chapter about Old Testament priests who bore the sins of the people, and about Ezekiel, the prophet-priest who bore successively the sins of the House of Israel and the sins of the House of Judah, now suggests a further observation: It is as a priest that the Servant comes before us "bearing our sufferings" and "carrying our sorrows" (Verse 4) and "bearing the faults of many" (12). In other words, the prophetic description in Isaiah 53 has, almost throughout, a priestly character.

W. Zimmerli has made a close study of the use of the expression "to bear the sin" (*nasa 'awon*) in the Old Testament.[10] The expression occurs thirty-five times, if we include the two somewhat divergent uses in Ezekiel 18:19–20 (where *'awon* is preceded by the preposition "in": to bear responsibility *in* the sin of someone). The uses may readily be divided into two groups. There are, first of all, eight passages that belong neither to the priestly code nor to Ezekiel. In these, the phrase almost always means to put up with the sin of another forgivingly; that is, to pardon it (Ex. 34:7; Nb. 14:18; Is. 33:24; Ho. 14:3; Mi. 7:18; Ps. 32:5; 85:3). The only passage causing difficulty is the reply of Cain in Genesis 4:13; it can be taken to mean either "my sin is too great to be pardoned," or "my sin is too great for me to bear."

Of the other twenty-seven passages eighteen belong to the priestly code and nine to Ezekiel; all have a context that deals with priesthood. The meaning in these passages is either that a person is responsible for the sanctuary or the priesthood (Nb. 18:1, 23), or, very often, that he has violated various regulations concerning worship (Ex. 28:43; Lv. 5:1, 17; 7:18; 17:26; Nb. 5:31; 30:16; Ezk. 44:10, 12), or, finally, that he takes away the sins committed by others (in these instances, Aaron, the scapegoat, or Ezekiel is the subject of the verb; Lv. 10:17; 16:22; Ex. 28:38; Ezk. 4:4, 5, 6).

The conclusion with regard to the Servant is clear: when Isaiah 53 emphasizes, in almost identical terms, that the Servant bears the moral wretchedness of sinful mankind, the author is transposing the priestly language of the Old Testament; for this transposition the prophetic experience of Ezekiel had already paved the way. Other spiritualizations of the same type in Isaiah 53 confirm the one we have just pointed out. For example, the traditional formulas "to see a posterity" and "to prolong one's days" acquire a new meaning when applied to the Servant (Is. 53:10). Throughout Isaiah 53 the Old Testament liturgy undergoes a considerable transformation because of the fact that the Servant of Yahweh is not content to carry the faults of others in a purely ritual way but identifies himself wholeheartedly with sinners, adding intercessory prayer to his sacrifice and thus entering the prophetic mainstream.

What we have been saying expresses only very imperfectly the unique greatness of the Servant's sacrifice and therefore of his priesthood as well. We must now attempt to pinpoint what is radically new in this sacrifice and priesthood.

The newness is to be seen, first of all, in the fact that in order to effect the reconciliation of sinners with God the

Servant accepts unheard of suffering and endures it in silence. Before him, Jeremiah too had been dragged like a sheep to slaughter, but he had called down God's vengeance on his persecutors. Jeremiah spoke the moving words: "The wound of the daughter of my people wounds me too" (8:21), but it would not have occurred to him that his tribulations, if generously accepted, might help save Israel and that for this reason Yahweh himself had willed them as part of his plan for saving men.[11]

The newness of the Servant's sacrifice and priesthood is also due to the fact that the sinners for whom he atones are not only Israelites but a sinful multitude of men without distinction or limitation. Those for whom the Servant suffers are several times called "many" (Hebrew: *rabbim;* LXX: *polloi*): cf. Isaiah 52:14; 53:11–12. In these passages, "many" were appalled at the sight of him; he will justify "many"; he will have "many" (men) for his heritage;[12] he bore the faults of "many." The context shows that these "many" were in fact "the crowds" (52:14; 53:12), or even all sinners (53:6, where "all of us" occurs twice): "We had all gone astray like sheep, each taking his own way, and Yahweh burdened him with the sins of all of us." The universalist perspective has already been established in the first two Servant songs. In 42:3, 6 we learn that the Servant is to be mediator of a revelation and a covenant that will profit the pagan nations. In 49:6 we are told that the limited task of achieving Israel's political restoration would be unworthy of him, since Yahweh intends to "make you the light of the nations so that my salvation may reach to the ends of the earth." It cannot be too often repeated that the Servant's role is purely religious, not political, and that it embraces all of mankind.[13]

Finally, and above all, the radical newness of the Servant's sacrifice and priesthood is due to the fact that he voluntarily offers himself as an expiatory victim and that God himself intends this sacrifice and makes it part of his plan for salva-

tion. Such an unimaginable conception was enough to dumb-
found the prophet's contemporaries. That is why Isaiah 53
begins with the question: "Who could believe what we have
heard, and to whom has the power of Yahweh been revealed?"[14]

We must bear in mind at this point that Israelite worship
would have nothing to do with human sacrifice. The question
asked by the people in Micah must therefore be taken as a
purely rhetorical one: "With what gift shall I come into
Yahweh's presence and bow down before God on high?
. . . Must I give my first-born for what I have done
wrong, the fruit of my body for my own sin?" (6:6–7). It is
true enough that now and then in the Old Testament the
punishment merited by an individual is extended to the group
of which he is a member. But these are simply cases of collective retribution, which, according to the mentality of the
time, were justified by the fact that the guilt weighs on all
members of the group. Before the Servant poems were written Ezekiel had already stressed the individual nature of responsibility. It could only be very odd, then, to hear, in
Isaiah 53, of a just man carrying out the plan of Yahweh by
freely atoning and giving his life for sinners. How much more
astounding when this just man is presented to us as being the
Messiah, the eschatological Saviour!

It is sometimes said that we have an earlier example of such
extraordinary generosity in the passage in Exodus where
Moses seems to offer himself as a victim to win pardon for
the guilty: "And yet, if it pleased you to forgive this sin of
theirs . . . ! But if not, then blot me out from the book that
you have written" (32:32). But, in fact, Moses is here simply
presenting alternatives: let the Hebrews be spared, or else let
him share their fate and perish with them.[15] In this passage we are far from the tragic situation of Isaiah 53.

There is another very important aspect to the amazing shift
in Old Testament sacrificial ideas. The Levitic ritual required

that any animal to be offered must be without physical blemish. In Isaiah 53, too, the expiatory victim is without blemish, but here it is the Servant's moral holiness that makes him acceptable to God.

There is another transposition of the same kind that would be highly significant if solidly established. The Massoretic text of Isaiah 52:14–15 reads: "Just as many were appalled at the sight of him—his disfigured appearance was no longer that of a man, his disfigured look was no longer that of men —so he will sprinkle many peoples." As J. Skinner[16] points out, this enigmatic text may mean that although the multitude looks down on him as an impure man (later he seems implicitly to be compared to a leper), the Servant will nonetheless purify multitudes of sinners. In this interpretation, the sprinkling performed by Moses in sealing the covenant at Sinai is here transposed: "Half of the blood Moses took up and put into basins, the other half he cast on the altar. And taking the Book of the Covenant he read it to the listening people, and they said, 'We will observe all that Yahweh has decreed; we will obey.' Then Moses took the blood and cast it towards the people. 'This' he said 'is the blood of the Covenant that Yahweh has made with you, containing all these rules" (Ex. 24:6–8).

Moses had sealed the covenant of Sinai by sprinkling the chosen people with the blood of the victims. The Servant will sprinkle, in a spiritual way, many nations with the purifying blood of his martyrdom. Such a transposition is antecedently all the more plausible since in Isaiah 42:6 the Servant is explicitly said to be, like Moses, the mediator of a covenant, and since, in addition, Ezekiel foresees a metaphorical sprinkling as a means of communicating a share in the blessings of the Messianic age: "I shall pour clean water over you and you will be cleansed; I shall cleanse you of all your defilement and all your idols. I shall give you a new heart, and put a new spirit in you" (36:25–26). Here the ritual cleansing with purifying water is transposed to the eschatological period. Ezekiel may simultaneously be alluding to the liturgy for the Day of Atonement (cf. Lv. 16:16, 19, 30).[17] Psalm 51 is undoubtedly referring to what Ezekiel says, while making it apply to the present situation of the Psalmist himself: "Purify me with hyssop until I am clean; wash me until I am whiter than snow" (Verse 7).

The question must be asked, however: Are we justified in accepting the reading of the Massoretic text—"he will sprinkle many peoples"—as the original? In the past most commentators have emended the text in accordance with the Septuagint, which reads: "So will the crowds be astonished (*thaumasontai*) at him." But E. Dhorme says that the authors of the Greek version "are suspect of having guessed at the meaning from the context, as they often do in other passages."[18] It is difficult, in fact, to see what Hebrew words lie behind their translation. Furthermore, the Massoretic reading is confirmed by the Isaiah text from Qumran and by the Syriac version which understands the words to mean: "He will purify many peoples." For these reasons we side with those who retain the Massoretic text, undeterred by grammatical difficulties which are far from insoluble.[19] This reading is increasingly favored by present-day commentators, who are more and more avoiding emendations.[20]

THE SACRIFICIAL AND PRIESTLY CONCEPTIONS OF ISAIAH 53 AND THE NEW TESTAMENT, ESPECIALLY THE JOHANNINE WRITINGS

IT HAS SEEMED NECESSARY to spend some time on the Old Testament preparations that led up to the great oracle in Isaiah 53. This last passage is very important if we are to understand what happened to the ideas of sacrifice and priesthood in the new religion that Christ began. The spiritualization that Christ himself carried out was irreversible, and the New Testament writers take it over and complete it, in an extraordinary manner.

Before going into what the Johannine writings have to say to us in this regard, we must say a few words about the accounts of the Last Supper in St. Paul (1 Co. 11:23–25) and the synoptic gospels (Mk. 14:22–25; Mt. 26:26–29; Lk. 22:14–20), for all these accounts clearly link up with the transposition already effected in Isaiah 53. The fourth gospel contains several echoes of these accounts.

A characteristic of these accounts, and one that we shall find in the Johannine texts as well, is the reference both to the Mosaic institutions that are being transformed and to the prophecies that are being fulfilled. We are referred, to begin with, to the oracle in Jeremiah 31:31–34 on the new covenant, and to the Servant of Yahweh who gives his life for the sins of the many. Even though it lacks the Matthean addition "for the forgiveness of sins" (Mt. 26:28), the formula used in the second gospel, "the blood . . . which is to be poured out for many" (Mk. 14:24) is a clear allusion to Isaiah 53. The Pauline formula (almost identical with that of Luke), "This cup is the new covenant in my blood" (1 Co. 11:25), picks up the expression "new covenant" which Jeremiah had coined.

In addition, these accounts recall the rites performed at the sealing of the Sinai covenant, as described in Exodus.[21] The last meal of Jesus with his disciples is one that seals a covenant through table fellowship and thus is of one kind with the sacred meal shared by Moses, Aaron, Nadab, Abihu, and seventy elders of Israel on the holy mountain in the presence of Yahweh (Ex. 24:9–11). In addition, the words of Jesus, "This is my blood, the blood of the covenant" (Mt. 26:28), use the language Moses used when he sprinkled the people with the blood of the sacrificial victims and said: "This is the blood of the Covenant" (Ex. 24:8).

However, all these echoes should not make us lose sight of the fact that the Eucharistic mystery as such did not exist in the Mosaic religion. It is one of the radically new things in the Christian dispensation, and is connected with the redemptive incarnation. This newness does not mean, on the other hand, that there were not numerous preparations for the Eucharist in the Old Testament.[22]

We may turn now to those elements in the fourth gospel that point in the same direction and allow us to see in Jesus the sacrificial victim and priest of the new covenant. We shall concentrate on four such elements: the designation of Christ as a lamb, his consecration by the Father, his consecration of himself in John 17, and the great prayer for unity of John 17.

There has been a great deal of discussion of the Baptist's words about the lamb of God who takes away the sins of the world (Jn. 1:29, 36).[23] The best explanation is undoubtedly the one that distinguishes the meaning given the words by the Baptist himself from the deeper meaning intended by the evangelist. On the lips of the Baptist, the title "lamb of God" may simply refer to the lamb of the apocalypses who takes moral evil away from the world; cf. Testament of Joseph 19:8; Enoch 90:38 (according to the most probable reading); Revelation 17:4. But in the mind of the evangelist the same title certainly has a much deeper meaning, and the parallel text, 1 John 3:5, allows us to determine it. In this latter text we read that Christ "appeared in order to abolish sin, and that in him there is no sin." The context (cf. 2:2 and 4:10: Christ as expiatory victim; 1:7 and 5:6: the blood of Christ) forces us to think of Christ as the Servant who exercises the priestly office of taking upon himself the sins of mankind in order to remove them; who lets himself be led as a sheep to slaughter, though he has done no wrong; who offers himself in expiatory sacrifice (Is. 53:4, 7, 9–10). In addition, the symbolic name "lamb" seems intended to remind the reader of the Passover lamb of the Jewish liturgy (cf. 1 Co. 5:7: "Christ, our passover, has been sacrificed"). The two references to the Pentateuch and to Isaiah 53 are analogous to those found in the accounts of the Last Supper. They are deeply meaningful and complement each other, since it is by acting as the Servant of Isaiah 53, who is both priest and victim—that is, by giving his life for men—that Christ will become the Christians' Passover lamb.

The Johannine account of the passion confirms our exegesis. Jesus is condemned to death about the sixth hour (19:14); that is, at the moment when the priests were beginning to sacrifice the Passover lambs in the temple. In the hyssop stick which holds the vinegar-soaked sponge offered to Christ by one of the soldiers (19:29), we are perhaps intended to see an allusion to the spray of hyssop dipped in lamb's blood that was used to mark the doors of Israelite houses (Ex. 12:22).[24] In any case, when John says of the soldier who does not break the legs of the dead Jesus that by his action the words of Scripture are being fulfilled: "Not one bone of his will be broken," he is referring both to the ritual prescription for the Passover lamb (Ex. 12:46) and to the divine protection promised in Psalm 34:24 to the persecuted just men of whom the Servant of Yahweh is the perfect example. In the next Verse (Jn. 19:37), the suffering Servant is even more clearly set before us by the citation of the related prophecy of Zechariah: "They will look on the one whom they have pierced" (12:10).

The consecration that Christ received from his Father (Jn. 10:36) has been explained in two ways. Some have connected it with the consecration of Jeremiah before his birth (Jr. 1:5; Si. 49:7).[25] In both instances God sets someone apart, even before his coming into this world, because God intends to speak to men through this individual; thus, after speaking to us through the prophets, God now speaks to us through his Son (Heb. 1:1–2). But, as we noted in Chapter 1, other commentators prefer to think of priests and to say that Jesus was consecrated a priest. As in Hebrews 5:5, so in John, Jesus receives the high priestly dignity from his Father. And, in point of fact, in New Testament times people thought of priests when they spoke of consecrated individuals.[26]

These two interpretations are by no means exclusive of each other since Jesus was conscious of being the Servant of God who resembled both prophets and priests. Nonetheless, the priestly perspective is certainly to the fore in John 10:36, for there is an evident connection between the consecration meant here and the consecration in 17:19. In short, if the Father consecrates Christ, it is that Christ may then consecrate himself and offer himself as a victim.

This view is confirmed by the immediate context of John 10:36. In the parable of the Good Shepherd, Jesus repeats as many as five times that the good shepherd gives his life (literally: "lays [down] his soul") for his sheep (10:11, 15, 17, and twice in 18). This very un-Greek expression is simply a transcription of Isaiah 53:10, where the Servant is said to offer himself in expiatory sacrifice. Now it is clear that the consecration of Jesus by the Father in 10:36 is closely connected with the description Jesus has just given of his role as good shepherd (Verses 26–30). This amounts to saying that the good shepherd of John 10 is the Servant of Isaiah 53 who is priest and victim. Need we be reminded that this extraordinary oracle expresses the idea that the Servant's atonement will restore the spiritual unity of the scattered flock? "We had all gone astray like sheep, each taking his own way, and Yahweh burdened him with the sins of all of us" (Is. 53:6).

It must be emphasized that the conception of priesthood implicit in Isaiah 53 greatly extended in John 10:36. For, to say that the Son of God was consecrated a priest at the moment of his being sent into the world amounts to saying that he is a *priest in his very being as the incarnate Son of God*. The two concepts of priest and mediator are closely connected. A mediator acts as intermediary between two or more parties with which he has something in common. A priest is "consecrated" for the purpose of acting as intermediary between the holy God and men. By the very fact that divinity and manhood are united in him, the incarnate Son of God is already the perfect priestly mediator and infinitely superior to all other priests.

The same reference to Isaiah 53 and the same transcending of that oracle are to be found even more clearly in the priestly prayer of John 17. On earth Jesus has glorified his Father; now he asks the Father to glorify him in turn "with that glory I had with you before ever the world was" (17:1–5). If he, Jesus, is glorified, he will be able to continue and bring to perfection among men his great work of glorifying the Father. This idea of mutual glorification had already been anticipated to some degree in Isaiah's Servant poems. Yahweh says to the Servant: "You are my servant in whom I shall be glorified" (49:3). Then, in the final poem, Yahweh says that in recompense for the humiliations and sufferings the Servant had endured, the Servant "shall be lifted up, exalted" (52:13; the LXX translates *hypsōthēsetai kai doxasthēsetai sphodra*). There is every reason to believe that Isaiah 53 is to be connected with the "lifting up" (*hypsoun*) and "glorification" (*doxazein*) of the Son of Man, of which the fourth gospel so often speaks (lifting up: 3:14; 8:28; 12:32, 34; glorification: 7:39; 8:54; 11:4; 12:10, 23, 28, etc.).

In John 17:19 Christ expresses his sacrifice by saying, in terms that remind us of the Servant's sacrifice, "for their sake I consecrate myself." But, once again, the already beautiful conception of Isaiah 53 is greatly surpassed and transformed by the fact that the sacrificial victim in John 17 is no longer just a very holy man, like the suffering Servant, but the incarnate Son of God.

We showed above that in Isaiah 53 the sacrificial liturgy of the Old Testament has been spiritualized, and back in Chapter 2 we showed at some length that the prayer in John 17 represents a transposition of the Jewish liturgy of the Day of Atonement. What we must now do is show how the prayer also christianizes that liturgy. The purpose of the festival of atonement was to expiate the sins of the priests and God's people as a whole, and thus restore to Israel its holiness. In this way the divine requirement laid on the chosen people— "Be holy because I am holy"—would be met. What Christ requires of his Church, however, is something much higher, in keeping with the revelation the Son of God has brought and with the new covenant he has established (cf. the mention of the new covenant in the accounts of the Last Supper).

E. Malatesta rightly observes that the prayer of John 17 is the prayer of Christ, not simply as one who restores the covenant of Sinai, but as one who mediates a new covenant in which there is a new knowledge of God, as Jeremiah had foreseen (31:31–34).[27] The liturgy of the Day of Atonement restored the people of God to a condition that satisfied the requirements of the Sinai covenant. The prayer of Jesus in John 17, on the other hand, intends that all the disciples of Jesus, the future Church, shall live in harmony with the new revelation that the Son of God has brought to men. This revelation teaches them that from all eternity the Father has a Son and that between the Father and the Son there reigns, in the Holy Spirit, the most perfect conceivable unity and communion. As a result, the people of God under the new covenant may no longer simply reflect the divine holiness as the people of the old covenant did ("Be holy because I am holy"). They must also, thanks to the sanctifying action of the Spirit and their own resultant unity in love, reflect the unity of Father and Son.[28] That is the principal object of Jesus' prayer: "Holy Father, keep those you have given me true to your name, so that they may be one like us. . . . May they all be one. Father, may they be one in us, as you are in me and I am in you. . . . I have given them the glory you gave to me, that they may be one as we are one. With me in them and you in me, may they be so completely one that the world will realize that it was you who sent me" (17:11, 21, 22).

The first letter of St. John evidently supposes the ideal existence of the Christian community such as it had been defined in John 17 by the high priest of the new covenant who fulfilled and went infinitely beyond the oracle in Isaiah 53. The first letter starts from, and in fact reminds its readers of, the essential points in the prayer. The Christian is a person who, in principle, lives in communion with the Father and the Son and therefore in communion with his brothers (1 Jn. 1:3–7; the word *koinōnia,* "communion," occurs four times in this passage). As priest and victim of the new covenant, Christ is, in this writer's eyes, an intercessor ("paraclete") and "the sacrifice that takes our sins away" (1 Jn. 2:1–2). Or else he is a living throne of mercy, as other commentators would prefer to put it, since they regard the *hilasmos* of this passage as a reference to the throne of mercy or mercy seat that the high priest sprinkled on the Day of Atonement.[29]

But the Christian can become deluded, and this danger is aggravated by the teaching of the false teachers who disturb the community.[30] The problem 1 John seeks to resolve is a very practical one; it can be formulated in this way: What are the criteria that make it possible to distinguish the Christian who lives in genuine communion with God from the Christian who is living by an illusion? John's answer is twofold. God is light (1:5); the Christian who walks in the darkness of sin and in whose life God the Light is not mirrored, is living under an illusion. God is love (4:8, 10); the Christian who does not love and in whose life the God of love is not reflected, is living under an illusion.

John uses formulas that remind us of the great Old Testament rule: "Be holy because I am holy." Now, however, the divine model to be imitated has drawn very close to us in

Jesus. The author likes to speak of this Jesus who fills his thoughts, simply as "that one" or "he," a manner of speaking that "shows an attitude of familiarity and affection toward the savior of the world."[31] The authentic Christian "is living the same kind of life as Christ [literally "he"] lived" (2:6).[32] The authentic Christian "must try to be pure as Christ [again, literally "he" or "that one"]" (3:3). The latter prescription represents a transposition into the moral order of the ritual purity required in the Old Testament for sharing in worship.[33] John gives the reason for his prescription in language that recalls both the Lamb of God in the fourth gospel and the Servant of Yahweh in Isaiah 53 (Verse 9, for example): "Now you know that he appeared in order to abolish sin, and that in him there is no sin" (3:5). The authentic Christian is "to live a holy life" and "to be holy just as he is holy" (3:7); here we have another allusion to the Servant who, according to the Hebrew text of Isaiah 53:11, is called "the just one, my servant." The authentic Christian is to give his life for his brothers, just as "he gave up his life for us" (3:16); the phrase is the usual Johannine one, "lay [down] his soul," that is, sacrifice his life, which derives directly from Isaiah 53:10 where the Servant is said to offer his life in atonement.

There is one final text that uses "that one" or "he." "Love will come to its perfection in us when we can face the day of Judgement without fear; because even in this world we have become as he is" (4:17). The passage is a difficult one, but the meaning becomes clear if we read it in the light of John 17. John, in his letter, wants to see Christians possessed of the assurance that is the effect and sign of perfect love (cf. 2:28; 3:21; 5:14). When Jesus was departing from this world but leaving his disciples behind in it, he had prayed: ". . . that the world will realize that it was you who sent me and that I have loved them as much as you loved me. . . . so that the love with which you loved me may be in them, and so that I may be in them" (John 17:23, 26). Under the old covenant the people had had the duty of becoming like the thrice holy God. The disciples of Jesus must be caught up, even in this world, in the very love with which the Father eternally embraces his Son: ". . . because even in this world we have become as he is" (1 Jn. 4:17). That is the source of their confidence. Only those who refuse nothing to Love can have such confidence.[34]

While clearly connected with the rest of the Johannine literature, the Apocalypse is nonetheless a special kind of book and needs to be studied separately. However, in what concerns the concepts of sacrifice and priesthood, it evidently follows the same line as the fourth gospel and the first letter of St. John. We think it right, then, to attempt to show, in brief form, the basic Christian meaning of this difficult book. We shall be making a somewhat more extensive use of the Apocalypse at the end of the next and final chapter.

The Apocalypse is a message of comfort and hope to the Church that is being tested by persecution. As such, the Apocalypse is essentially "the Book of the Lamb" who was sacrificed and is now triumphant and who "loves us and has washed away our sins with his blood" (Rv. 1:5). Although it is not a form of address or a Christological title in the strict sense of the term, the word "lamb" occurs with unusual frequency throughout the Apocalypse, about thirty times in all. This cannot be a simple accident. This fact of vocabulary is enough by itself to prove that the book makes fully its own one of the most important elements in early Christian Christology: the application to Jesus of the poems about the suffering Servant, and especially the last of them, Isaiah 53.

Though the words for lamb are different in gospel and Apocalypse (*amnos* in the former, *arnion* in the latter),[35] there is every reason to believe that, like the word "lamb" on the lips of the Baptist in John 1:29–36, the name "lamb," so often attributed to Christ in the Apocalypse refers not only to the Passover lamb, but also, and even primarily, to the Servant who "like a lamb . . . is led to the slaughter-house" (Is. 53:7).[36]

There is no doubt, of course, that some passages of the Apocalypse definitely recall the warlike and victorious lamb of the Jewish apocalypses. Revelation 6:16 speaks of the anger of the Lamb. We also read: "They will go to war against the Lamb; but the Lamb is 'the Lord of lords and the King of kings,' and he will defeat them and they will be defeated by his followers, the called, the chosen, the faithful" (17:14). Such passages have led some exegetes to think that there is a real opposition between Christ the Lamb of the fourth gospel (where "lamb" suggests only innocence and holiness), and the Lamb of the Apocalypse (who is "mighty and wrathful"[37]).

In fact, however, as J. B. Caird has shown in admirable fashion,[38] such an opposition is contrived in the commentator's mind, inasmuch as the Apocalypse is careful to correct the warlike images borrowed from the Old Testament by means of references to the suffering Servant of Isaiah 53. Christ is presented to us as the Lion of the tribe of Judah and *simultaneously,* even if quite paradoxically, as the Lamb who has been sacrificed and still bears the marks of his immolation: "One of the elders said to me, '. . . the Lion of the tribe of Judah . . . has triumphed. . . . Then I saw . . . a Lamb that seemed to have been sacrificed" (Rv. 5:5–6). It is as if St. John were saying to us: "Each time the old Testament tells us of the Lion, the victorious Messiah, and the defeat of his enemies, you should think of the Lamb who was sacrificed, for the Christian dispensation knows of no victory save that of the cross." The Lamb slain is shown to us with "seven horns, and . . . seven eyes, which are the seven Spirits God has sent out all over the world" (Rv. 5:6). The seven horns are the symbol of omnipotence, the seven eyes the symbol of omniscience, and the seven spirits a way of describing the full gift of the Holy Spirit.[39] Once again, it is as if St. John were saying to us: "It is as the one who was sacrificed that the Lamb will exercise all his divine prerogatives, and his triumphs will be modelled on that of Golgotha."

We can interpret the Apocalypse in this way because there is no doubt that the book does refer to the suffering Servant who is both priest and victim. The emphasis put on the blood of the Lamb as a sign and means of salvation certainly does make us think of the Passover lamb, but only the reference to Isaiah 53 can explain the great stress on the voluntariness of the Lamb's sacrifice and on its saving power. Above all, only in the light of Isaiah 53 can we understand the paradoxical idea that runs through the Apocalypse: The violent death of the Lamb was also his way to life and victory. The persecuted Church is thus urged to see that all its real triumphs will resemble the triumph of the Lamb who was sacrificed. The 144,000 confessors of the faith on Mount Zion (Rv. 14:1–5) are surely being assimilated to the suffering Servant. They are virgins because they have refused to prostitute themselves through idolatry; they, like the Servant (Is. 53:9), "never allowed a lie to pass their lips" (Rv. 14:5), when it came to confessing or denying their Christian faith.[40]

The Apocalypse shows us Christ as king, priest, and sacrificial victim of the new covenant. He is a king, and even the king of kings and lord of lords (1:5, 17:14). This represents a strong warning to tyrants who wish to be adored and who therefore persecute the disciples of Christ.

Christ is also a victim: As we have already seen, he is the Lamb who was sacrificed. The blood of Christ or of the Lamb is often mentioned in the Apocalypse. It has rescued men from their sins and gives Christians the strength to confess their faith, even if this means the shedding of their blood. The Apocalypse, therefore, often likens the blood of the Lamb to the blood of the martyrs: "He loves us and has washed away our sins with his blood" (1:5); "You were sacrificed, and with your blood you bought men for God" (5:9); "They have washed their robes white again in the blood of the Lamb" (7:14); "They have triumphed over him [the persecutor] by the blood of the Lamb and by the witness of their martyrdom, because even in the face of death they would not cling to life" (12:11); "I saw that she [the scarlet woman] was drunk, drunk with the blood of the saints, and the blood of the martyrs of Jesus" (17:6); "In her [the city of Babylon] you will find the blood of prophets and saints, and all the blood that was ever shed on earth" (18:24); "His cloak was soaked in blood. He is known by the name, The Word of God" (19:13).

Finally, Christ is a priest: he appears to St. John, clad in a long priestly tunic. At the end of our next and final chapter we shall come back to the priestly dignity of Christ in the Apocalypse, for in it the "angels" of the Churches, these "stars" which Christ holds in his hand, have a share.

The three roles of Christ—king, victim, and priest—are closely connected with one another, since Christ became fully king of the world when he acted as priest and offered himself as victim. The three roles are also connected in the life of the Church, since, as in the fourth gospel and the first letter of St. John, so in the Apocalypse, Christ makes his disciples like himself. Thus, he makes all members of the Church into "a line of kings, priests to serve his God" (Rv. 1:6; 5:10), the two Christian dignities being inseparable. But Christ does so only on condition that his disciples confess their faith in him, even, if need be, by shedding their blood. We will recall that, whereas in the other New Testament writings the cross of Christ is only a prelude to his kingly glorification (Lk. 24:26: "Was it not ordained that the Christ should suffer and so enter into his glory?"), in the fourth gospel Christ already rules because of his cross. The Apocalypse extends the same principle to Christians. For them, trials are not a path to be followed in order some day to rule with Christ; rather, tribulation and

rule are the two sides of the same calling, since those who
suffer with Christ also rule with him; that is, they rule in the
midst of tribulation itself. All this is implicit in the simple
words of Revelation 1:9: "My name is John, and through
our union in Jesus I am your brother and share your sufferings, your kingdom, and all you endure." Suffering, kingdom,
and endurance are inseparably woven together.

THE TEACHING OF THE LETTER TO THE HEBREWS ON SACRIFICE AND PRIESTHOOD

AS WE POINTED OUT MUCH EARLIER, the Letter to the Hebrews is the only New Testament document to call Christ a
priest (*hiereus,* six times) or high priest (*archiereus*). We
chose, however, not to use the Letter as our starting point in
the attempt to define the priesthood of the new covenant; in
fact, the choice of a different starting point is what gives the
present book its specific character. But it is time now for us to
present in outline form a synthesis of what the Letter to the
Hebrews has to say about sacrifice and priesthood. We shall
see that on a number of points its teaching easily harmonizes
with the Johannine writings.

This comparison will show that, contrary to what has sometimes been said, especially in recent times, the conception of
priesthood in Hebrews does not occupy a purely peripheral
place in New Testament theology; this, if true, would supposedly severely limit the value and importance of that conception. In fact, however, the undeniable doctrinal novelty of the
Letter to the Hebrews is to be found much less in the teaching
given than in the terminology used to express the teaching.
Let us, then, turn first to a short summary of the teaching of
the Letter. Then we can compare it with that of the Johannine
writings.

Under the probable influence of Philonian thought, some

ancient writers (Clement of Alexandria and Gregory Thaumaturgos are said to be among them) imagined that Christ, the Word of God, was from all eternity a priest and mediator between God and men; they understood this to be the meaning of the words from Psalm 110 which the Letter to the Hebrews often quotes: "You are a priest . . . for ever" (Ps. 110:4). In point of fact, however, the Letter suggests that Christ is a priest because of his two natures, the divine and the human, and therefore a priest only from the moment of his incarnation. Several statements in the Letter make this point clear. The priest, who exists only for the sake of men, is to be taken from among them (Heb. 5:1). The priest and those he sanctifies must be of the same stock (2:11); the mediatorial role so often assigned to Christ the priest (8:6; 9:15; 12:24) implies that he is both man and God. The words of Psalm 110: "You are a priest . . . for ever" imply only that Christ's priesthood will have no end, not that it had no beginning.

It is true enough, however, that the transcendence of Christ's priesthood and its uniqueness (Christ being the only priest of the new covenant) are set in sharp relief. These characteristics of Christ's priesthood are due to the fact that he is the only Son of God, "radiant light of the Father's glory and the perfect copy of his nature" (1:3), who played a role in the creation of the world. Hebrews 5:5 closely connects Christ's priesthood and his divine sonship: "Nor did Christ give himself the glory of becoming high priest, but he had it from the one who said to him: 'You are my son, today I have become your father.'" This association means that the priesthood of Jesus acquires its dignity, efficacy, and duration from the fact that he is the Son of God. The statement that Christ "offered himself as the perfect sacrifice to God through the eternal Spirit" (9:14) expresses the same truth.

At a given moment in history God made his Son the priest and victim par excellence. He gave his Son a human body so that he might replace the powerless sacrifices of the Old Testament: "Bulls' blood and goats' blood are useless for taking away sins, and this is what he said on coming into the world: 'You who wanted no sacrifice or oblation, prepared a body for me. You took no pleasure in holocausts or sacrifices for sin; then I said, just as I was commanded in the scroll of the book, "God, here I am! I am coming to obey your will"'" (10:4–7). The scroll of the book means the whole of the Scriptures, which were put on a roller for use in the synagogue services. The author is saying that the Scriptures bear witness to God's plan of inaugurating through the Messiah a worship that is acceptable to him.

The text continues: "And this will [of God] was for us to be made holy by the offering of his body made once and for all by Jesus Christ" (10:10). Here we have a clear allusion to Christ's self-oblation at the Supper: cf. "This is my body which will be given for you" (Lk. 22:19). The thought also moves back quite naturally to the martyrdom of the Servant in Isaiah 53, since at the Supper Jesus himself refers explicitly to this passage.

The incarnation of the Son of God means that he is made lower than the angels: "For a short while you have made him lower than the angels" (2:7, citing Ps. 8); "but we do see in Jesus one who was for a short while made lower than the angels" (2:9). Moreover, during his earthly life, instead of the joy offered to him, Christ "endured the cross, disregarding the shamefulness of it" (12:2). The joy he thus renounces is triumph on earth, not the glory he enjoys as the Son within the Trinity. This state of lowliness leaves untouched, of course, the divine sonship of Jesus, as is shown by the statement in Hebrews 5:8 (which matches with numerous elements of New Testament Christology): "Although he was Son, he learnt to obey through suffering."[41] In addition, the abasement of Christ was only temporary: "Now that he has destroyed the defilement of sin, he has gone to take his place on heaven at the right hand of divine Majesty" (1:3).

The words of Hebrews 10:5–6: "You who wanted no sacri-

fice or oblation, prepared a body for me. . . . Then I said
. . . '. . . I am coming to obey your will,'" have led some
theologians to speak of a sacrifice offered by Christ at the
moment when the mystery of the incarnation becomes a reality. From this viewpoint, the sacrifice of Calvary would simply have been the ritual, external expression of an interior
sacrifice that comprehended the whole earthly career of Christ
from the moment of the incarnation on. Christ, these writers
say, constantly had the will to offer himself as a victim. The
cross was simply the culminating point of the earthly life of
Jesus as priest and victim.[42]

What are we to think of this view? It is certainly a beautiful
theological conception that unifies Christ's life in terms of his
interior sentiments and, as such, is quite plausible. But what
we are concerned with here is the exact thought of the Letter
to the Hebrews. Hebrews 10:5-6 certainly does suggest that
from the first moment of his human existence Jesus offered
himself as a sacrifice. But, like the rest of the New Testament,
the Letter seems to connect the sacrifice in the strict sense with
the event of Golgotha. A grammatical observation lends support to this view. When the author is speaking of the repeated
sacrifices of the Old Testament, he uses the present tense
which readily expresses an action as repeated. But when he
speaks of the sacrifice Christ offered once and for all, he uses
the aorist tense, and this aorist (which relates to a determined
point in the past) usually refers quite clearly to Golgotha,
not to the incarnation (cf. Heb. 5:1, 7; 7:27; 9:7, 14; 9:25–
28).[43]

If taken literally, several statements in Hebrews might urge
a position contrary to the one we just explained. They could
easily lead us to think that on earth Christ was only called to
the priesthood and that he became a priest only once he had
ascended into heaven. Numerous writers have thought that
since Christ has a heavenly priesthood, he must also have a
heavenly sacrifice; in other words, the glorified Christ forever
offers himself to his Father as a heavenly victim.[44]

Not a few texts seem to justify such a conception: "Having been made perfect, he became for all who obey him the source of eternal salvation and was acclaimed by God with the title of high priest of the order of Melchizedek" (5:9–10); ". . . beyond the veil where Jesus has entered before us and on our behalf, to become a high priest of the order of Melchizedek, and for ever" (6:19–20); "He is ever living to intercede for all who come to God through him" (7:25); "In fact, if he were on earth, he would not be a priest at all, since there are others who make the offerings laid down by the Law" (8:4); "These [other priests] only maintain the service of a model or a reflection of the heavenly realities" (8:5); "Christ has come, as the high priest of all the blessings which were to come" (9:11).

How are these statements to be understood? The last two with their references to "a reflection of the heavenly realities" and "high priests of the blessings which were to come" call for a general remark on the use of the adjectives "heavenly" (*epouranios*) and "future" (*mellōn*) in the Letter to the Hebrews. In this Letter all realities belonging to the Christian dispensation are described as "heavenly" or "to come." They are heavenly, not so much in a local sense (though that is not simply to be excluded) as in a qualitative sense: They are infinitely superior in nature to the more material realities of the old covenant. The two covenants are contrasted with each other as earth and heaven are. If the same realities are described as "to come," the sense is not strictly chronological, as though they were to be opposed to present realities; the real point is that the author looks at things from the standpoint of the Jewish expectation of the Messiah.[45]

With this general observation behind us, we may now attempt to explain the complicated thought of the Letter to the Hebrews on the priesthood of Christ. It seems clear, to begin with, that Christ is already a priest on earth. If God gave him a body and sent him into the world, it was that he might carry out a priestly function (10:4–5). It is as a priest that Christ on earth sympathizes with men in all their weaknesses (5:2). Above all, it is while on earth that Christ sheds his blood and thereby purges men of their sins (9:14; 10:29; 13:12, 20). Purgation from sins is an essentially priestly act, and Jesus does it by reason of the priesthood he has possessed since he came into the world; his very coming was motivated by the intention to substitute the offering of his own body for the sacrifices of the Old Testament (10:5–10). The Septuagint indeed occasionally applies the words *teleioun* and *teleiōsis* (which in themselves express the idea of completion) to the consecration of priests (cf. Lv. 8:22, 26, 28, 29, 31, 33). But it does not follow that the *teleiōsis* of Christ in Hebrews 5:9– 10 must refer to his consecration as priest. On the contrary, as Hebrews 7:11 and 19 show, the word is rather to be understood in the same sense as the completion of Jesus' work in the fourth gospel (cf. the use of *teleioun* in Jn. 4:34; 5:36; 17:4, 23, and the *tetelestai* of 19:30). It refers, then, to the perfecting of Jesus in his priestly office, not to the initiation of his ministry.

In addition, we must without qualification exclude any idea of a heavenly sacrifice that would be juxtaposed to the sacrifice of Calvary.[46] It can be said, however, that the Letter looks at the earthly life of Christ primarily in terms of his victimhood and that it links his priestly activity chiefly to his risen life. In heaven, Christ is for ever a perfect priest, not because he offers a new sacrifice but because he abidingly offers the sacrifice he offered once and for all on Calvary "through the eternal Spirit" (9:14). Under the old dispensation, the repetition of sacrifices shows that the latter were imperfect and that the priestly mediation they expressed was imperfect; the repetition showed that a certain distance always remained between God and the priest. For the risen and glorified Christ this distance does not exist; he always has access to God; more than that, he is seated at God's right hand (8:1; cf. 1:3).

The parallelism with the liturgy of the Day of Atonement,

which is elaborated in the Letter to the Hebrews, is a great help to understanding the viewpoint adopted in the Letter. According to Leviticus 16 the Jewish high priest sacrificed two victims for sin, then entered the holy of holies, and sprinkled the throne of mercy with the blood of the victims, This final action was the decisive one for the expiation of sins. The death of Christ on the cross corresponds to the immolation of the two victims by the high priest, and the ascension of Christ corresponds to the high priest's entrance into the holy of holies as well as to the sprinkling of the throne of mercy with the blood of the victims. In the eyes of the writer of this Letter, then, the climactic moment in the mystery of salvation is not the immolation of Christ on Golgotha but his glorious exaltation and entrance into the heavenly sanctuary where God greets him as high priest, "living for ever to intercede for all" (7:25). Our heavenly high priest constantly prays to God for the Church. He is always offering and interceding, just as on Calvary he offered "through the eternal Spirit" (9:14).

This exegesis of the Letter to the Hebrews has the advantage that it makes it possible for Catholic theologians to give a better account of the sacrifice of the Mass, which is the sacrament of Christ's ceaseless offering in heaven. It also explains the heavenly liturgy of the Apocalypse, which is a liturgy *now going on,* as well as the statement in 1 John 2:1–2, which represents the glorified Christ as the *present* intercessor and *present* expiatory victim for sinful men.

COMPARISON WITH THE JOHANNINE WRITINGS

NOW THAT WE HAVE SUMMARIZED THE IDEAS of the Letter to the Hebrews on priesthood and sacrifice, we would like to compare them in a more detailed way with parallel elements in the Johannine writings. The comparison will take up the following points: the transposition and spiritualization of the

Old Testament liturgy, the reference to the suffering Servant of Isaiah 53, the linking of Christ's priesthood to the mystery of the incarnation, and, finally, the importance assigned to the intercessory prayer of Christ the priest.

St. Paul, who is in conflict with the Judaizers, likes to contrast the two dispensations: the Mosaic law and grace.[47] St. John and the Letter to the Hebrews, however, both see in the Mosaic dispensation a preparation for and an anticipation of the Christian dispensation, so much so that "it is possible to transpose and apply to the new priesthood the liturgical prescriptions of the Mosaic Law."[48]

We have already shown that the Johannine writings present, in outline, a complete spiritualization of the Old Testament liturgy: Christ is the expiatory victim and Passover lamb of Christians; throughout the drama of redemption Christ's action is implicitly compared to that of the high priest on the Day of Atonement. Some authors have even supposed that the evangelist intends to use the major Jewish festivals (Passover, Pentecost, Tabernacles, Dedication) as a means of dividing his material; he would thus be suggesting that Jesus fulfilled and by so doing put an end to the liturgy of the old covenant.[49] In any case, it is beyond doubt that according to the fourth gospel the risen and glorified Lord is to replace the temple at Jerusalem.

In the Letter to the Hebrews a great deal more emphasis is put on the transposition of the Levitic cultus. The priesthood and liturgy of the old dispensation are declared to have been ineffective; the Holy Spirit intended them to point ahead to what the author calls the "time to reform them" (Heb. 9:10, reform=*diorthōsis*); that is, to the Christian dispensation. The use to which Psalm 110 is put, as well as the bold typology based on the person of Melchizedek, help to show that the Levitic priesthood must give way to the incomparably superior priesthood of Christ.[50] The Letter expounds at length the parallelism between the festival of atonement and the drama of redemption. That parallelism makes it clear that in the Letter to the Hebrews the entrance of Jesus into heaven assumes the same importance as the return of Jesus to the Father has in the fourth gospel.

In the gospels, including that of John, the reference to the suffering Servant of Isaiah 53 plays a very important role. It makes it possible to show that for the New Testament, and especially for the Johannine writings, Jesus is a priest who offers himself as an expiatory sacrifice after the fashion of the Servant in Isaiah 53:10. We might expect that the New Testament book most concerned with priesthood would be filled with allusions to the Servant. Yet it must be admitted that the Letter to the Hebrews refers only indirectly to Isaiah 53, the direct reference being to the evangelical tradition concerning the Supper, which is recalled several times. We may refer the reader to the offering of Christ's body of which Hebrews 10:10 speaks ("This will was for us to be made holy by the offering of his body made once and for all by Jesus Christ"), and to the frequent mentions of the new covenant and the blood of the covenant (8:13; 9:15; 10:29; 12:24; 13:20). The last of the texts just listed speaks of "the blood that sealed an eternal covenant" and is especially important. It seems to tell us, in an indirect way, that the doctrine of Hebrews on sacrifice and priesthood is already to be found implicitly in the gospels.

In addition to these indirect references, some direct references or allusions may be discovered.[51] The clearest reminiscence is in 9:28: "Christ . . . offers himself only once to take the faults of many on himself" (the *polloi,* or "many," is a characteristic of Isaiah 53). We may also point to 7:25: Christ "is living forever to intercede for all who come to God through him"—an allusion to the intercession of the Servant in Isaiah 53:12. Still other allusions may be seen. The ability to sympathize with the ignorant and the uncertain, specified as an essential priestly quality in Hebrews 5:2 is also one of

the major traits of the suffering Servant according to the first
and third poems (Is. 42:3; 50:4). The stress on the absolute
sinlessness of Christ, whether as priest (7:26: "holy, innocent
and uncontaminated, beyond the influence of sinners") or as
victim (9:14: "the perfect sacrifice"), reminds us of the innocence of the martyred Servant (Is. 53:9).

The fourth gospel (10:36) and the Letter to the Hebrews
also have in common that they go immeasurably beyond the
already lofty conceptions of sacrifice and priesthood to be
found in Isaiah 53 when they connect the priesthood of Christ
with the mystery of the Incarnation. From this connection it
follows that the priesthood of Christ is as permanent as the
incarnation; it is eternal, not in the sense that it had no beginning but in the sense that it will never end. The Letter to the
Hebrews links this teaching to Psalms 110:4: "You are a
priest of the order of Melchizedek, and for ever."

On the basis of the intimate relationship between Christ's
incarnation and his priesthood, the Letter to the Hebrews proclaims the supereminent value of the sacrifice of the cross,
but it does so in unusual terms: Christ "offered himself as the
perfect sacrifice to God *through the eternal Spirit*" (9:14).
On this point we cannot do better than to quote the commentary of C. Spicq: to say that Christ offers himself "through
the eternal Spirit" means that he offers himself

> in virtue of his very personality or his own power, which is
> infinite in value and guarantees him eternal life and an eter-
> nal priesthood despite the rupture of death; we are justified
> by Hebrews 7:16, 24 in identifying this spirit with the divine
> nature (cf. Rm. 1:4; 1 Tm. 3:16; St. Ignatius of Antioch,
> *To the Smyrnaeans,* 3:2, 3; *To the Magnesians,* 1:2; *Second
> Epistle of Clement,* 9:5). . . . The addition of "through the
> eternal Spirit," which is motivated by the desire to stress
> once again the contrast between the sacrifice of Jesus and
> Levitic worship, allows us, on the one hand, to conclude to
> the identity of the eternal priest and the spotless victim and
> to understand how the former can survive the immolation of

the latter, and, on the other hand, to highlight the unparalleled value of this sacrifice (because of the hypostatic
union). Because it is willed and undergone in this "eternal
Spirit," the immolation cannot but have an everlasting effectiveness.[52]

Like the Johannine writings, the Letter to the Hebrews
lays great importance on the prayer of Christ, whether at the
climax of the redemptive drama (cf. the moving words in
5:7–8), or as the ongoing terminus of that drama (cf. 7:25).
Because of this, the Letter, again like the Johannine writings,
clearly links up with the great tradition of intercessor prophets
of whom we spoke earlier, a tradition in which Isaiah 53
represents an extraordinary and wholly surprising climax.
When we read in Hebrews that Christ's "power to save is ut-
terly certain, since he is living for ever to intercede for all who
come to God through him" (7:25), it is difficult not to
think of the prayer which Jesus utters in John 17 as he goes to
the Father, and of the glorified Christ who, according to
1 John 2:2, has become "our advocate." Both passages of
John were probably present in the mind of the author of Hebrews when he wrote the lines just quoted. He was undoubtedly thinking as well of the prayer offered by the Levitic
priests, and especially of such a passage as: "By means of the
pectoral of judgement, when Aaron enters the sanctuary, he
will bear the names of the sons of Israel on his breast to call
them to mind continually in the presence of Yahweh" (Ex.
28:29).[53] But he must have remembered even more clearly
the prayer of the suffering Servant, as it is referred to in Isaiah
53:12: "praying all the time for sinners."

Here again, however, we find the same highly significant
phenomenon that drew our attention earlier: The use of Isaiah
53 is only indirect, being mediated through the Christ of the
gospels. Hebrews 5:7–8 shows us Christ, the high priest, praying on earth for his fellow men: "During his life on earth, he
offered up prayer and entreaty, aloud and in silent tears, to

the one who had the power to save him out of death, and he submitted so humbly that his prayer was heard. Although he was Son, he learnt to obey through suffering." It was as a priest that Christ prayed thus; the verb for "offer" is *prospherein,* which is also used for sacrificial offering.[54] In this passage the author is not referring us directly to the Old Testament but to the gospel tradition. It is as if the author were saying to us: "It is from that tradition that I chiefly derived my teaching on priesthood, for Christ in the gospel tradition acts as a priest, even if he does not expressly apply the name to himself." This point is so important for us and so wonderfully justifies our decision to use the gospel tradition as the basis for defining the priesthood of Christ, that we shall spend a few moments on it as we end this chapter.

Hebrews 5:1–10 seems at first sight to be concerned with a general definition of priesthood on the basis of Levitical priesthood; the author would then go on to show that the definition finds its most perfect application in the priesthood of Christ. It seems we might sum up his thought in the following syllogism. (1) Verses 1–4: Since a priest is destined to be an intermediary between God and men, especially in presenting God with offerings and sacrifices for sin, he must have certain traits, which include being taken from among men, being capable of sympathy for the ignorant and uncertain men for whom he must intercede, and being called by God, since God cannot accept the offerings and intercession of a mediator whom he himself has not chosen. (2) Verses 5–8: But Christ has these characteristics—he was chosen by God as two of the Messianic Psalms tell us (Ps. 2:7 and 110:4), he possesses human nature ("during his life on earth"), he sympathizes with sinners and prays for them. (3) Verses 9–10: Therefore Christ is the perfect high priest and the source of eternal salvation for those who obey him.

In fact, however, only the surface of the text is touched by this syllogism with its major premise in the form of a definition of priesthood based on the Levitic priesthood, and with its minor premise in the form of a statement that Christ fulfills the definition. Thus, when the Letter speaks of the necessity of the priest showing indulgence and compassion for sinners, it is difficult to find any texts in the Levitical legislation to which he could be referring. "Moreover it is well known that since the second century before Christ, and especially during the period of Roman overlordship, the high priests owed their office to the favor (frequently purchased) of princes and procurators. The divine call was therefore simply a theoretical condition, and was fully operative only in Aaron and Jesus."[55]

We are thus led to a conclusion the significance of which will not escape the reader: Even though some elements in the picture drawn in Hebrews 5:1–10 do not apply to Christ (the priest "has to make sin offerings for himself as well as for the people"), it is in the light of what the Christ of the gospels really was that the Letter defines the priestly ideal. The author really tells us the chief source of his thought of perfect priesthood when he recalls the scene in Gethsemani in Verses 7–8. It is impossible to doubt that the writer really is referring to the scene in the Garden of Olives. But we must add that the author "does not mean to refer only to the moments in Gethsemani" and that he "has in mind the life-long self-abasement, trials, and sufferings of the incarnate Son of God."[56] The language he uses reminds us chiefly of the Lukan and Johannine traditions; recall, for example, "In his anguish he prayed even more earnestly" (Lk. 22:44), and "Now my soul is troubled. What shall I say: Father, save me from this hour? But it was for this very reason that I have come to this hour. Father, glorify your name!" (Jn. 12:27–28). The Letter to the Hebrews thus gives us to understand that such prayers as the living Jesus uttered during his earthly life, and not only the so-called priestly prayer of John 17, were all prayers of Christ the priest. There is every reason to believe, moreover, that the Letter is not referring to this or that passage in the gospels but only to the oral tradition. It also uses some stereotyped expressions borrowed from the Old Testament.

Once we are aware of the connection of the passage with the gospel tradition, one statement of the author becomes surprising. He tells us that Jesus was heard when he prayed to him who could save him from death. Yet the synoptic gospels show us that in Gethsemani Jesus was not heard when he asked, conditionally indeed, that the Father might take the cup of suffering from him. How can we account for this seeming contradiction?

Since it is not our purpose here to offer a detailed exegesis of the Letter to the Hebrews, we can go directly to the essential point. First of all, we must reject the radical solution that would make the text read: "Although he was the Son, he was not heard."[57] Such a reading has no basis in the manuscript tradition. We think we must also reject another translation which some commentators propose: "having been heard and freed from fear." That is: Jesus was freed from fear, and this enabled him straightway to abandon himself to the Father's will: "Let your will be done, not mine."[58] This translation cannot be justified because analysis of the *eulabeia—eulabeisthai* word group as used in Hebrews (cf. 11:7; 12:28) shows that the basic sense is "fear of God,"[59] and because we have no right to make the preposition *apo* mean "freed from."

In our opinion, the true solution of the problem is as follows.[60] What we are shown in the Letter to the Hebrews is the prayer of Christ as high priest. When Christ prays "to the one who had the power to save him out of death," he is not praying only for himself. His prayer is essentially a priestly one and must therefore be for the benefit of all those with whom he has identified himself and whom he represents, all those who "share the same flesh and blood" with him (2:14) and whom he wants to set free from the fear of death (2:15).

There is another, equally essential point to be made here. The death from which Christ asks to be delivered in Hebrews 5:7 is not simply bodily death, nor even the torments of crucifixion. "Death" must be understood as in 2:14 where it is the supreme catastrophe behind which the power of the devil lurks. This had already been in 2:9: "We do see in Jesus one who was 'for a short while made lower than the angels' and is now 'crowned with glory and splendour' because he submitted to death; by God's grace he had to experience death for all mankind."

By his bodily death, then, Jesus freed men from spiritual death which is the normal companion of bodily death and makes the latter so fearful. He was heard in the sense that, thanks to him, God removed a fearful evil from mankind, and the devil, involved in that evil, was repulsed. It is not only or even chiefly to Gethsemani that we should relate Christ's priestly prayer in Hebrews 5:7; it is also, and above all, to the prayer of Jesus reported in John 12:27–28, a prayer that ends in a victory song: "Now sentence is being passed on this world; now the prince of this world is to be overthrown. And when I am lifted up from the earth, I shall draw all men to myself" (Jn. 12:31–32). Once again, the Letter to the Hebrews turns our minds to what is said in John.

In summary: The synoptic accounts of the Last Supper and the Johannine tradition concerning Jesus are the chief source of the teaching in the Letter to the Hebrews on priesthood and sacrifice. It is principally through this twofold gospel tradition that Hebrews refers back to Isaiah 53.

Chapter 4

The Priesthood of Christ's Ministers

AT THE END OF THE PRECEDING CHAPTER we emphasized the numerous similarities between the teaching of the Letter to the Hebrews on sacrifice and priesthood and the teaching we believe we can discern in the Johannine writings, especially in the priestly prayer of John 17.

But amid the likenesses there is one major difference. The Letter to the Hebrews asserts very emphatically that there is only one priest, Christ, and only one sacrifice, the one Christ offered on Golgotha. It delights in drawing the contrast between, on the one hand, the successive priests of the old covenant and the constantly repeated sacrifices of the Levitical liturgy which were each time ineffective, and, on the other hand, the eternal priesthood of Christ, the Son of God, and the infinite value of his self-oblation, *once and for all*, on Calvary. The Letter to the Hebrews gives no hint that in addition to the incarnate Son of God, ordinary men could be considered as priests in the Christian dispensation.

On the contrary, according to the priestly prayer of Christ, as we understand it, Christ gives his apostles a share in his own twofold consecration as priest and victim. Obviously, this is an extremely important gesture and one that is highly relevant to the present situation in the Church.

The present urgency, as well as the permanent value, of a study of Christ's action recently found very forceful expression. By way of introduction to this chapter we cannot do better than to quote some sentences from a manifesto that hits off nicely the very purpose of the present book:

> It is useful to draw up a list of different kinds of ministry as the basis for choice and distribution of them among priests and laity. It is even more important, however, to determine and set apart what is essential to the priestly ministry. The decreasing number of vocations presses us to put the emphasis on the essential tasks of the priest. Isn't it startling to see priests looking for various professions while neglecting such essentially priestly tasks as the teaching of religion at all levels and the celebration of the sacraments in the spirit of the Church? These essential tasks must be presented in the light of the gospel and the Acts of the Apostles and in connection with the actions and words of Christ. Christ alone is a priest. The people of God as a whole is priestly. Each member of God's people shares through baptism and confirmation in the royal priesthood of Christ. The priesthood of the faithful, however, and the priesthood of the ordained priest are not of the same order. This must be forcefully reasserted and *given a theological, and especially a scriptural, basis* that will be crystal clear and thus put an end to the efforts to reduce the ministerial priesthood to the universal priesthood of all Christians. The distinction between the common priesthood and the ministerial priesthood must be put forward more strongly.[1]

We shall begin by explaining those passages of the priestly prayer that speak of the consecration of the apostles. We shall speak later of two passages in the fourth gospel that we think have the same doctrinal significance: the washing of the feet (13:1–20), which we will show can be taken as a kind of prelude to the consecration of the apostles; and the gift of the Holy Spirit to the apostles in the Easter Christophany of John

20:19–23, which is a consequence of or complement to their consecration.

The fourth gospel speaks only of the apostles. But once Christ had willed the Church to be a lasting society, the apostles had to provide for successors to themselves who would share, as they did, in the priestly consecration of Jesus in a way that would distinguish them from the rest of the Christian community. Our main task, then, is to give solid proof that the apostles were really priests, after the model of Christ, the supreme priest; many today tend to doubt that they were. Yet it is not without interest that in the Johannine writings themselves the apostles are already providing successors to themselves in their role as leaders of the Church. With this perspective as our guide, we shall, in the final section of this chapter, tackle the difficult problem of the "angels" of the Churches in the letters of the Apocalypse (Chapters 2–3).

We shall limit ourselves here to an examination of the Johannine writings. The Pauline corpus provides numerous valuable indications concerning the hierarchical Church, but we shall deliberately leave them aside or, at most, speak of them only in passing and by comparison with what we find in the Johannine literature.

THE PRIESTLY CONSECRATION OF THE APOSTLES
(JN. 17:17, 19)

A POINT OF PHILOLOGY will serve us as a springboard. The Letter to the Hebrews and the prayer in John 17 both apply the same verb "to sanctify" (*hagiazein*) both to Christ who "sanctifies" and to other men who "are sanctified" by Christ. But the meaning of the verb is not quite the same in both documents.

Consider, first of all, the various uses of the verb "to sanctify" in the Letter to the Hebrews: "The one who sanctifies, and the ones who are sanctified, are of the same stock" (Heb. 2:11);[2] "And this will was for us to be made holy by the offering of his body made once and for all by Jesus Christ" (10:10); "By virtue of that one single offering, he has achieved the eternal perfection of all whom he is sanctifying" (10:14);[3] "Anyone who disregards the Law of Moses is ruthlessly 'put to death on the word of two witnesses or three'; and you may be sure that anyone who tramples on the Son of God, and who treats the 'blood of the covenant' which sanctified him as if it were not holy . . . will be condemned to a far severer punishment" (10:28–29); "And so Jesus too suffered outside the camp to sanctify the people with his own blood" (13:12).

There is also 9:13–14: "The blood of goats and bulls and the ashes of a heifer are sprinkled on those who have incurred defilement and they restore the holiness of their outward lives;[4] how much more effectively the blood of Christ, who offered himself as the perfect sacrifice to God through the eternal Spirit, can purify our inner self from dead actions so that we do our service to the living God." This text is of special interest to us because it shows the Letter to the Hebrews undertaking the same kind of transposition which we observed earlier in the fourth gospel. The author is deliberately shifting sanctification from the ritual to the moral sphere.

We turn now to the three uses of "sanctify" in John 17: "Consecrate them in the truth; your word is truth. As you sent me into the world, I have sent them into the world, and for their sake I have consecrated myself so that they too may be consecrated in truth" (17:17–19). The difference between Hebrews and John 17 is manifest. In the Letter to the Hebrews all Christians without distinction are sanctified, and the sanctification is clearly of the moral order. In John 17 Jesus asks the Father only for the sanctification of the apostles;

he is clearly thinking only of them, and he does not repeat this petition when he comes to the third part of his prayer and prays for all the faithful (17:20–26).[5]

There is a further point. The consecration or sanctification of the apostles is closely connected with that of Christ and is in the image of his: "For their sake I have consecrated myself so that *they too* may be consecrated in truth." Now, as we saw above, Christ's "consecration" of himself in 17:19 is a consecration as victim, and depends on the consecration as priest which he had received from the Father (10:36). The consecration by the Father was, in turn, connected closely with the mystery of the hypostatic union, which is a permanent reality; consequently the priesthood of Christ is necessarily eternal.

Against this background we are already in a position to determine the exact nature of the consecration that Jesus asks his Father to bestow on the apostles. It can only be a consecration to priesthood. For, as W. Thüsing has accurately observed, when Christ, *acting as a priest,* consecrates himself as a victim (Jn. 17:14–19), the dominant idea is that of the very real assimilation or conformation of the apostles to Christ.[6] Like Christ, the apostles have been sent into the world; *like Christ, and in the same sense as he, they too* must be consecrated. J. H. Bernard refers us to the command given to Moses in Exodus 28:41: "You will . . . consecrate them [Aaron and his sons] to serve me in the priesthood" (consecrate is *hagiazein*).[7]

There can be no question for the apostles, any more than for Christ, of being set apart only temporarily. The consecration the apostles receive marks them forever; a merely temporary consecration would not really assimilate a man to the eternal priest of the new covenant. In 17:19 Christ says: ". . . so that they too may be consecrated in truth." Here the perfect participle (literally: "[men] having been consecrated") indicates a permanent state already acquired; we shall see further on that the words "in truth" contrast this permanent reality with the imperfect and temporary institutions of the Old Testament. Although the point being made is different, the same basic meaning is expressed in Revelation 21:14: "The city walls stood on twelve foundation stones, each one of which bore the name of one of the twelve apostles of the Lamb." The permanent Jerusalem of the end of time will forever keep the hierarchic structure given it by Christ.

Max Thurian proposes other Scriptural and theological arguments for the permanence of the priestly character:

> The gifts and choice of God are irreversible, St. Paul tells us (Rm. 11:29). It is impossible to imagine the apostles thinking their ministry to be limited in time. . . . God is faithful, despite the possible infidelities of his ministers. God does not repent of his gifts and his call (another way of rendering Rm. 11:29). If we are unfaithful, he remains faithful, for he cannot deny his own nature (2 Tm. 2:13). Christian tradition is fully justified in holding the pastoral ministry to be a lifelong commitment and in speaking of the permanent character given to the minister at his ordination."[8]

The connection which Christ makes between his own consecration as victim and the consecration of the apostles as priests ("I have consecrated myself so that they too may be consecrated in truth") shows clearly that, like all the other blessings of the new covenant, the priesthood of the apostles is the fruit of Christ's self-giving on the cross as an expiatory victim that men may have eternal life. By this very fact, that priesthood is also connected in a special way with the eucharistic mystery in which Christ, who has already given himself on Calvary for the life of the world, now gives himself to each of his disciples as food: "The bread that I shall give is my flesh [already given] for the life of the world" (Jn. 6:51).

In our first chapter we showed that even if the prayer of Jesus in John 17 does not speak directly of the eucharist, it is nonetheless uttered in a eucharistic atmosphere. As W. Thüsing writes, the two essential themes of John 17—glory and unity—are:

> two key-terms in the whole work of salvation, and not simply in the eucharist. But in the work of salvation there is neither the glorification of Jesus nor the unity of the Church without the eucharist. Is the eucharist not part of the glory given to Jesus? In the eucharist the Holy Spirit is given, and the love which unites Jesus to his Father is breathed into the hearts of believers, so that they may be one in this love and their unity may lead the world to faith.[9]

The eucharistic mystery is at the very center of Christian worship. It is suitable, then, but also very meaningful, that the eucharist should provide the context within which Jesus asks his Father to consecrate the apostles as priests.

That petition, with its eucharistic context, can be easily related to an element in the synoptic accounts of the Last Supper to which the Council of Trent and speculative theology rightly attach great importance.[10] When Jesus institutes the eucharist, in which he gives himself as food and drink and thereby anticipates his self-giving on the cross (what he gives as food and drink is his body broken on the cross and his blood poured out on Calvary), he asks those at the table with him, that is, the Twelve (who alone share the meal with him) to repeat in their turn his eucharistic action. It is evident that they must at the same time be enabled to repeat this wonderful gesture. The words of Luke (22:19) and Paul (1 Co. 11:24–25): "Do this as a memorial of me," and the words of John (17:17–18): "Consecrate them . . . I consecrate myself," clarify and complement each other: The Father consecrates the apostles as priests, and one of the essential purposes of the consecration is to enable them to act "in the person of Christ" and to consecrate him as a victim under the signs of bread and wine, as a memorial of the one sacrifice of Golgotha ("as a memorial of me").

The reader may be inclined to object that Paul's two ex-

plicit references to the celebration of the Eucharist (1 Co.
10:16–21; 11:17–27) make no mention of anyone presiding
over the gathering and rather show the eucharist to be essentially a community action. But the silence is, in fact, not total,
inasmuch as the words "the blessing-cup that we bless" (1 Co.
10:16) probably allude to the formula of consecration as
pronounced by the president of the meeting; note that in
1 Samuel 9:13 the words "bless the sacrifice" (*eulogein tēn
thysian*) mean "consecrate the victim."[11] In any event, the
silence is not a sure proof that no one presided over the gathering, for another explanation is preferable. Paul's language,
especially "the table of the Lord" as contrasted with "the table
of demons" (1 Co. 10:21), shows that he regards the eucharist as a true sacrifice. But, since there can only be one sacrifice in the new covenant, Paul can only think of the true celebrant of the eucharist as Christ himself. If, then, there are
men who repeat the gestures of the Last Supper in the presence
of the assembled Church, they can only be living signs of the
invisible presence and permanent mediatorial action of the
Christ the priest.[12]

It is clear, however, that the role of priests in the new covenant cannot be limited to the eucharist, however important
the latter may be. Their mission, being a sharing in that of
Christ, must be coextensive with his. It must therefore include
the preaching of the word of God, from which indeed the
eucharistic mystery itself is inseparable, as the discourse on
the bread of life in John 6 shows. As Jesus indicates in John
17:20, it will normally be through the mediation of Christ's
ambassadors and thanks to their preaching that men through
the centuries will believe in Jesus. It is true enough that the
Council of Trent did not stress this important aspect of Christian priesthood, although it had been prefigured in the Old
Testament inasmuch as priests were charged with the religious
education, unfortunately often overlooked, of the people of
God. The reason for Trent's onesidedness is that its aim was

to oppose the errors of Luther, who denied the existence of a special priesthood communicated through the sacrament of orders, as well as the sacrificial nature of the Mass. In his view, there could only be delegates of the community, and their only function was to preach the gospel.

In both John 17 and the accounts of the Last Supper, we see men being specially set apart by Jesus for functions strictly reserved to them. There is nothing surprising about this if we remember the structure of Jesus' prayer in John 17 (cf. Chapter 2, above). In this tripartite prayer the apostles occupy a special section, set between the prayer of Jesus for himself and his prayer for all believers. In other words, they occupy the same middle place as the Levitical priests in the liturgy of the Day of Atonement, when the high priest offers a threefold expiation: for himself, for the other priests, and for the whole people of God.

We also saw earlier, at the end of Chapter 3, that according to the Apocalypse, Christ makes "kings and priests" of all his faithful disciples. In fact, if we take all the scriptural data into account, and especially the triple link of the Servant of Yahweh with the Davidic line, the prophets, and the priests, we must say even more of the disciples of Christ. As Max Thurian writes:

> Christ came as the Servant who fully carries out the old covenant: he is the perfect successor of the prophets, the priests, and the kings of the chosen people; he brings to completion the work they had begun in the service of the living God. Once Christ has come, there will be no more prophets, priests, and kings, as the old covenant knew these, but only a prophetic, priestly, and kingly people.[13]

But analogy with the Old Testament also makes it clear that the priesthood of all God's people under the new covenant does not exclude a priestly ministry strictly reserved to certain individuals. In Exodus 19:5–6 Yahweh says that although all the earth and all peoples belong to him, he has nonetheless determined to make of Israel alone "a kingdom of priests." That is the reason for his choice of them. The meaning is doubtless that Israel will be a kind of intermediary between God and the other nations; Israel will be the normal place where he manifests himself, and the means by which he will communicate his salvation to other men. And, in fact, it was indeed through Israel that the gentiles came to know the one true God. But this choice of Israel does not prevent a further setting apart of men within the bosom of the chosen people for the exercise of liturgical functions that are strictly reserved to them. Later on, the third part of the Book of Isaiah foretells the resacralization of the whole chosen people: "But you, you will be named 'priests of Yahweh,' they will call you 'ministers of our God'" (61:6). But once again the same oracle foretells also the choice of priests and Levites for the purpose of helping the people to maintain its sacred character: "Of some of them I will make priests and Levites, says Yahweh" (Is. 66:21).

The two settings apart, of the first people of God and of priests in the narrow sense of the term, are neither exclusive of each other nor identical with each other. In fact, the serious sin of Korah, Dathan, and Abiram, which led to their death, was to deny the distinction between the two kinds of priesthood. "Korah . . . Dathan and Abiram . . . joined forces against Moses and Aaron saying to them, 'You take too much on yourselves! The whole community and all its members are consecrated, and Yahweh lives among them. Why set yourselves higher than the community of Yahweh?' . . . The moment he [Moses] finished saying all these words, the ground split open under their feet, the earth opened its mouth and swallowed them, their families too, and all Korah's men and all their belongings" (Nb. 16:3, 31–32).[14]

In order, probably, to express the difference between the two priesthoods, the Septuagint uses for the priesthood of all the people the word *hierateuma* (Ex. 19:6; 2 M. 2:17; the *-ma* ending points to the result of the action). For the priesthood in the narrower sense, it regularly uses the term *hierateia* (Ex. 29:9; 39:19; 40:15; Nb. 3:10; 18:1, 7; 25:13; Jos. 18:7; 1 K. 2:26; Ezr. 2:62; Ne. 7:64; 13:29). The same distinction of terms is found in the New Testament: *hierateia* is used for the priesthood of Zechariah (Lk. 1:9) or the sons of Levi (Heb. 7:5), and *hierateuma* for the priesthood of the Christian people in 1 Peter 2:5, 9: "so that you too, the holy priesthood that offers the spiritual sacrifices which Jesus Christ has made acceptable to God, may be living stones . . . You are 'a chosen race, a royal priesthood, a consecrated nation . . .' "[15]

We need not enter here into a lengthy discussion of the nature of the distinction. But we can, even while staying within the Johannine writings, show that the distinction has a solid basis. All the disciples of Christ must love one another as Christ has loved them, and must sacrifice themselves as he has done before them. They must even be ready to give their lives ("lay [down] their souls") as he did. It is undoubtedly through such self-sacrifice and readiness to die that they chiefly carry out their priestly office (cf. Jn. 12:24–26; 13:34; 15:12; 1 Jn. 3:16; Rm. 12:1–2; 1 P. 2:5). But how are they to fulfill their duty and reach such heights of generosity if they do not have at their disposition the redemptive and sanctifying power of Christ? It is by means of Christ's ambassadors and agents and the exercise of their ministerial priesthood that his power is normally present with and given to his disciples. From such texts as John 13:20; 17:18; and 20:21, it follows that Jesus hands on his own mission of sanctification to the Twelve and thus also to their successors.[16]

PRIESTHOOD AND MISSION

WHEREAS THE PRIESTS of the Old Testament were not the messengers of Yahweh, priesthood and mission are closely connected for the apostles: "Consecrate them in the truth . . .

As you have sent me into the world, I have sent them into the world." Priestly consecration by the Father and mission go together in the life of the incarnate Son of God: "someone the Father has consecrated and sent into the world." Priestly consecration by the Father and mission will also go together in the lives of the apostles. In fact, due allowance being made, the apostles will be, as it were, other Christs! It is true, of course, that while it is the Father who sends his Son into the world, it is Christ who sends the apostles. Yet through Christ it is the Father, origin of all things, who does the sending since the sole reason for their being sent is that they may carry on the mission of the incarnate Son of God.

In the strict sense of the terms, Christ is the only one sent by the Father into the world in order to save it; he alone is the Saviour of the world. If, then, the apostles are also sent into the world to labor for its salvation, it can only be as the ambassadors or stewards of Christ, who act in his name and in dependence on him.[17] Similarly, Christ alone is, in the strict sense, the priest of the new dispensation. He is priest by nature and for ever because he is the incarnate Son of God; he can have neither rival nor successor. If, then, the apostles and those who continue their work become priests, it can only be as the agents of Christ the priest, who depend on him and act "in his person."

What we would like to do here is to analyze more exactly, in the light of the data provided in the gospel, the relations between the priesthood of the apostles and their mission. The consecration of Christ as priest precedes his being sent into the world: "someone the Father has consecrated and sent into the world" (Jn. 10:36). So, too, the priestly consecration of the apostles (17:17–19) precedes their being definitively sent out into the world, an event that takes place only after the resurrection of Jesus: "As the Father sent me, so am I sending you" (20:21). The end of the first gospel harmonizes with the Johannine presentation: "All authority in heaven and on earth has been given to me. Go therefore, make disciples of all the nations" (Mt. 28:18–19; cf. Mk. 16:15).

In John 17, however, the mission is also presented as an accomplished fact, an event in the past: "As you sent me into the world, I have sent them into the world" (17:19). Does not mission therefore seem to have preceded priestly consecration, since Jesus is just now asking the Father for this consecration: "Consecrate them in truth"? How is this discrepancy to be explained? The answer is that in John 17 Jesus is anticipating the future, as though he had already returned to the Father. At the same time, however, we must not forget that consecration and definitive mission were preceded by a lengthy preparation that began when the Twelve were appointed or chosen.

In John 17, Jesus alludes to this preparation. For, whereas in Verses 2 and 24 the formula "that which you have given me" applies to all the disciples of Jesus, present and future, in Verse 6, which speaks only of the apostles, the latter are described as "the men you took from the world to give me." In John 15:19 this setting apart from the world is attributed to Christ himself: "Because you do not belong to the world, because my choice withdrew you from the world, therefore the world hates you."

The appointment of the Twelve is highlighted in the three synoptic gospels (Mk. 3:13–19; Mt. 10:1–4; Lk. 6:12–16); it is already a setting apart. The text of Mark is especially clear: "He appointed twelve; they were to be his companions and to be sent out to preach, with power to cast out devils" (3:14). The idea that the apostles were to represent the whole people of God and should therefore be twelve in number seems to be a priestly rather than a prophetic idea. Thus, in the pectoral of the high priest twelve precious stones were set, bearing the names of the twelve tribes of Israel (Ex. 28:17–21), and in the shoulder straps which supported the ephod were set two more precious stones, each inscribed with the names of six of the twelve tribes (Ex. 28:9–11). The language of Mark in 3:14 is unusual: *kai epoiēsen dodēka,* literally "he made twelve." The use of the verb "make" to mean "appoint" is non-classical, but it is found in 1 Kings 12:31: "he appointed priests" (*epoiēsen hiereis;* cf. 13:33; 2 Ch. 2:18), and again in 1 Samuel 12:6: "he [Yahweh] who raised up Moses and Aaron." In these passages the reference is not to prophetic vocations but to the cultic institutions of the Old Testament.

The appointment of the Twelve means two things: They are to leave their present familial and social milieu and remain with Jesus; they are to share in his ministry. It is clear that even though the other disciples of Jesus cannot be disinterested in the cause of God's kingdom, the Twelve are now bound to make it their special concern. This is why as time passes we see the Twelve often receiving special instruction. The consecration for which Jesus prays in John 17 is thus the climax of a long preparation that has already set them apart from the mass of disciples.

If we prescind from Luke 6:13, the fourth gospel is the only one to speak of choice (verb: *eklegesthai*) with regard to the Twelve: 6:70; 13:18; 15:16 (twice), 19. The five occurrences of the term are the more noteworthy in that John rarely mentions the Twelve as such. The great Old Testament prophets were not instructed by Yahweh in the same way that the Twelve are instructed by Jesus, nor were they said to be chosen. The objects of a divine choice or election were the kings, the chief agents in the history of salvation (Abraham, Moses), places of worship, the priests, and the Levites.[18]

This fact about "choice" helps us realize how complex and difficult it is to define the idea of "apostle." Since the Twelve are appointed or chosen by Jesus, we are reminded of the cultic institutions of the Old Testament, and especially the priesthood. On the other hand, the appointment of the Twelve as a group was preceded by individual callings which remind

us of the calling of the prophets: the calling of the four fisher-
men (Mk. 1:14–20 par.), the calling of Levi (Mk. 2:13–14
par.). There is also the remark that immediately precedes the
listing of the Twelve: "He went up into the hills and sum-
moned those he wanted" (Mk. 3:13).

The fact that the apostles are sent by Jesus turns our
thoughts in the same direction. Just as Yahweh had his envoys, the prophets, who were his greatest servants, through
whom he spoke to the chosen people and in whom he was, as
it were, present to his people, so Jesus too (and this is a mark
of his transcendence) has his envoys and servants. The latter
are the apostles, in whom he is, as it were, present, so that
whoever receives them receives Jesus himself, and whoever
rejects them rejects Jesus himself (Mt. 10:24–25, 40;
Jn. 13:20; 15:20–21).

In short, like the suffering Servant of Isaiah and like Christ
himself, the apostles resemble both the priests and the prophets of the old covenant. It is a well-known fact that St. Paul
thought of, and expressed, what we call his conversion, in
terms of a prophetic calling; he had in mind more especially
the calling of Jeremiah (cf. Ga. 1:15 and Jr. 1:5). But his
case is not to be regarded as an exception; what is true of him
is basically true of all the apostles.

When St. Paul writes that the foundation of the Church,
God's holy temple, is the apostles and the prophets (Ep. 2:
20–21), we can hardly take this as referring to the Old Testament prophets since these would not be named after the
apostles and, great though they were, do not form part of the
Christian building but only prepare for it. Nor can we take the
word "prophets" as referring only to the prophets of the New
Testament; these figures are too shadowy to be given such importance. "Prophets" must include, at least in part, the apostles themselves: the apostles who are also prophets (we note
that there is but one article with the two nouns: "the apostles
and prophets").[19]

Admittedly, if the priesthood passes from the apostles to their successors, it does not follow that the latter are also prophets in the same way and the same degree. After all, St. Paul had just reminded us that the apostles play a unique role in the history of salvation; there is a sense in which they have no successors.[20] But we must at least maintain that the priesthood of the new covenant is in the line of the priesthood of Isaiah 53 and of Christ himself; that is, priesthood in the New Testament is a synthesis of both the priestly and the prophetic conceptions of the Old Testament.

When we bear in mind that the mission of the apostles is like that of the prophets, it becomes easier to understand how John 17 can suggest that, alongside the high priest of the new covenant, there are other priests, the "consecrated" individuals of Verses 17 and 19. The Old Testament knew only one divine revealer: Yahweh alone teaches; Moses and the prophets have no real successors.[21] But the one revealer does communicate through numerous prophets who are his spokesmen; the one God speaks through these many instruments. Similarly, in the New Testament there is only one priest, the incarnate Son of God, but he speaks and acts in the Church through many priests who are simply his instruments. The latter may act as priests only in dependence on Christ, for their priesthood and mission derive from the priesthood and mission of Christ.

CONSECRATION IN THE TRUTH (JN. 17:17), ASSIMILATION TO CHRIST THE TRUTH, AND THE SPIRITUAL LIBERATION OF MANKIND●THE PRIEST AT THE SERVICE OF MEN THROUGH THE WORD OF GOD AND THE SACRAMENTS

WE MUST NOW TURN to the very important and difficult formulas of John 17:17 and 19: consecration "in the truth" and consecration "in truth." Though they seem almost identical, they are not to be taken as synonymous. Grammatically, they differ since the first has the definite article and the second does not. We must take each formula separately.

But first, what does the word "truth" mean? Despite the opinion of some exegetes,[22] it is difficult to maintain that the Johannine idea of "truth" is wholly reducible to the "fidelity" (*'emet*) of the Old Testament. Other commentators have often derived the meaning of the term from Platonism or Gnosticism, in which truth has to do with what is hidden from the senses and is permanent, in contrast to what is superficial and changing. I. de la Potterie rightly rejects this approach.[23]

Without entirely forgetting the Greek world (cf. Jn. 8:32: "liberation through the truth" is a commonplace of Hellenistic philosophy), we must certainly start with the fact that in the Old Testament truth is not atemporal and suprahistorical, as in Hellenism, but bound up with the history of salvation and the covenant. At the same time, however, we must take into account the partly new meaning the word "truth" receives in the apocalyptic and sapiential literature as well as in the Qumran writings.

In the sapiential and apocalyptic literature "truth" is synonymous with revealed teaching, mystery, or the divine plan of salvation. A glimpse of this meaning may be caught as early as Proverbs 8:6, to be translated as, "My mouth proclaims the truth" (cf. 23:23). In Daniel 11:2 "truth" refers to the revelations brought to Daniel by an angel; in Daniel 10:21 "the Book of Truth" is the book in which the divine plan of salvation is written down. The promise of Wisdom 3:9, that the just "will understand the truth," does not mean that they will experience God's fidelity or that they will see God, but that they will at last understand God's mysterious plan.[24]

Especially important for us here is the sapiential Psalm 119, in which the Law (or the Word) signifies the whole of divine revelation considered as a rule of life, and in which Law, knowledge, and truth are very closely interconnected.[25] In a

rather remarkable way, the Psalm several times makes Word
(or Law) and truth equivalent (cf. Verses 43, 142, 151,
160). Jesus will later do the same thing in the very passage we
are now studying: "your word is truth" (Jn. 17:17), and John
does it in the prologue of his gospel where "the Word" is the
very person of Jesus. The conclusion to be drawn is clear: the
incarnate Son of God, the Word made flesh, brings the truth
because his coming into this world, his teaching, and his action all are the definitive revelation of the divine plan for salvation.

In the Book of Wisdom the revelation of Wisdom's action
in history brings with it the revelation of Wisdom's own nature: "What Wisdom is and how she came to be, I will now
declare, I will hide none of the secrets from you; I will . . .
set out knowledge of her, plainly, not swerving from the
truth" (Ws. 6:22). So, too, in the fourth gospel, the understanding of Christ's saving intervention in the world depends
on the understanding of his origin and nature and thus of the
very mystery of God. In the last analysis, truth in the fourth
gospel is something christological and eschatological, for it
is the mystery of the divine being and the divine plan for salvation insofar as these have been revealed in the person and
work of Jesus Christ. The invisible, transcendent God has
spoken in his only Son who is now incarnate. Consequently,
"truth" has its ultimate basis in the very person of Christ; in
Christ truth has entered the world.[26]

Exegetes have sometimes seen a relationship between the
prologue of the fourth gospel and the priestly prayer of Chapter 17.[27] One of the most striking resemblances between the
two is the fact that the word "truth" occurs twice in the prologue and three times in Chapter 17 and that in both places it
is connected with the word. There is an obvious parallel between "your word is truth" (Jn. 17:17) and "The Word was
made flesh . . . full of grace and truth. . . . grace and truth
have come through Jesus Christ" (Jn. 1:14, 17). It is a fact,

of course, that in John 17:17 "word" does not directly refer
to the person of God's only Son, as it does in the prologue.[28]
But is there any doubt that in 17:17 the person of the Son is
what is ultimately being referred to, as the living synthesis of
the revelation that Christ brought to the world? In recording
the statement in 17:17 could the evangelist have forgotten
what he himself had written at the beginning of his gospel?

We are now in a position to explain more fully what is meant
by the consecration of the apostles "in the truth." According
to M.-J. Lagrange, it is not enough to say simply that the
apostles are to be at the service of the truth; the meaning is
rather that they are to be "penetrated and interiorly changed
by the truth."[29] W. Thüsing comments: "The Father consecrates the disciples of Jesus in the truth by keeping them
within the sacred space formed by his revelation and by bestowing on them the power of his revelation, which is the
power of the Holy Spirit."[30]

Thüsing's final words here suggest that we should connect
the petition "consecrate them in the truth" with the statement:
"When the Paraclete, the Spirit of truth, comes, he will lead
you into the path of truth in its entirety" (Jn. 16:13).[31] The
various promises concerning the Paraclete show that his role
is to make them understand from within the teachings of
Jesus; it is to be the interior teacher of the disciples, enabling
them, as it were, to get inside the truth that Jesus reveals; that
is, to get inside Jesus himself. For he is in his very being the
Way which leads to the Father (14:6), as well as the Truth
(ibid.), and sums up in his own person the whole revelation
he brings concerning what God is and what men are or ought
to be in relation to God.

We should remember at this point that the promises of the
Paraclete have a double reference.[32] They certainly refer to
future history and the Church of all the ages since they herald
the fulfillment of the prophecies uttered by Jeremiah (31:31–
34: divine teaching to be given within man's heart) and

Ezekiel (36:26–27: communication of God's spirit) concerning the new covenant. But, first of all, and in a very special way, the promises refer to the apostles, who alone hear the discourses after the Supper. They are the first to be introduced to the truth in its entirety, so that they may establish the apostolic tradition which the later Church will not change but simply explain and make explicit. As eyewitnesses of Christ the Truth, the apostles have a unique role in the Church.

In asking, then, that the Father consecrate the apostles in the truth, Jesus is, for all practical purposes, asking that the Father make them like him ("the priest is another Christ"), prolongations, as it were, of he who is by his very being the Truth. Moreover, the connection between consecration in the truth and the promises voiced in 16:13 suggests that the assimilation to Jesus the Truth will be effected by the Holy Spirit. Commentators have wondered at times that the priestly prayer should say nothing about the Holy Spirit; but, in fact, the Spirit's action is presupposed at several points and especially at the point of which we are now speaking.[33]

Jesus the Truth, to whom the apostles are to be assimilated in a special way by their consecration, is the one Savior given men by the Father. The Father was looking to the salvation of mankind when he consecrated Jesus and sent him into the world. So, too, it is with the salvation of men in view that Jesus asks the Father to consecrate his apostles. As M.-J. Lagrange says in commenting on 17:17: "In order to act upon the world without being of the world, that is, without being contaminated by it, the disciples must receive a consecration which will complete their separation from the world and bring them close to God."[34] Their being set apart and separated from the world is not intended to isolate the apostles from the world, but only to assimilate them to the Truth that sets men free, to the one Saviour who lived in the world without being of it. In this way, they will be better fitted to work for the salvation of mankind by the same means that the one Saviour of men used.

We must emphasize this twofold orientation which the priest of the new covenant has in his mission among men. Being "consecrated in the truth," he is to bring the saving truth to the world, and he is to work for the world's salvation by using the same means as were used by Christ, the Truth to whom he has been assimilated.

The truth in which the apostles are consecrated is, as we have seen, the revelation brought by Jesus Christ; it is, in the last analysis, the very person of Christ the revealer. The two claims: "the truth will make you free" (8:32) and "the Son makes you free" (8:36) are set side by side by Jesus himself; he offers them as equivalent statements, synonyms that are quite evident in view of all we have been saying here. Chapter 8 must be read carefully if we are to understand what it is that Christ the Truth intends to free men from, first in his own person and later on through his representatives.

The liberation Christ brings is first and foremost a liberation from sin. Sin is the great enemy of God and by that very fact the great enemy of men; it is the only thing that truly enslaves men: "Everyone who commits sin is a slave" (8:34). Of course, as the gospel makes clear, Christ is also concerned with other aspects of liberation. He did not look upon physical ills with an indifferent eye. He had compassion on all human wretchedness, including the wretchedness of the body, and cured many who were ill. How could we forget that the message of the gospel has, more than anything else, roused love for the poor and oppressed and given men a sense of social justice? Nonetheless, it is clear that liberation from physical suffering of whatever kind is not the main thing with which he who was the great sufferer among men was concerned.

Moreover, the Christ of the gospels had no intention of establishing the rule of God on earth by using violence. Recall in this connection the third temptation in the desert (Mt.

4:8–11; cf. Lk. 4:5–8), the "Give back to Caesar what belongs to Caesar" (Mk. 12:17 par.), Jesus' refusal to call down fire from heaven on the Samaritans (Lk. 9:54), his refusal to let himself be made a king (Jn. 6:14), his rejection of violent resistance to evil (Lk. 22:38; Mt. 26:52), and his statement that his kingdom is not of this world (Jn. 18:36). Respectable commentators even claim that during his public ministry Jesus had constantly to fight against any compromise with the politico-religious ideals of the Zealots who were preaching a holy war and dreaming of bringing Roman overlordship to an end by force.[35]

Whatever is thought of this last hypothesis, one thing is clear: The essential aim of Christ was always the spiritual liberation of his brothers. The early Church understood this and followed the example of the Master. Thus, although its members often came from the lowest strata of society, and even from among slaves, it never preached rebellion. It did, however, preach a revolutionary message which would in the long run put an end to slavery: Slaves and masters alike, when converted, came to realize that in God's sight they were brothers, called to the same sharing in the life of God.

The representatives of Christ must therefore always bear in mind that their primary concern must be to change the souls of men and turn them to God, and that a mixture of religion and politics, in which politics gains the upper hand, is a betrayal of the gospel. This is not to say that the religion of Christ is content to rule over souls alone. On the contrary, the Apocalypse shows that this religion sets limits to the authority men exercise in this world; it sets its face against that authority when it becomes tyrannical and leagued with Satan. Historians have often noted that the religion of Christ is destructive of all tyranny and that wherever Christ has truly ruled the hearts of men, violence has subsided. But to this we must add that the authentic Christian message is not directly concerned with the well-being of the earthly city; it contributes to the latter, but it looks to something higher.

The poems of the Servant had already taken the same view, and in very eloquent fashion.[36] In the Old Testament political liberation and moral liberation are ordinarily closely connected and indeed inseparable. But the Servant of Yahweh is to be a purely spiritual liberator: "It is not enough for you [that is, it is unworthy of you] to be my servant, to restore the tribes of Jacob and bring back the survivors of Israel; I will make you the light of the nations so that my salvation may reach to the ends of the earth" (Is. 49:6). In Isaiah 40–55 Cyrus is to free Israel from its Babylonian captivity; the Servant, on the other hand, is to free men, be they Israelites or gentiles, from a purely spiritual captivity and imprisonment: "I, Yahweh . . . have taken you by the hand and formed you; I have appointed you as covenant of the people and light of the nations, to open the eyes of the blind, to free captives from prison, and those who live in darkness from the dungeon" (42:6–7). M.-J. Lagrange astutely observes in commenting on this passage: "Since the Servant's preaching is concerned with religion, it is clear that the servitude from which he frees men is the ignorance of religious truths . . . and from sin which is the usual consequence of such ignorance."[37]

In earlier prophecies, and notably in Ezekiel 34, the image of the straying and scattered flock is applied to the chosen people in their Babylonian captivity. But Isaiah 53 (probably having in mind a time when many Israelites have returned from exile to the holy land unaware of having been spiritually liberated) gives us to understand that the real diaspora does not arise from spatial separation from the home country but from spiritual distance away from the Lord, a distance caused by sin. Only from this diaspora, which consists for a man in following his own way and not that of the Lord, is the Servant commissioned to free men. That will also be the mission of Christ the Truth who fulfills to the letter the astounding oracle in Isaiah 53, which one might think had been written at the foot of the cross: "We had all gone astray like sheep, each taking his own way, and Yahweh burdened him with the sins of all of us" (53:6).

In the fourth gospel Christ the Truth saves the world through his word and through the sacraments he institutes. The latter are prolongations, as it were, of the mysteries of the incarnation and the redemptive passion. They will make their appearance once the incarnate Son of God, the great living sacrament who brings God to men, has returned to the Father. As long as he is on earth, there is no reason for the sacraments.[38] In reaction against some commentators (R. Bultmann, G. Bornkamm, E. Lohse, E. Schweizer), the dimension of reference to the sacraments in the fourth gospel has been heavily stressed, at times in what is clearly an excessive way.[39] It is impossible to doubt that John is interested in the sacraments and that the highlights, in particular, the basic importance of baptism and the eucharist. The close relationship between the word of God, which is in itself an authentic food, and the sacrament of the eucharist has long been a traditional teaching of the Church; that teaching has the most solid of foundations in the discourse in John 6 on the bread of life.

Having been by their consecration assimilated in a special way to Christ whom the Father has sent into the world to save it (Jn. 17:18: "As you sent me into the world, I have sent them into the world"), the apostles must labor, through preaching and the administration of the sacraments, for the salvation of the world. The two tasks must be as closely linked in their ministry as the word of Jesus and the sacraments are in the fourth gospel. Need we remind ourselves here that the atmosphere of John 17 is entirely eucharistic?

In his commentary on John 17, Lagrange is quite right to protest against A. Durand's statement that "the chief ministry of the apostle is to preach the gospel; the Old Testament was chiefly concerned with cultus, the New Testament must be concerned, *first of all,* with teaching."[40] As Lagrange says, the "first of all" is true only in the order of execution; that is, first must come the teaching, which gives rise to and nourishes faith, then come the sacraments.[41] Moreover, Lagrange goes on to say, Durand's view of things has been unduly influenced by the special vocation of St. Paul who writes: "Christ did not send me to baptise, but to preach the Good News" (1 Co. 1:17). The work of the other apostles, as defined by Christ, includes not only preaching but the sacraments, as two inseparable functions of the same ministry. "Go, therefore, make disciples of all the nations; baptise them in the name of the Father and of the Son and of the Holy Spirit" (Mt. 28:19). We may note, too, that St. Paul did occasionally baptize (cf. 1 Co. 1:14–16) and that it must have been chiefly for practical reasons, especially the lack of time, that he preferred to leave this task to others.[42]

Nor may we forget that the Apostle of the gentiles understands his missionary work to be an act of worship and priesthood:[43] "The reason why I have written to you . . . is to refresh your memories, since God has given me this special position. He has appointed me as a priest [*leitourgon*] of Jesus Christ, and I am to carry out my priestly duty [*hierourgounta*] by bringing the Good News from God to the pagans, and so to make them acceptable as an offering [*prosphora*] made holy by the Holy Spirit" (Rm. 15:15–16).[44] And: "If my blood is to be shed as part of your own sacrifice [*thysia*] and offering [*leitourgia*]—which is your faith—I shall still be happy and rejoice with all of you" (Ph. 2:17).[45] We must also mention the text in which St. Paul compares workers for the gospel with the Jewish priests who drew their livelihood from the altar because they had Yahweh for "their inheritance" (cf. Dt. 18:1–2; Nb. 18:20–24): "Remember that the ministers serving in the Temple [*ta hiera ergazomenoi*] get their food from the Temple [*ta ek tou hierou*] and those serving at the altar can claim their share from the altar itself. In the same sort of way the Lord directed that those who preach the gospel should get their living from the gospel" (1 Co. 9:13–14). In commenting on this passage P. Grelot rightly observes:

> It is also true that Paul's reflection here on the calling of the Christian clergy and their condition as men living on earth looks as much to the example of the prophets as to that of the levitical clergy. The title "prophets" for the apostles is not unknown to the gospels (Mt. 23:34; Lk. 11:49), and the account of St. Paul's vocation recalls the visions with which the prophets began their work. So too the charismatic side of the apostolate and other ministries reminds us very much of the charismatic side of Old Testament prophetism.[46]

Here we come back to a point made several times in earlier chapters of this book: like the priesthood of the suffering Servant, which prophetically points to the priesthood of the new covenant, the latter looks back to both the Levitical and prophetic traditions of the Old Testament.

CONSECRATION IN TRUTH (JN. 17:19) AND ASSIMILATION TO CHRIST AS PRIEST AND VICTIM•CONSECRATION IN TRUTH AND WORSHIP IN SPIRIT AND IN TRUTH•THE THEOCENTRIC NATURE OF PRIESTLY CONSECRATION

THE CONSECRATION OF THE APOSTLES "in truth" is closely dependent on the consecration of Christ himself: "For their sake I consecrate myself so that they too may be consecrated in truth" (Jn. 17:19). In consecrating a victim Jesus acts as a priest; in consecrating himself he also acts as the expiatory victim which replaces the animal sacrifices of the Old Testament. In so doing he carries further the thought of Isaiah 53, as we have frequently noted in the preceding pages.

The surprising thing in John 17:19 is that the fruit of the

redemptive sacrifice seems to be limited to the apostles alone. Elsewhere in the Johannine writings, Christ is given by the Father and offers himself in sacrifice for the salvation of the whole world (Jn. 3:16; 6:51; 1 Jn. 4:10). But the narrowing of perspective in the present passage is readily explained once we accept the priestly interpretation of the prayer in John 17 as a whole and the transposition of the liturgy of the Day of Atonement which the chapter represents. Jesus' intention in the verses under consideration is to show his redemptive suffering to be the wellspring of the priesthood of the apostles, just as elsewhere in the fourth gospel the same suffering is clearly shown to us as being the source of the sacraments of baptism and the eucharist.

The consecration received by the apostles is to assimilate them to Christ as priest. The Father had first consecrated his Son as priest (10:36); now Jesus asks him (17:17) to consecrate his apostles in the same way. At the next moment (17:19) Jesus stresses the fact that like the other blessings of the new covenant this consecration will be the fruit of his redemptive sacrifice: The Father will consecrate the apostles through Jesus. It is evident that their consecration will be connected with his own: "For their sake I consecrate myself so that *they too* may be consecrated."

Here we may recall the commentary given earlier (Chapters 1 and 3) on John 10:36, as well as the connection we showed between the consecration of Jesus in 10:36 and the one in 17:19. It is with a view to the sacrifice he must offer to save men that the Father consecrates Christ as a priest; that is, it is with a view to the voluntary gift of his own life for the sins of all mankind. Jesus shows himself a priest first and foremost by fulfilling the oracle of Isaiah 53 on the suffering Servant. The Servant himself is the climactic figure in the long and splendid line of prophets who committed themselves wholeheartedly and heroically to the service of God, generously pouring out their energies and, if need be, sacrificing their lives for the cause of God's kingdom and the salvation of their brothers. The representatives of Christ the priest could not be worthy instruments of his if they were content to share in his saving power without at the same time sharing his outlook as victim and without trying to rouse in themselves something of the generosity of the ancient prophets.

In the Old Testament priestly consecration did not indeed bestow moral holiness, but it did call for such holiness in everyday life because of the holy actions priests had to perform. The prophets on occasion reproached priests for not living in a way that corresponded to their calling (Ho. 4:4–5; Ml. 1:6–7). The setting apart of the prophets likewise did not effect a moral holiness in them, and it is wrong to understand the "consecration" of Jeremiah before his birth as a purification from original sin.[47] It is true, however, that the call to be a prophet was also a special call to holiness and to a life wholly dedicated to the service of God. Moreover, this requirement on God's part brought with it promises of special divine help: God committed himself to make his demands possible of fulfillment through his grace, as we see in the model case of Jeremiah.

The same is true of the priestly consecration of the apostles which, like that of the Servant, is connected with both the Levitical and the prophetic traditions. Such a priestly consecration brings with it a special demand for holiness in the line of Isaiah 53 and the suffering of Christ; at the same time it is a guarantee that the divine energies needed for such holiness will be given along the way.

Bossuet expressed all this in a very rich text:

> Christ was holy and consecrated to God not only as a priest but also as a victim. That is why he sanctifies himself, offers himself, and consecrates himself like an object that is holy and dedicated to the Lord. But he adds: "I consecrate myself for their sake" (meaning his apostles), so that, sharing through their ministry in the grace of his priesthood, they

may also make their own his condition as victim, and, not having in their own power the holiness needed in order to be the envoys and ministers of Jesus Christ, they may find it in him.[48]

Numerous commentators have realized that the phrase "in truth" (17:19, without the definite article) cannot have exactly the same meaning as the phrase "in the truth" (17:17), which we explained earlier. Lagrange thinks that the words "in truth" mean "truly, in all truth," as in 2 John 1 and 3 John 1; that is (as he adds with a reference to St. John Chrysostom), "not by a purely external consecration, as in the old Law."[49]

Lagrange's remark is accurate enough as far as it goes, but we think it incomplete. It is hardly thinkable that there should be no connection at all between the "truth" meant in 17:17 and the words "in truth" of Verse 19. To determine what the connection is we cannot do better than to go to the "worship in spirit and in truth" of which Jesus speaks in his conversation with the Samaritan woman (4:23–24). We say this because the priestly consecration of the apostles "in truth" has to do with liturgy and must therefore have reference to the new worship in spirit and in truth which the "Christian dispensation" brings with it. R. E. Brown has noted the fact that 4:23–24 and 17:17–19 shed light on each other.[50]

What does adoration "in spirit" and "in truth" mean? In the past most commentators (Lagrange may serve as an example) gave the words "in spirit" and "in truth" a chiefly subjective meaning. These commentators prefer to think here of human psychology: "in truth" would mean "in a sincere disposition with regard to the truth one knows and possesses," and "in spirit" would mean "a human disposition: the spirit of a man is the part of him that is purest and most like God; man must use this faculty to seek and worship God."[51] Most modern exegetes rightly reject this kind of explanation. For, even prescinding from the fact that the expression "in spirit" is connected with the statement that "God is spirit" (4:24), the phrase "true worshippers" (4:23) must be connected with a number of similar formulas in the fourth gospel that have a precise meaning. Moreover, the immediate context concerns the complex relations between Old Testament worship and the new worship brought by Christ. These various facts direct us to an interpretation that is theological and not simply psychological.

The fourth gospel frequently uses the adjective "authentic, genuine" (*alēthinos*), which is not to be confused with "true, real" (*alēthēs*).[52] The adjective "genuine" expresses the fact that something corresponds to the meaning of the name given it; "real" expresses the fact that a person does not lie or that a thing is not lying or deceptive.[53] In 6:55 the statement that "my flesh is real food" (with *alēthēs*) means that the food is not imaginary. On the other hand, the genuine (*alēthinos*) light of 1:9 is not opposed to a false light but to the imperfect revelations of the Old Testament. The genuine bread that comes down from heaven (6:32) is opposed to the manna that was likewise a bread that came from heaven. The genuine vine (15:1) is opposed to the vine that was Israel and had so often been reproached by the prophets. Similarly, the genuine worshippers who will worship the Father in spirit and in truth (4:23) are contrasted not with a false worship but with the imperfect worship of the Old Testament. The context also makes this clear: Jesus heralds the cessation not only of the schismatic worship of the Samaritans on Mt. Gerizim but also of the legitimate worship offered in the Temple at Jerusalem. Yet the latter was based on a genuine, even if imperfect, revelation; in God's plan it paved the way for the definitive kind of worship, since "salvation comes from the Jews" (4:22).

This data will help us understand what is meant by worship in spirit and in truth. Worship in truth is worship in conformity with the definitive revelation brought by Jesus, a revelation that is in the last analysis summed up in his own person. But worship in truth is inseparable from worship in spirit, inasmuch as it is possible only through a rebirth which the Spirit effects (3:5). In other words, worship in spirit is possible only because of a basic fact of the new dispensation: The new spirit that is given by the Holy Spirit.[54] Consequently, the words "worship the Father in spirit and in truth" imply the Trinity.

The "consecration in truth" of 17:19 must be explained along the same lines. It is a consecration that is in harmony with the definitive revelation given by Christ to mankind. This consecration is not effective without the intervention of the Holy Spirit, so that "consecration in truth" is also a "consecration in spirit." This consecration is contrasted with priestly consecration in the Old Testament, not as if the latter were false, but inasmuch as it was imperfect. Thus, we are led to compare the two dispensations in this respect. In fact, John 17 itself invites us to make such a comparison.

The fact that consecration in truth must be explained by reference to worship in spirit and in truth has important consequences. The priest of the new covenant, who is consecrated in the truth and thus assimilated to Christ the Truth, is certainly called to work for the salvation and spiritual liberation of mankind; this we showed above. But this more-or-less man-centered aspect of priesthood must not make us lose sight of another, essentially God-centered aspect. That the priesthood should have this other side to it is only to be expected, when we recall the transcendence of God and the fact that man exists only in dependence on God. The priests of the new dispensation are consecrated for the sake of a new worship; that is, for the sake of winning for the Father those worshipers in spirit and in truth whom Jesus tells us the Father seeks as though he had need of them (though he needs nothing and no one) and as though that were the highest goal of his plan of salvation. How could the priest win such worshippers for the Father if he did not try in his own prayer to become such a worshipper himself?

The theocentric character of priestly consecration in truth can also be established in another way. In the Old Testament the setting apart and consecrating of priests was an eloquent proclamation of God's rights and awesome holiness. "They shall be consecreated to their God and must not profane the name of their God. For it is they who bring the burnt offerings to Yahweh, the food of their God; and they must be in a holy condition" (Lv. 21:6); "Let no one enter the Temple of Yahweh except the priests and the Levites on duty, since they are consecrated and may enter" (2 Ch. 23:6). Now, it can be shown that in the same way the priestly consecration of the apostles is closely connected, in John 17, with God's holiness.

The prayer contains three forms of address to the Father: simply "Father" in Verses 1, 5, 21, 24; "Holy Father" in Verse 11; and "Father, Righteous One" in Verse 25. Some exegetes see a progression in the three forms of address. According to E. C. Hoskyns the progression reflects the movement of Jesus' prayer that begins with thoughts of his coming death and ends with thoughts of the glorification of the Church.[55] B. Schwank thinks that "Righteous One" represents a step beyond "holy"; for support he appeals to 1 Corinthians 6:11: "now you have been washed clean, and *sanctified,* and *justified* through the name of the Lord Jesus Christ and through the Spirit of our God."[56]

We cannot agree with this approach to the text. "Father," without a qualifying adjective, is the highest form of address conceivable, and it occurs at the very beginning of the prayer; it is not the starting point for an ascending series. "Father" corresponds to the Aramaic *abba,* a familiar term used by children in addressing their father. It is quite unusual to find it used in a prayer to God, yet it does express the spirit of Jesus' prayers as well as his awareness of being the Son of God in the strictest sense of the terms (cf. Mk. 14:36; Mt.

11:25–26; Lk. 11:2; Jn. 11:41; 12:27).[57] The address, "Father, Righteous One," in Verse 25, is easily explained, as R. E. Brown notes, by what comes immediately after. The Bible habitually speaks of the "justice" of God when he intervenes to punish the guilty or save the innocent; Verse 25 implicitly describes a divine judgment, since it contrasts two groups of men who stand before the Father: the world that has not known him and those men who have.[58]

But what of "Holy Father" in Verse 11? It occurs in the second part of the prayer; that is, the part that concerns the apostles and in which Jesus asks that they be set apart in a special way, that they be preserved from evil (or the evil one),[59] and that they be consecrated as priests and as victims. As we see it, there is surely a deliberate connection between the *hagios* (holy) addressed to the Father in Verse 11 and the three occurrences of *hagiazein* (sanctify or consecrate) in Verses 17 and 19. Lagrange cogently observes: "If Jesus addresses his Father as 'holy,' it is because he is going to ask his Father to sanctify his disciples"[60] and to make them, as it were, manifestations of his own holiness.

But what conclusion are we to draw from the fact? The conclusion that the priests of the new covenant are not simply men who dedicate themselves, or are dedicated by God, to the service of other men in a special way. Before they are directed toward men, they are directed toward God. Like the priests of the Old Testament, they are by their consecration to recall to men the unconditioned rights and moral demands of a God who is completely transcendent to the world and thrice holy.

We must add, however, that in the Christian dispensation the proclamation of the thrice holy God is internalized and sublimated in a way that is pregnant with consequences. It would take too long to demonstrate this, and in any case such a demonstration is not relevant to our purpose in this book.

We must content ourselves with a few convergent observations which are based on all that we have said up to this point.

The high priest of the old covenant wore a diadem on which were engraved the words "Consecrated to Yahweh" (Ex. 28:36). This does not mean, of course, that it was only through the diadem that the high priest reminded men of God's holiness and his own consecration. When Peter says that Jesus is "the Holy One of God" (Jn. 6:69), is this an allusion to the high priest's diadem and thus a figurative way of saying that Christ is a priest?[61] In any event, not by any diadem but by his innermost being Jesus proclaims the divine holiness with which he is associated in a unique and strictly incommunicable way. That association is what makes him the one and only priest of the new covenant. But since he has decided that weak men who are sinners like the rest of mankind are to represent him in his priesthood, he also wills that these men, far more than the priests of the old covenant, are to reflect God's holiness in their moral conduct and everyday lives. This is why he asks for them of the Father a "consecration in truth" which is far superior to the priestly consecration known in the former dispensation. Christ himself decided that there should be consecrated priests. And he wanted, not melancholy, fearful souls who would give themselves grudgingly, but joyous men who trust that they are sustained by the word of Christ and who are sure of the love he has for them: "While still in the world I say these things to share my joy with them to the full" (Jn. 17:13).

The priests and victims of the Old Testament had to be without physical defect. Isaiah shifts this requirement to the moral level and shows the suffering Servant to a just and sinless man who is therefore fully acceptable to Yahweh as priest and as sacrificial offering. The Christ of the gospels fulfills in an infinitely perfect way the prophetic statement of Isaiah 53, for he has no connection whatsoever with sin. More than other Christians, priests who represent Christ by reason of their priestly consecration should be deeply concerned with moral purity; they must "try to be as pure as Christ" (1 Jn. 3:3). This is why in John 17 Jesus offers a special prayer for them that they be protected from evil.

The purification Christ requires of all his disciples and in a special way of his priests is much more far-reaching than that which the sacrifices of the old covenant were thought to effect. Hebrews 9:13–14 brings out this point very strongly. At a much earlier time, Isaiah 53, as we showed earlier, a radical transformation of the sacrificial liturgy of the Old Testament portends, and the transformation is accomplished when Christ dies as expiatory victim for the sins of all mankind.

In keeping with this transformation, John 17 transposes and spiritualizes the solemn liturgy of the Day of Atonement. Jesus' ideal is not simply that of the festival of atonement; namely, that the people of God, through the mediation of its priests, should recover the purity required if they are to be a genuine mirror of God's holiness. There is now a new priesthood which, being consecrated "in truth" and closely linked with Jesus the Truth, shares in the divine love that brought about the incarnation and Calvary. Consequently, the people of God in the new covenant must reflect not only God's holiness but also the love that eternally unites the divine persons with one another.

Bearing in mind the tripartite structure of the prayer in John 17, we see that there are two distinct requests for unity. The first, in Verse 11, looks only to those disciples who will share in the priesthood of Jesus; only toward the end, in Verses 21–23, does Jesus ask, with no less intense a longing, for unity among all the members of the Church. He acts as if the unity of the Church would depend on unity among those whose task it will be to direct the Church.

The basic goal of the prayer in John 17 is that the Church should be as it were a mirror in which the unity of Father and Son is reflected. By this fact the perspectives adopted in the Old Testament are greatly transcended. Here we have valuable pointers given us as we try to recover an authentic priestly spirituality. To this point we shall return in the Conclusion of this book.

THE WASHING OF FEET (JN. 13:1–20): THE HUMBLE EX-
ERCISE OF AUTHORITY IN THE CHURCH AND THE PREPARA-
TION OF THE APOSTLES FOR THEIR CONSECRATION AS PRIESTS

NUMEROUS INTERPRETATIONS have been offered of the washing of feet in John 13 (Verses 1–20), and we have no intention of examining them in detail.[62] We need only recall here that the interpretations may be reduced to two types. There are the moralizing interpretations according to which Christ is giving us an example of humility by performing an action usually left to slaves; many commentators add that Christ's act is but a symbol of the great abasement of his passion. Then there are the sacramental interpretations, such as some of the Fathers were already providing:[63] these consider Christ's action to be either symbolic or an act of purification or communion, and they connect the action sometimes with baptism, sometimes with penance, sometimes with the eucharist.

Those who back the moralizing interpretation usually accept the passage as a unit. The unity is challenged, on the other hand, by a number of those who defend the sacramental interpretation; we may mention F. Spitta, W. Bauer, R. Bultmann, and M.-E. Boismard.[64] These critics differ a good deal in their explanations of the passage; we shall restrict ourselves to the arguments offered by Boismard. In his view, the present text of John is a combination of two complete accounts from two divergent and temporally successive traditions concerning the washing of feet. Verses 1–2, 4–5, 12–15, 17, and 18–19 belong to the moralizing tradition, and Verses 3, 4–5, 6–10, 11, and 21–30 to the sacramental tradition. Verses 16 and 20 have no direct connection with their immediate context and were added by the final redactor.

There are several objections to Boismard's conjecture. Verses 1 and 3 do indeed constitute two introductions, but we are not therefore justified in speaking of a doublet. Verse 3 introduces only the washing of the feet, while Verse 1 also serves as an introduction to everything that follows, including the death of Jesus. In fact, the words of the dying Jesus, "It is accomplished" (19:30), seem to be an intentional recall, in the form of an inclusion, of the words "now he showed how perfect his love was" (13:1), the death of Jesus being the supreme proof of that love.[65] Moreover, since Verses 21–30 are made up of elements that largely correspond to things found in the synoptics, there is no reason for considering them to be an integral part of the episode of the washing of feet and for seeing in them an extension of the sacramental tradition; most exegetes rightly think of Verse 21 as the beginning of a new development.

This leaves us with the chief argument proposed by those who deny the unity of the passage and by Boismard in particular. Before speaking of this argument, however, we must take a stand on an important problem of textual criticism. With a number of authors, Boismard among them, we think that in Verse 10 the short reading, "No one who has taken a bath needs washing," is to be preferred to the longer reading, ". . . needs washing except for his feet." The short reading has in its favor the impressive agreement of the Codex Sinaiticus, Origen, Tatian, Tertullian, and the great majority of early Latin Fathers. In itself, moreover, the short reading seems the better, for several reasons: Copyists tend to lengthen rather than abridge; the words "except for his feet" contradict the words immediately following, "he is clean *all over*"; the words were probably added later on to justify Christ's action.[66]

Now to the chief argument against the unity of the passage. According to Boismard, two distinct and irreconcilable meanings are successively given to Christ's action by the evangelist. According to 13:8, if Peter does not let Jesus wash him, he will not be admitted into the company of Jesus in the next world, but will damn himself; this meaning corresponds to John 3:3: "Unless a man is born from above, he cannot see the kingdom of God." But according to 13:12–16 a man need only imitate the humility of Christ and he will have eternal life; there is no allusion here to the need of any sacramental rite. According to 13:8 if one is to be saved, one must be washed and purified by Christ. According to 13:12–16 one is saved by imitating Christ and washing the feet of others; that is (in view of the hidden reference to the Servant of Yahweh and to the passion of Christ), by loving others to the point of giving one's life for them.

What is to be thought of this exegesis? To suppose that the text is incoherent is a solution born of desperation, and it is not to be accepted unless it is absolutely forced on us. In fact, however, no contradiction exists between the two parts of the passage (Jesus' dialogue with Peter and the following discourse), unless we accept a strict sacramental interpretation of the dialogue with Peter. But an objective examination of the text shows that such an interpretation is not necessary.[67] The whole episode can be understood quite differently if we keep two facts in mind. First, the washing of feet can symbolize the passion not only insofar as the latter is an abasement of Jesus, but also insofar as it is a purifying bath for sinful mankind (with Christ suffering the purification of mankind's sins). Second, the dialogue between Jesus and Peter recalls the dialogue that follows upon the first prediction of the passion in the synoptics (Mk. 8:32–33; Mt. 16:21–23): In both cases Jesus warns Peter that if he rejects the mystery of the cross, he can no longer be a companion of Jesus.[68]

We could rest satisfied with this general explanation of the passage. But several points about the episode urge us to complete the explanation along lines that contribute to our purpose in this book. Moreover, if we do not attend to these points, we are likely to miss the main purpose behind the writing of John 13.

The first point that invites us to look for a more precise and profound explanation is the twofold fact that Jesus washes only the feet of his apostles and that the lesson of humility is addressed primarily to them.

The washing of the feet is an introduction to the farewell discourses which seem to have been addressed only to the Twelve. This would agree with the fact that according to the synoptics only the Twelve are present at Jesus' last meal (cf. Mk. 14:17; Mt. 26:20; Lk. 22:14). In John 13–17 the only persons who are named or who speak are part of the apostolic group: the traitor Judas, Peter, Thomas, Philip, another Judas (cf. Lk. 6:16; Ac. 1:13), and the beloved disciple. The same conclusion emerges if we compare 13:18: "I know the ones I have chosen," with 6:70: "Have I not chosen you, you Twelve?"[69]

Given such a context, there is no difficulty in understanding that the lesson Jesus himself draws from the washing of the feet is not a general lesson in humility addressed to all disciples without distinction but rather a lesson on humility in the exercise of authority. This is why he insists so strongly on the startling contrast: He, the lord and master, without ceasing to be lord and master, has washed his own disciples' feet. Christ has chiefly in mind those who will exercise his authority in the Church. It is the same important lesson that is to be found in the parallel passage in Luke (22:24–27; cf. Mk. 10:42–44; Mt. 20:25–28): The greatest in the Christian community must, like Christ, act as if they were the youngest and the servants of the others.[70]

The parallel texts in Matthew and Mark are placed after the request made by the sons of Zebedee (or by their mother, according to Matthew). Here is what Mark says:

> When the other ten heard this they began to feel indignant with James and John, so Jesus called them to him and said to them, "You know that among the pagans their so-called rul-

ers lord it over them, and their great men make their authority felt. This is not to happen among you. No; anyone who wants to become great among you must be your servant, and anyone who wants to be first among you must be slave to all. For the Son of Man himself did not come to be served but to serve, and to give his life as a ransom for many (Mk. 10:41–44).

Luke's text is put in the context of Jesus' last meal:

A dispute arose also between them about which should be reckoned the greatest, but he said to them, "Among pagans it is the kings who lord it over them, and those who have authority over them are given the title Benefactor. This must not happen with you. No; the greatest among you must behave as if he were the youngest, the leader as if he were the one who serves. For who is the greater: the one at table or the one who serves? The one at table, surely? Yet here am I among you as one who serves!

Both in John 13 and in the passages from the synoptics there is in the background the poignant figure of Christ the Servant who fulfills to the end the prophecy of Isaiah 53. The idea expressed in all the passages is the very important one that authority in the Church means humble service. Authority is for the service of the community. It can be exercised in the right way only if its possessor tries constantly to share the sentiments that inspired Christ the Servant in his suffering.

Christ is in advance denouncing and fighting against the serious danger that today we call clericalism. The apostles, having their authority from Jesus himself, are certainly not simply delegates of the community. They cannot be conceived in this way because they were chosen by Jesus at the beginning of his ministry to be the nucleus of the Church and they are prior to the fully constituted Christian community. Nonetheless, they must constantly be on the watch not to put themselves outside or above the Church for they are entirely at the service of the Church. This is the basic lesson Jesus is teaching them in John 13, and he does it by bringing before their eyes in advance the act that can both illustrate and make possible for them the very difficult exercise of authority as service: his own passion.

This analysis of the passage explains several points that at first reading surprise us in the scene of the washing of feet. The washing is much more than a lesson in humility, despite what the explanatory discourse following it (Verses 13–16) may suggest; it is first and foremost a symbol of the very source of our salvation, as the dialogue with Peter (Verses 6–11) suggests. Yet when Jesus comments on his action, the only lesson he draws is that of humble service. Comparison with the parallel passages in the synoptics explains the anomaly. In Mark 10:42–44 the passion in which the Son of Man will give his life as a ransom for the multitude is proposed to the disciples as an example for them, and we might say that it is brought in only as an example for the sake of comparison (cf. Mt. 20:28: *"just as* the Son of Man . . ."), whereas in fact it is infinitely more than that, being the very source of sinful mankind's reconciliation with God.

It is too quick and superficial a judgment to say that Verse 16 does not belong in this context; this is the verse in which Jesus says that a servant is not greater than his master nor a messenger (literally an apostle) greater than the person who sent him. For, even if the word "apostle" is not to be taken in its technical sense, Jesus is always thinking of his apostles and trying to make them understand that their seemingly privileged position in the Church must not prevent them from humbling themselves as he had done.

It is more difficult to connect the unexpected Verse 20 closely to its context. Christ here states the dignity of the apostles, which is measured by his own dignity: "Whoever welcomes the one I send welcomes me, and whoever welcomes me welcomes the one who sent me." There is, however, at least this connection with the washing of the feet, that Jesus is still addressing his apostles. Lagrange supposes that Jesus was going "to begin a discourse on the apostolate and its dignity . . . But this new discourse was interrupted by the feelings which swept over Jesus when he thought of his betrayal by one of the apostles, and his instructions, like his consolations, moved on to a different path."[71] Whatever we may think of this hypothesis, there is in any case no need of regarding Verse 20, much less Verse 16, as later redactional additions.

The rest of what we have to say on the washing of the feet is newer. The threat Jesus utters to Peter if he refuses to let himself be washed by the Master takes a quite significant form: "you can have nothing in common with me" (13:8), or, more literally, "you have no share with me." The words are a Hebraic formula (*haya heleq le* or *im*) often found in Deuteronomy (cf. 10:9; 12:12; 14:27, 29; 18:1–2; cf. Nb. 18:20), and *always and exclusively refer to the Levites who have no share or inheritance with the rest of the Israelites, since Yahweh himself is their share and inheritance.* R. Bultmann rightly notes that the formula on Jesus' lips should not be given a psychological interpretation; in other words, the threat is not that Peter will be deprived of the friendship of Jesus or communion with him, but that he will not share in a specific blessing that belongs to Jesus.[72]

M.-E. Boismard argues from the fact that in Deuteronomy "share" and "inheritance" go together and that in the New Testament the concept of inheritance is spiritualized by being identified with the blessings of that eternal life which is promised to the just (for *klēronomein,* cf. Mt. 5:5; 19:29; 25:34; 1 Co. 6:9; etc.; for *klēronomia,* cf. Ga. 3:18; Ep. 1:14, 18; 5:5; etc.).[73] He concludes that the words, "you have no share with me," in John 13:8 mean, "you cannot share eternal life with me in the Father's presence."[74] But we must point out that the word "part" (*meris* or *meros*) has not acquired this limited meaning in the New Testament. On the other hand, the word "inheritance," which elsewhere in the New Testament does mean eternal life, is absent from John 13:8. What is the justification for supplying it?

A rather different explanation comes to mind when we realize that Jesus' language is inspired not by the Old Testament texts on inheriting the promised land but only by those passages that define the lot or share of the Levites. In an incomparably deeper sense than the Levites, Jesus can say that he has no share except God the Father. That the apostles are in principle "to have a share with him" or "to have the same share as he" can mean that they will share in a special way in his mission and priestly consecration.[75] Thus, their lot is comparable to that of the Levites: Like the Levites and like Christ, the apostles have God alone for their inheritance.

If this interpretation be accepted, the passage contains the equivalent of and a preparation for what is said in 17:16–19 in a way that is both negative and positive: "They do not belong to the world *any more than I* belong to the world. Consecrate them in the truth; your word is truth. *As* you sent me into the world, I have sent them into the world, and for their sake I consecrate myself so that *they too* may be consecrated in truth." It is striking that immediately after the passage in Luke that corresponds to the washing of feet and ends with the words, "Yet here am I among you as one who serves!" (Lk. 22:27), Jesus goes on to foretell a very special (even if not easily definable) participation of the apostles in his own privileges: "You are the men who have stood by me faithfully in my trials; and now I confer a kingdom on you, just as my Father conferred one on me: you will eat and drink at my table in my kingdom, and you will sit on thrones to judge the twelve tribes of Israel" (Lk. 22:28–30).[76]

The application to the apostles of the Levites' share, which seems to us in the background of John 13:8, leads to a further conjecture along the same general lines. Struck no doubt by the fact that from the washing of feet Jesus draws a lesson for the apostles on how authority is to be exercised in the future Church, Max Thurian would see in the washing "a kind of ordination of the apostles to their ministry, which will be the sign and instrument of the ministry of Jesus himself."[77] E. Lohmeyer had already suggested something similar: In his view, through the washing of feet Jesus makes his apostles the priests and leaders of the eschatological community and his own associates in the final kingdom.[78] These interpretations, however, return by a different way to a strictly sacramental interpretation of Jesus' action; but the sacramental interpretation, as we have noted, makes the text as a whole incoherent and is in no way necessary.

Yet we can retain something of Thurian's idea, especially if we bear in mind the close relations between Chapters 13 and 17; Bultmann has brought out these relations, although with some exaggeration. In Chapter 17 Jesus asks the Father to consecrate his apostles, and he consecrates himself as a victim so that they may be consecrated. We may argue that the washing of the feet is a symbolic preparation for this consecration.

In the Old Testament we find Moses being ordered to wash Aaron and his sons in preparation for their consecration as priests, the point being that physical purity symbolizes the purity of soul required for liturgical service: "You are to bring Aaron and his sons to the entrance of the Tent of Meeting and they are to be bathed" (Ex. 29:4; cf. Lv. 8:6; Nb. 8:6–7). Elsewhere, regular ritual ablutions are connected with the exercise of priestly functions (Ex. 30:17, 21; 40:30–32). It is permissible to think that the washing of feet represents a transposition of the ritual bath that prepared Levitical priests for their consecration, just as in John 17 we have a transposition of the liturgy for the Day of Atonement. The washing done by Jesus has, of course, a much deeper meaning than that of the bath required in the Old Testament of candidates for the priesthood; Jesus' washing of feet prefigures his purifying passion.

In the light of all the points we have been making, we can express the significance of Jesus' threat to Peter in this way: If you do not agree to let me wash you, and if you rebel against the redemptive abasement that will win for you the dispositions needed for sharing in my priesthood and especially for overcoming your pride and your desire to dominate; in short if you reject the mystery of the cross that will purify you, then you will not share in my priesthood.

Clearly, this is only a working hypothesis. We have no intention of offering these partly new views as certain; they are worth as much as the arguments that back them up. They do have two advantages. They make clearer the connection between the washing of feet, which is an introduction to the farewell discourses, and the priestly prayer that concludes the discourses. They also clarify Christ's choice of this particular symbolic action. The idea that Christ *washes* men of their sins is, of course, an authentically scriptural theme, but the image of the purifying bath, which is relatively rare, is more Pauline (cf. 1 Co. 6:11; Ep. 5:26; Tt. 3:5) than Johannine, especially since the reading, "he . . . has washed away our sins with his blood" (Rv. 1:5) is uncertain and disputed.[79] Consequently, if the allusion is to the ritual bath of the Levites, we can make sense of the somewhat unexpected symbolic action in John 13.

From the *christological* viewpoint, the scene of the washing of feet reminds us of the christological hymn in Philippians 2:6–11 in which we see Christ humbling himself without losing his divine prerogatives, just as in John 13 he washes his apostles' feet while remaining lord and master. A good number of modern exegetes, ourselves among them, find in this hymn, no less than in John 13, allusions to Isaiah 53.[80] The hymn is also to be connected with the transcendent Son of Man in the gospels who becomes a servant and humbles himself to accept death by crucifixion for the salvation of sinful mankind.

The *pastoral* significance of the washing of the feet is best illustrated by the recommendations of St. Peter:

> Now I have something to tell your elders: I am an elder myself, and a witness to the sufferings of Christ, and with you I have a share in the glory that is to be revealed. Be the shepherds of the flock of God that is entrusted to you: watch over it, not simply as a duty but gladly, because God wants it; not for sordid money, but because you are eager to do it. Never be a dictator over any group that is put in your charge, but be an example that the whole flock can follow. . . . All wrap yourselves in humility to be servants of each other (1 P. 5:1–5).

In the final recommendation, "wrap yourselves in humility," the Greek text uses the verb *egkombōsasthe* (tie something on oneself; wrap oneself by tieing or buttoning), which is quite unusual in such a context. The text should be translated literally, with C. Spicq: "tie around yourselves the overall of humility." The image is probably of the coarse apron workmen and slaves donned so as not to dirty their tunics. But the word almost certainly also alludes to the slave's garment Christ put on in the astounding scene of the washing of feet. Peter, who had initially been repelled by this gesture of humility, did not forget the lesson he learned.[81]

THE COMMUNICATION OF THE HOLY SPIRIT TO THE APOSTLES (JN. 20:19–23) AND THE PRIESTLY MINISTRY OF RECONCILING MEN WITH GOD

ACCORDING TO JOHN 20:19–23, on the evening of Easter day Christ appeared to the gathered disciples ("the doors were closed . . . for fear of the Jews") and communicated the Holy Spirit to them. The appearance must be the same as the one recounted in Luke 24:36–46. But in Luke the manifestation of Christ seems intended for the Eleven and "their companions," at least if we are to rely on Verse 33 just before. In any case, it is only in John that we can seek the identity of those to whom the Spirit is given, for only he speaks of this giving. The account in the fourth gospel is independent and must be interpreted in its own terms. The case is quite different from the account in the third gospel.[82]

As most commentators recognize, the beneficiaries of Christ's appearance in John 20:19–23 are identical with the men who heard the farewell discourses. In other words, those present on Easter evening are the apostles alone, except of course for Thomas whose absence is explicitly stated in 20:24 and motivates the well-known episode concerning the incredulity of this apostle. Moreover, the manifestation of Christ in 20:19–23 certainly is to the apostles alone, for it corresponds to the promises made to them during the farewell discourses.

Jesus had told the apostles he would come to them: "I am going away, and shall return" (Jn. 14:28). Now, while Luke (24:36) says only that the risen Jesus stood in the midst of the disciples, the fourth evangelist makes event correspond to promise by writing: *"Jesus came* and stood among them" (Jn. 20:19).

Jesus had said: "My peace I give you" (14:27); the risen Lord brings with him the peace that abides. Of course, the words "peace to you" could, of themselves, be a simple everyday greeting. But the solemnity of the occasion requires that we give the word "peace" here the deep religious meaning it often has in Scripture, both in the Old and in the New Testaments. A few biblical parallels come more readily to mind. "Yahweh answered him [Gideon], 'Peace be with you; have no fear; you will not die.' Gideon built an altar there to Yahweh and called it Yahweh-Peace" (Jg. 6:23–24). " 'Do not be afraid,' he [the angel] said [to Daniel], 'you are a man specially chosen; peace be with you; play the man, be strong!' And as he spoke to me I felt strong again" (Dn.

10:19). In John 20:21 we should translate "Peace is yours," rather than "Peace be with you," as though the risen Christ were simply expressing a wish, for as a matter of fact he intends to confirm the priceless gift of Messianic peace which he had already conferred upon them in 14:27. He says, "Peace is yours," twice (Verses 19 and 21), just as he had used the word "peace" twice in 14:27.[83]

Jesus had also predicted: "You will be sorrowful, but *your sorrow will turn into joy. . . . I shall see you again, and your hearts will be full of joy*" (16:20, 22). The words certainly have a very comprehensive meaning which can be fully matched only by the eternal happiness of heaven; but they receive their initial fulfillment in 20:20: *"The disciples were filled with joy when they saw the Lord."*

When Jesus was speaking to the Father in his priestly prayer, he was anticipating and thinking of himself as already back with the Father. For this reason he spoke of the sending of the apostles as having taken place in the past; in addition, he must have been thinking of the preparation for that mission that went on during his public ministry: "As you sent me into the world, I have sent them into the world" (17:18). In John 20 Christ expresses himself in the present tense, but he uses almost the same words as earlier (there is no difference of meaning between *apostellein* and *pempein*), and the same turn of phrase (a comparison between his own mission and that of the disciples). It is evident then that the reality of which he speaks is the same in both passages: "As the Father sent me, so am I sending you" (20:21). This last-mentioned correspondence is significant: Coming as it does after the other three correspondences already cited, it is a valuable confirmation of the structure we discovered earlier in John 17. That is, contrary to what some commentators have claimed, the consecration and mission of 17:17–19 are meant not for all the disciples without distinction but only for the apostles, as is the mission in 20:21.

The scene we have been analyzing is a highly important one, for it provides the decisive proof that Jesus intended to bestow upon his apostles powers reserved strictly to them and a ministerial priesthood essentially distinct from the common priesthood of all the faithful. For this reason we must give careful attention, first to the details of the Johannine text, then to the various parallel passages. The latter consist, first of all, in Matthew, in which Christ himself forgives sins (9:1–8) and in which he confers special powers on Peter and the Twelve (16:19; 18:18). There is, secondly, the account of Pentecost in the Acts of the Apostles; a number of commentators believe that John 20:19–23 corresponds to, or is a transformation of, the account of Pentecost in Acts. Finally, we shall say a few words about 2 Corinthians 5:17—6:1.

In John 20:22 Jesus breathes upon his apostles. The action is described in the rare verb *emphusaō,* which had been used by the Septuagint in translating Genesis 2:7 which tells of Yahweh breathing a breath of life into the first man. The verb occurs again in Wisdom 15:11, which also speaks of the creation of the first man: "he misconceives the One who shaped him, who breathed an active soul into him and inspired a living spirit." Once again referring to Genesis 2:7, Ezekiel describes the eschatological resurrection of the dry bones with the same word: "Come from the four winds, breath; breathe on these dead; let them live!" (37:9).

These verbal parallels cannot be coincidental; they teach us to see in the symbolic action of Jesus in the Supper room an act of eschatological creation that corresponds to the original creation. The risen Christ shows himself, in dependence on the Father, the source of a new creation, which completes and goes infinitely beyond the original since the Holy Spirit is now given whereas originally only the spirit that gives bodily life was infused.[84]

The idea we receive of the Holy Spirit in this passage is

rather different from the idea that emerges in the promises after the Last Supper in which the Spirit Paraclete is presented to us as the interior master, the divine teacher who will instruct the disciples from within their hearts and enable them to penetrate into the truth Jesus has brought. On the other hand, we should not conclude that there is in John 20 a special conception of the Spirit not found elsewhere in the fourth gospel.[85] In fact, the Spirit in John 20 is closely connected with the new birth through water and the Holy Spirit of which Jesus speaks in the conversation with Nicodemus (Jn. 3:3–8). We may note that the prediction in John 3 is also inspired by the prophecies of Ezekiel and especially by the one that occurs just before the vision of the dry bones: "I shall give you a new heart and put a new spirit in you; I shall remove the heart of stone from your bodies and give you a heart of flesh instead. I shall put my spirit in you, and make you keep my laws and sincerely respect my observances" (36:26–27). We may refer also to Ezekiel 11:19 and to the *misérere* (Ps. 51:9, 12–13), which in all probablity depends upon Ezekiel.

Once again in dependence on Ezekiel, a similar role of eschatological purification is attributed to the Spirit of God in the instruction on the two spirits, which is part of the Manual of Discipline, or Rule of the Community, in the Dead Sea scrolls:

> Then, too, God will purge all the acts of man in the crucible of His truth, and refine for Himself all the fabric of man, destroying every spirit of perversity from within his flesh and cleansing him by the holy spirit from all the effects of wickedness. Like waters of purification He will sprinkle upon him the spirit of truth, to cleanse him of all the abominations of falsehood and of all pollution through the spirit of filth; to the end that, being made upright, men may have understanding of transcendental knowledge and of the lore of the sons of heaven, and that, being made blameless in their ways, they may be endowed with inner vision. For them God has chosen

to be the partners of His eternal covenant, and theirs shall be all mortal glory. Perversity shall be no more, and all works of deceit shall be put to shame.[86]

J. Schmitt sums up nicely the similarities between the Qumran text and the fourth gospel:

In both, the theme of eschatological purification is further determined by the idea of a new creation which represents the victory of Light over Darkness. In both, the disciple's purity has its source in the Holy Spirit, while its agent and model is the risen Christ or the Messianic man. In these respects the pericope in John is almost a replica of the Zadokite passage.[87]

Schmitt points out that the parallelism will not surprise anyone who bears in mind the links of the apostle John with baptist groups and even with Qumran:

There is nothing extraordinary about such a convergence of thought. . . . The Jewish idea of holiness must have played a much more important part in the reflection that went on in various apostolic circles than the exegesis of bygone years would lead us to believe. That idea underlies the exhortations in the gospels and letters and is also attested in the earliest traditions of Jerusalem or Palestine (cf. Ac. 5:3; Rm. 1:4). In its Judeo-Christian expression, it seems to go back beyond Jesus (cf. Mt. 5:3) to John the Baptist (cf. Mk. 1:8 par.). That it therefore became a category of Johannine thought (cf. Jn. 3:5) is at least an extremely probable hypothesis for anyone who remembers the strong links between John, author of the traditions recorded in the fourth gospel, and John the Baptist, the baptist groups, and even the Zadokites. The Palestinian theme of the *Geber-Anthropos* suggests analogous remarks. . . . This theme was very soon applied to the risen Christ, and to a large extent it dominated the postresurrection reflection of the early Christ. Romans 1:3–4 and 1 Corinthians 15:42–52, among other passages, provide clear testimony on this point. They are controlled by the idea of Christ as "second Adam" (cf. 1 Co. 15:45–46) and emphasize that Jesus owes his prerogative as eschatological man to the "spiritual" condition (cf. ibid.) or "spirit of holiness" (cf. Rm. 1:4) which is his due to his resurrection from the dead (cf. ibid.).[88]

The Council of Trent has quite legitimately applied John 20:21–23 to the sacrament of penance.[89] But the foregoing observations on the passage lead us to assign a much broader meaning to the power of forgiving sins that Christ is here bestowing on his apostles. As a matter of fact, the Church Fathers of the first three centuries related the forgiveness of sins in John 20:23 to baptism. And we recall the Creed: "one baptism for the forgiveness of sins."[90] We may say, then, in general terms, that in John 20:19–23 Christ is associating his apostles with the great work of creating a new race of men, a work that necessarily requires the gift of the Holy Spirit.

The association is equally evident in the cure of the paralytic at Capernaum as recounted in Matthew 9:1–8. Here we see Christ claiming for himself the power to forgive sins which was regarded as reserved strictly to God himself. The latter belief is expressed by the scribes more fully in Mark's account of the scene: "How can this man talk like that? He is blaspheming. Who can forgive sins but God?" (2:7; the parallel text in Matthew has simply, "This man is blaspheming"). But this does not prevent Matthew from ending his account with the implication that the power to forgive sins had been granted to men generally, to every man: "A feeling of awe came over the crowd when they saw this, and they praised God for giving such power *to men*" (Mt. 9:8). How is such a statement to be explained?

The history-of-forms school has taught us to look upon the gospels less as biographies in the modern sense of the term than as testimonies to the faith of the early Christian community. Provided that the proper limits of such an approach be respected, it can be a fruitful way of reading the gospels. When

Matthew shows us the crowds praising God "for giving such power to men," a power which in the context can only be that of forgiving sins, he is not for a moment losing sight of the difference between the Son of Man and his fellow men any more than Daniel indentifies purely and simply the Son of Man with the saints of the Most High. The point is rather that for Matthew as for Jesus the idea of a Messiah and that of a Messianic community or people of God are inseparably connected. We think, therefore, with R. Bultmann, A. Schlatter, P. Benoit, and numerous other exegetes, that the evangelist has in mind the Christian community of his day and the ministers who continue to exercise in the Church the power of forgiving sins in Jesus' name.[91]

Following Luther's lead, some commentators have wanted to limit the forgiveness of sins in John 20:23 solely to the ministry of preaching.[92] But the text itself makes such a limitation untenable since it adds to the power of forgiving sins the power of retaining them as well: "For those whose sins you forgive, they are forgiven; for those whose sins you retain, they are retained." The act of retaining sins implies the exercise of a genuinely juridical power, such as exercised, for example, in the sacrament of penance. To the sacramental interpretation the objection has been raised that in the best Greek text the verb *apheōntai* ("they are forgiven") is in the perfect passive tense, as though the apostles' role were simply to proclaim a forgiveness of sins that has already been effected; but the objection has no validity.[93] In a conditional proposition such as we have in John 20:23 (cf. the initial Greek particle *an*), a perfect tense in the apodosis or main part of the sentence can well refer to an action that is still in the future; such a tense in such a position need not express an action that takes place prior to the action named in the protasis or "if" part of the sentence.[94]

There is evidently a relationship between the power of forgiving and retaining sins in John 20:23 and the power of binding and loosing in Matthew 18:18, and it raises many complicated problems. Both passages use a literary device found in all languages: the statement of two contraries as a way of expressing a totality.[95] We shall limit ourselves here to such aspects of these two antitheses as directly relate to our purpose in this book.

First of all, the two antitheses must be compared. It would be inaccurate and simplistic to maintain that the Johannine antithesis forgive-retain is simply a transcription into good Greek of the Matthean antithesis bind-loose. In John, the Greek verb that expresses the idea of forgiveness (*aphienai*) offers no difficulty, but the same is not true for its antithesis, the verb *kratein;* the sense in which the latter is used here ("to retain [sins]") is quite unusual; it is difficult to determine what its Hebrew equivalent would be (*shamar* or *natar?*). The Matthean antithesis, on the contrary, has its equivalent in rabbinic literature (*'asar* and *hittir* [hiphil of *natar*] or *sharah*).[96] Moreover, the Matthean antithesis is more comprehensive than the Johannine for it means not only to forgive or refuse to forgive sins, but also to authorize or prohibit a teaching and to allow or exclude a practice.

With P. Benoit,[97] we must distinguish two successive uses of the bind-loose antithesis: in Matthew 16:19 and 18:18. In the incident at Caesarea Philippi, the power of binding and loosing goes with the power of the keys; that is, of opening or shutting the door into the kingdom of God; this power is given to Peter alone as steward of the house of God.[98] In such a context, the antithesis bind-loose becomes as comprehensive as possible.

The discourse on the Church in Matthew 18 repeats the antithesis but in a rather different context. Here there is question of sins committed in the community and of brotherly correction. Jesus requires that the offender be reported to the community. He then adds: "I tell you solemnly, whatever you bind on earth shall be considered bound in heaven; whatever

you loose on earth shall be considered loosed in heaven"
(Mt. 18:18). We have every reason for thinking that in this
context the bind-loose antithesis acquires the same specific
meaning as the forgive-retain antithesis in John. The passive
construction used in the fourth gospel ("are forgiven," "are
retained") is a roundabout way of designating God as the
source, just as in Matthew heaven ratifies what has been done
on earth. Commentators ask in connection with Matthew
18:18: To whom is Christ here giving the power of binding
and loosing? Some (chiefly Catholics) answer: to the apostles
alone. Others answer: to the community as a whole or even
to each Christian. The immediate context does not resolve
the dispute. But we must add that the connection of the
saying in Matthew 18:18 with this context is very loose and
evidently secondary; like the Sermon on the Mount in Matthew 5–8, the discourse on the Church in Matthew 18 is a
synthesis of teachings that Christ gave on various occasions.
In fact, as we read Matthew 18:18 we cannot help but be
reminded of the ending of the first gospel (Mt. 28:18–20)
where, just as in John 20:19–23, the risen Christ, invested
with "all authority in heaven and on earth," gives the eleven
apostles (Mt. 28:16) a share in his mission of teaching
and sanctifying. Moreover, the close parallelism between
Matthew 18:18 and John 20:23, crowns our conviction that
in the Matthean text only the apostles are the recipients of
the power to bind and loose.[99]

A very important problem in regard to John 20:19–23 is
the relationship of this passage to the outpouring of the Spirit
on Pentecost as narrated in the Acts of the Apostles (2:1–13).
No one today would accept the opinion of some commentators of the distant and not too distant past (Theodore of
Mopsuestia, Euthymius, Theophylact, Grotius, Tholuck,
Lampe) that John is depicting only a preparation for and
pledge of the future gift of the Spirit on Pentecost. Such an
interpretation goes counter to the explicit language of the

fourth gospel which points to a real reception: "Receive the Holy Spirit." This interpretation was condemned by the Fifth Ecumenical Council.[100]

Two interpretations are upheld today. A number of modern exegetes see in John's account a scene that corresponds to or is the equivalent of the Pentecost which Luke narrates. These exegetes maintain that John is describing the same event as Luke; Luke paints a more brilliant scene, John a more spiritual one. According to X. Léon-Dufour, "the same event is evidently being presented in two different ways; there is contradiction between the two accounts only on the point of the date when the gift was given."[101] Archimandrite Cassien Besobrasoff tries to eliminate the discrepancy in date: He claims that John, like Luke, puts the sending of the Spirit fifty days after Easter; in his view, the words "that day" in John 20:19 are a technical formula referring to the return of Christ in the person of the Holy Spirit.[102] No serious commentator will allow such a forced harmonization, but it is certainly true that today, even among Catholics, the opinion is becoming ever more widely accepted that despite the considerable difference between the two accounts not only as to date but even as to content, John and Luke are both relating the same event. These exegetes think that it would be artificial to distinguish two successive gifts of the Spirit to the apostles and that, if the two descriptions are as divergent as they are, it is because they have quite different theological perspectives behind them.[103]

Nonetheless, some excellent commentators are unconvinced and maintain that the two accounts report different events. M.-J. Lagrange oberves: "The act described here by John does not fulfill the conditions John himself had mentioned (14:16, 26; 16:7, 13) for the mission of the Spirit, since the Spirit is to be sent by the Father (or by the Son) but after the Son's return to the Father and in order to make up for the absence of the Son."[104] But the ever more numerous exegetes

who think that in the perspective adopted by John the chris-
tophanies of the Easter period are manifestations of a Christ
who comes from his place at the Father's side, will not be
persuaded by Lagrange's argument.[105] There is good reason
for preferring the view expressed by P. Benoit:

> How does it come about that, according to John, the Holy
> Spirit is given to the apostles on the very evening of Easter
> Day? This is really a false problem since there is no opposi-
> tion between the Holy Spirit of John who pardons sins and
> the Holy Spirit of Luke who presides over the universal proc-
> lamation. They are two different aspects of the same infi-
> nitely rich reality, which is the breath, the power, of God.
>
> John emphasizes the inward and sanctifying aspect of the
> Spirit who in fulfillment of the promises of the prophets
> comes to purify the soul of the sinner, to restore him to in-
> nocence and give him that justice, that life with God which is
> the life of Grace. It is the Spirit promised by Ezekiel (36:
> 25–27), a promise renewed by Jesus in his discourse after
> the Supper, the Spirit who comes to the inward soul of every
> Christian to enlighten him, to remind him of the words of
> God, and to purify him by pardoning his sins.
>
> Luke, on the other hand, in the story of Pentecost, is talk-
> ing about the Spirit under his "charismatic" aspect. It is the
> Spirit that God gives the faithful for the welfare of the
> Church as a whole, not now for inner holiness, but for out-
> ward action and the spreading of the gospel.[106]

Approaching the matter from a different angle F.-M. Braun
stresses the considerable difference between the *imperceptible*
gift of the Spirit in the fourth gospel, and the *ecstatic* experience of Acts that brings about the preaching of the gospel.[107]

These various answers require a complement, for they leave
obscured the most important difference of all between Acts
2:1–13 and John 20:19–23. In Acts, the beneficiaries of
the wonderful event of Pentecost (a group not composed
exclusively of the apostles[108]) are personally transformed
by the Spirit and "filled" with him: "they . . . began to speak

foreign languages" (2:4). This amazed those who heard them and caused the apostles to be taken for drunken men. The circumstances of the gift of the Spirit (to the apostles alone) in John 20:19–23 are very different. The gift does not throw the recipients into ecstasy; moreover, it does not correspond exactly to the promises of the Paraclete as made by Jesus after the Supper, for the gift is directly intended, not for the transformation and interior sanctification of the apostles, but for the transformation and sanctification of others who through their mediation will believe in Christ. We have here a paradox. The action of Jesus in breathing on the apostles undoubtedly symbolizes the coming into existence of a new race of men. Yet the apostles, to which the action is directed, are considered by Jesus, not as the nucleus of this new creation, but rather as the collaborators of Christ and the Holy Spirit in carrying out the great plan, inasmuch as in the normal course of events they will be the intermediaries through whom men will be rescued from the captivity of sin and will receive divine life. B. F. Westcott rightly observes that the absence of the definite article before "Holy Spirit" justifies us in taking "Receive the Holy Spirit" to mean: "Receive a gift of the Holy Spirit, a spiritual power."[109]

We are thus in a very clear way brought back to the basic theme of the prayer in John 17, where the apostles are consecrated to carry on the work of Christ. We can only agree, therefore, with F. Prat when he sees in John 20:23 "the complement of the priesthood" that Christ had bestowed on his apostles in sacrificing himself, the complement of their priestly consecration.[110] We ourselves remarked at an earlier point in this book that while the Holy Spirit seems to be absent from the priestly prayer, his intervention is presupposed at every point. It is presupposed especially by the consecration in the truth, since it is the Spirit Paraclete who leads men into the whole truth. It is also presupposed by the consecration in truth which is inseparable from the consecration in spirit, just as worship in truth is inseparable from worship in spirit. In the pericope we are now studying, the action of the Holy Spirit is, of course, set forth in explicit and powerful fashion.

It would be very interesting to compare John 20:19–23 with the way in which St. Paul describes the apostolic ministry throughout his second letter to the Corinthians. We may cite at least one text:

> For anyone who is now in Christ, there is a new creation; the old creation has gone, and now the new one is here. It is all God's work. It was God who reconciled us to himself through Christ and gave us the work of handing on this reconciliation. In other words, God in Christ was reconciling the world to himself, not holding men's faults against them, and he has entrusted to us the news that they are reconciled. So we are ambassadors for Christ; it is as though God were appealing through us,[111] and the appeal that we make in Christ's name is: be reconciled to God. For our sake God made the sinless one into sin, so that in him we might become the goodness of God. As his fellow workers, we beg you once again not to neglect the grace of God that you have received (2 Co. 5: 17—6:1).

There are evident similarities between John 20:19–23 and the passage just quoted which deal with the role not only of Paul but also of "all his fellow apostles and fellow workers."[112] In both passages the redemptive work is thought of as the creation of a new race of men. In both, the apostles are associated with the divine work as messengers or ambassadors of Christ; Christ or, what amounts to the same thing since Christ is God, God himself acts in them and through them appeals to men. In both, the apostles carry out in Christ's name (cf. the two *hyper Christou* phrases in 2 Co. 5:20) the strictly priestly ministry of reconciling men with God. While the fourth gospel shows us the apostles invested with the power to forgive sins, St. Paul tells us that God has put into their mouths "the news that they [men] are reconciled." Paul, too, is speaking of a message that is effective, for it is a fruit and application of the great reconciliation of mankind with God that Christ brought about on Calvary. In this passage Paul does not actually mention the Holy Spirit, as John does, but a little earlier Paul had laid great stress on the fact that the ministry of the new covenant is essentially a ministry of the Spirit and not of the letter (2 Co. 3).

CHRIST THE PRIEST AND THE "ANGELS" OF THE CHURCHES IN THE APOCALYPSE ● THE PROBLEM OF APOSTOLIC SUCCESSION ● THE HIERARCHIC LEADERS RESPONSIBLE FOR THE SPIRITUAL STATE OF THE CHRISTIAN COMMUNITIES

IN CHAPTER 3 we dealt briefly with the Apocalypse; the time has come to speak of it at greater length. We want especially to draw attention to the splendid letters to the Churches (Chapters 2–3), concerning which W. Bossuet wrote: "Despite their awkwardness of expression, these letters are among the greatest things in the New Testament."[113] The letters are closely connected with the subject of this book, for they show us Christ the Priest holding in his hand seven stars which are the "angels" of the Churches; that is, in our view, the hierarchic leaders of these Churches—men who are in turn ruled by apostolic authority. The fervor of these leaders and the fervor of their communities are intimately linked. It seems to us that there is a substantial doctrinal contact between these letters and John 17, even if this contact has hardly been noticed by the commentators. These are the points we shall now explain as briefly as possible, limiting ourselves to the essentials.

The opening vision (1:13–20) of John is usually offered as a sign, if not a compelling proof, that in the Apocalypse Christ shows himself to us clad in his priestly dignity. And, in fact, the Son of Man there appears to John dressed in a long robe (*podērēs* or garment reaching to the feet), such as the high priest of the Old Testament wore (Ex. 28:4). We may refer to Zechariah 3:4 (LXX), which tells of the robes of state worn by the high priest Joshua, and especially to Wisdom 18:24, which says that the greatness of Aaron the high priest—a man united in a special way to the creator of the world—was symbolized by his long robe on which the whole universe was represented.[114] The fourth gospel furnishes a valuable confirmation of this exegesis. For, as we noted above at the end of Chapter 1, the "seamless" garment of Jesus, "woven in one piece from neck to hem," which the soldiers decided not to tear (Jn. 19:23–24), has also been taken as a sign of his priestly dignity.

J. B. Caird attributes priestly significance also to the golden girdle which the Son of Man wears in the opening vision of the Apocalypse (1:13).[115] But in Exodus 39:29, to which Caird refers, the high priest's girdle is actually made of fine twined linen. Other commentators think the golden girdle of the Son of Man is rather a sign of his royal dignity; Allo refers to 1 Maccabees 10:89, where King Alexander sends Jonathan a golden brooch of the kind usually given only to princes of the royal blood.[116]

It is usual, of course, for the Apocalypse to link closely the priestly and royal dignities; thus, elsewhere it lays great stress on Christ being a king. It teaches us, in addition, that Christ makes kings and priests of his disciples (1:6; 5:10); he must himself, therefore, be both priest and king, for in the Apocalypse, perhaps more clearly than elsewhere in the New Testament, we see him rewarding his faithful followers with a share in his own privileges. Once again the fourth gospel is enlightening: In the account of the Passion the scene of the seamless robe follows directly on that in which Pilate unwittingly proclaims the royalty of the crucified Jesus, by having a trilingual inscription (in Hebrew, Greek, and Latin) affixed to the cross with the words, "Jesus the Nazarene, King of the Jews," and by answering the high priests when they object, "What I have written, I have written" (Jn. 19:19–22).[117] In John 19:18–24, then, as in the Apocalypse, Christ is implicitly declared to be both priest and king.

The fourth gospel suggests a further important point. The ending of John's account of the passion shows Jesus as both the priest and the sacrificial victim of Christians. For, just as John highlights the title "Lamb of God" given to Jesus by the precursor, so in 19:35–37 he refers us both to the Passover Lamb of the Jews and to the martyrdom of Servant of Yahweh, after having alluded a few lines before (19:19–24) to the priesthood of Christ. This close association of priesthood and victimhood is taken for granted, as it were, since it is already present in Isaiah 53, the prophecy that Christ is fulfilling. Like the Servant, Jesus is priest of the sacrifice in which he offers his own life; in his person, priest and victim are inseparable.

From this fact a conclusion follows with regard to the Apocalypse: inasmuch as the focus of this book is the Lamb slain who had freed us from our sins by his death, the focus is also, implicitly, Christ the priest. This is, of course, only one aspect, even if a basic one, of the essentially liturgical character of the Apocalypse.[118] It becomes easier to understand why the life of the Christian community, whether in the next world, or already on earth, is conceived in the Apocalypse as a liturgy, an uninterrupted act of adoration: "They now stand in front of God's throne and serve him day and night in his sanctuary" (7:15);[119] "I saw that there was no temple in the city since the Lord God Almighty and the Lamb were themselves the temple. . . . The throne of God and of the Lamb will be in its place in the city; his servants will worship him, they will see him face to face, and his name will be written on their foreheads" (21:22; 22:3). As A. Gelin puts it, the life of the elect takes the form of an unending liturgy that is bound up with the blessedness of seeing God face to face.[120]

In the opening vision of the Apocalypse, the Son of Man, king and priests, appears surrounded by seven golden lamp stands and holding seven stars in his hand (1:12, 16). Later on, we learn that the lamp stands are the seven Churches and the stars the "angels" of these Churches (1:20); John receives orders to write to them. Christ himself dictates to the seer the content of each of the seven letters. It is obvious that the "angels" of the Churches depend in some way on John and also that they have a special relationship to the Son of Man who holds the stars "in his right hand." But this does not yet tell us who these addressees are. Their identification is one of the greatest puzzles in a book that contains so much of the enigmatic.

A good many commentators think that the "angels" are angels in the proper sense, and more specifically the guardian or tutelary angels who watch over the Churches. Others think the "angels" are a personification or spiritual double of the Church; or that they are human messengers sent by the Churches of Asia to the exiled John on Patmos; or that they are the bishops or elders who direct the Churches; or that some combination of these explanations is required. Allo, for example, suggests that the symbol works at several levels: The angel is to be taken as the personified spirit of the Church in question, but a spirit that is embodied in the bishop who represents that Church.[121]

We need not discuss all these theories in detail and shall limit ourselves to a few observations on the subject. According to Theodor Zahn, the idea that each Christian community has a special guardian angel is unparalleled either in early Christianity or in Judaism.[122] This objection is, of course, not decisive. Nonetheless, it is impossible to make angels (in the strict sense of the term) truly responsible for the sins of men as the "angels" of the Churches are, inasmuch as Christ blames them for the poor spiritual state of the communities. Moreover, if the "angels" were truly angels, why should they be represented as present to Christ by means of a symbol (the stars he holds in his hand), instead of simply sitting at his side? The seer of the Apocalypse has a lofty conception of the angels, as we can see from his prostration before the angel who tells him of the fate of Babylon (19:10). Is it at all likely, then, that he would show us Christ reproaching the good angels? Finally, everywhere else in the Bible, including the Apocalypse, God makes use of the angels in order to speak to men and communicate his thought and will to them. Isn't this picture of reality turned upside down if in Revelation 1–3 God uses a man, John, to communicate his thought and will to angels in the proper sense of the term?

We must agree, therefore, with those exegetes who in ever growing numbers see in the "angels" the hierarchic leaders of the Churches.[123] Our intention here is simply to fortify this position with some important nuances which, we think, will render it much more solid.

In the Book of Daniel (10:12–13, 20–21; 12:1) the prophet speaks of the guardian angels of the various peoples. What he says provides the chief point of reference for those who see in the "angels" of the Churches the heavenly guardian angels of those Churches. The inference is mistaken, we believe, because the thought in the Apocalypse is very different from that of the passages in Daniel.[124] This does not mean, however, that John is not alluding to these texts. On the contrary, it seems that he is, for in this same passage of the Apocalypse he refers clearly to Daniel, Chapter 10 (cf. Rv. 1:13 and Dn. 10:5, 16; Rv. 1:14 and Dn. 10:6; Rv. 1:17 and Dn. 10:9, 12).

Generally speaking, the author of the Apocalypse is a deeply original thinker, who uses the Old Testament with great freedom, often radically transforming what he takes.[125] It is tempting to see such a transposition at work in the "angels" of the Churches. It is highly probable that John is thinking of the angel who is "the prince of the kingdom of Persia" (Dn. 10:13), of the angel who is "the prince of Javan" (Greece; Dn. 10:20), and of Michael, "the great prince who mounts guard over your people" (Dn. 12:1), when he calls the hierarchic leaders the "angels" of their Churches. He is suggesting the important truth that these men are indeed *the guardian angels of their Churches* and that their first duty is to watch over the faith and moral conduct of their communities.

It is to be noted that the Greek word *episkopos,* which in the letters of St. Ignatius of Antioch becomes the ordinary technical term for describing a bishop (more than forty times in the letters), expresses quite exactly the task of acting as guardian angel.[126] Both in secular usage and in the Bible, *episkopos* originally means an overseer, a guardian, a protector. Homer says that "the gods are the best witnesses and overseers of our agreement" (*Iliad* 22:255). According to Plato, the goddess Nemesis, who is the messenger of Dikē (Justice), is appointed to watch (to be *episkopos* of) our every action (*Laws* 4:717d). According to the Book of Wisdom, God sees and truly observes the hearts of men (he is the *episkopos alēthēs;* 1:6). Nehemiah speaks of Uzzi as the *episkopos* of the Levites (11:22). The function of the *episkopoi* of the Christian Churches is to watch over those concerning whom they will have to render an account to God, as is said of the leaders of the community (the *hēgoumenoi*) in Hebrews 13:17. In the Pauline letters the word *episkopos* admittedly does not yet have the very precise meaning it will have in the letters of Ignatius of Antioch. But there is only a short time lapse between these letters and the Apocalypse (the latter dates from around 95, the former from around 110); moreover, John and Ignatius are in the same geographical region. In our view, the "angels" of the Churches in the

Apocalypse can only be men, and they are identical with those whom Ignatius calls bishops.

A further observation will corroborate this exegesis. In the Old Testament Yahweh's messenger (*mal'ak Yahweh*) is usually an angel (in the proper sense) who descends from heaven to men. But the same title is occasionally given to men, and in these cases it refers either to prophets or to priests.[127] Against this background it is still easier to think of the hierarchic leaders being called the "angels" of their Churches, since the apostles, who are the nucleus of the hierarchy, resemble both the prophets and the priests of the Old Testament, as we showed earlier in this book.

In at least three passages of the Old Testament the messengers or angels of Yahweh are undoubtedly the prophets: "I am he who . . . makes the plans of my envoys succeed" (Is. 44:26); "Yahweh, the God of their ancestors, tirelessly sent them messenger after messenger (2 Ch. 36:15); "Haggai, the messenger of Yahweh, passed on the message of Yahweh to the people" (Hg. 1:13). In two other passages Yahweh's human messenger is the priest, not the prophet: "The lips of the priest ought to safeguard knowledge; his mouth is where instruction should be sought, since he is the messenger of Yahweh Sabaoth" (Ml. 2:7); "Better a vow unmade than made and not discharged. Do not allow your own words to bring guilt on you, nor tell your angel afterwards it was unintentional" (Qo. 5:4–5).[128]

In heaven the "angels" of the Churches are presented by the stars that the Son of Man holds in his hands. Why this symbol? Those who identify the "angels" with the hierarchic leaders of the Churches find a new argument in their favor here and refer us once again to Daniel where teachers will have starlike splendor in heaven as their reward: "The learned will shine as brightly as the vault of heaven, and those who have instructed many in virtue, as bright as stars for all eternity" (12:3).

Such an allusion is quite plausible, but it does not explain everything. In the opening vision of the Apocalypse, Christ shines like the sun (1:16) and later he is twice called "the Morning Star" (2:28; 22:16).[129] According to Allo, if the Churches are lamp stands (*luchniai*) or candelabra, and if their leaders are stars, it is because both transmit a light they have received from Christ, who is the Sun in the world of souls and the Morning Star that scatters the darkness of night.[130] Once again, there is undoubtedly more to it than that. Besides their numberlessness, two other traits make the stars in Scriptural allusions to them. They shine to the glory of their creator, and they obey his commands promptly: "The stars shine joyfully at their set times: when he calls them, they answer, 'Here we are'; they gladly shine for their creator" (Ba. 3:34–35; cf. Is. 40:26; Jr. 31:35; Jb. 38:31–33). Through the symbol of the star a lesson is being taught the leaders of the Churches: They are wholly dependent on the Son of Man, wholly "in his right hand," and bring light to men only thanks to him; they must labor solely for his glory.

These duties of the leaders are only the other side of their special privileges. Being set in the hand of the Son of Man, who is clad in the robe and dignity of high priest and is the sun and morning star of the whole Church, the stars mean that the hierarchic leaders share in their Master's priesthood and in his power of enlightening and sanctifying the Christian communities. These men are not simply the guardian angels of the Churches; they are also the messengers (or angels) of the Son of Man. He holds them in his hand and makes use of them as he wills, just as in the gospels the apostles are the messengers of Jesus and in the Old Testament the prophets are the messengers of Yahweh, speaking only in dependence on him.

Once we admit the identification of the stars and "angels" with the hierarchic leaders of the Christian communities, we find that the Apocalypse is very helpful in answering two other

questions of considerable importance. One of them is historical and theological: the question of apostolic succession.
The other is moral and pastoral: What is the relation between
the Christian community and the man who guides its des-
tinies? The Apocalypse highlights the fact that the moral and
religious worth of the Christian communities is in large measure proportionate to that of their hierarchic leaders. It is important that on the two questions just mentioned we should
show clearly what may be derived from the Apocalypse.

The important problem of apostolic succession may be put
in these terms: How was the transition made from the apostles
to the later hierarchic leaders; that is, to the bishops whom
we find at the head of the local Churches and who regard
themselves as the legitimate successors of the apostles? With
our eye on the limited object of the present book, we may
restate the problem: How did other men inherit the priesthood of the apostles which, as we have seen, is a participation in the priesthood of Christ, the high priest and only
priest of the new covenant? The problem is a very difficult
one historically and theologically; the Apocalypse shows the
inheritance already transmitted and the problem resolved at
the concrete level, provided, of course, that we recognize the
Apocalypse to be of apostolic and specifically of Johannine
origin. We must say a few words here on this prior question.

Notwithstanding the increasingly widespread rejection that
has become fashionable today and includes the fourth gospel
as well as the Apocalypse (many people would think themselves old-fashioned if they did not blindly and uncritically
accept the so-called critical position), we accept unhesitatingly the apostolic origin of the Apocalypse, which is so
solidly grounded in tradition. We think that one and the same
apostle, John, is at the source, though in somewhat different
ways, of the Apocalypse, the fourth gospel, and the three
letters.[131] We may fittingly remind ourselves here of A. von
Harnack's judgment: "I adopt the critical heresy which at-

tributes Apocalypse and gospel to one and the same author."[132]

To begin with, there are a large number of similarities that argue to the single authorship of gospel and letters. These likenesses cannot be offset by some differences between the writings; these differences are not to be denied, but their importance has been exaggerated. The special circumstances and, in particular, the need of fighting against certain heretical tendencies can well explain a number of the special characteristics of the letters.

The Apocalypse is a much more complex matter, and the question of its authorship is much less easy to answer. E. Renan summed up in a striking sentence the major difficulty many critics feel: "The Apocalypse is the most Jewish and the fourth gospel the least Jewish of New Testament writings."[133] We may add that a number of key ideas in the gospel are absent from or but weakly represented in the Apocalypse. Allo, a strong advocate of the Johannine origin of the Apocalypse, does not seem to have made enough of this fact, it does require explanation. At the same time, however, the likenesses between gospel and Apocalypse are at least as significant as the differences, and an objective study of the question must take account of both. E. Lohmeyer, who maintains the unity of authorship, rightly points out that the basic ideas of the Apocalypse—the Logos, the Lamb, the Bride of the Lamb, light, witness, life, death, hunger, thirst, victory, etc.—are Johannine.[134] The theme of the living water is found in both gospel and Apocalypse, but nowhere else in the New Testament. The theme of the pierced Christ is found in both writings, and in both it is supported by Zechariah 12:10: "They will look on the one whom they have pierced"; in both, the prophet is quoted from a translation that is different from the Septuagint and found only in these two passages.

Although we cannot here justify our position in full fashion, we maintain that the apostle John, author of the fourth gospel, was also the recipient of the visions of the Apocalypse. It is not a valid objection—quite the contrary—that he does not call himself an apostle in a work that is related to the prophetic writings of old. He was sufficiently well-known to the immediate readers that he had no need to add any qualifier to his name (cf. 1:4, 9; 22:8), whereas an unknown who wanted to pass himself off as the apostle John would surely have been fuller in self-designation. To prefer an unknown like "John the presbyter," whose very existence is doubted by some (Zahn, Gutjahr, Sickenberger, Michaelis, Schnackenburg),[135] to the son of Zebedee is "to rush to give credit to a weak hypothesis and refuse it to the witness of tradition."[136] The letters in the Apocalypse, to which we shall be turning in a moment, supply a further argument. As H. Lilje observes, "anyone who can address the Church with such priestly and apostolic authority is more than a mere compiler in the apocalyptic tradition."[137] We must go even further and say that from no one but an apostle would the "angels" of the Churches have accepted such stern reproaches and the reminder of such hard truths.

Once this last-mentioned point is accepted, the situation suggested by the letters in the Apocalypse is easy enough to define. The apostle St. John, who writes to the communities of Asia of which Ephesus is the chief, is at this time no longer directly governing the Church of Ephesus. This is understandable, since he is exiled on Patmos (1:9). The Church of Ephesus now has a residential leader, whom we may call a bishop, as have a number of other Churches, including at least the six mentioned in Chapters 2 and 3 of the Apocalypse. As we have already noted, the hierarchic organization depicted here reminds us of the one we see in the letters of St. Ignatius of Antioch. In this context, it is worthwhile to recall that the twenty-four elders (*presbyteroi*) gathered around the throne of God in Revelation 4:4 have been compared with the presbyters gathered around the bishop in the letters of Ignatius. It is as if the Apocalypse wanted to suggest that in the heavenly world there exists as it were a prototype of the earthly hierarchy and liturgy.[138]

The residential leaders which the letters of the Apocalypse presuppose must have been set at the head of the communities by John himself or by other apostles. For Ephesus the other could be St. Paul, if Timothy, who was "ordained" by Paul (cf. below), was still alive at this time, and if he remained bishop of Ephesus until his death.[139] In any case, it is only if the residential leaders did depend closely on the apostles, that we can explain why John, the last survivor of the apostolic college, should receive the command to write to them, pass judgment on them, and, if need be, admonish them.

It would be a misunderstanding to think that John acts as a purely passive instrument in these letters. He is the spokesman for Christ, but he is also the wideawake apostle and a responsible agent. There is clear evidence of this in the many literary and doctrinal similarities between these chapters of the Apocalypse and the rest of the Johannine literature; a little further on, we shall speak of the striking likenesses to the third letter of John.

One characteristic of the letters relates them to the prayer of John 17 in a special way. The distinguishing mark of these letters, as compared with all others in the New Testament, is that they are dictated by Christ himself. At the beginning of each letter Christ recalls what he is and his divine privileges in order that the Church may contemplate themselves in this mirror and correct what they find faulty in themselves.[140] The letters show a tripartite scheme: *Christ, the "angels" of the Churches, the Churches themselves*. The implication is that the moral and religious growth of the communities is closely connected with the worth of the leaders who govern the Churches; the leaders, in turn, must be faithful followers of Christ as king and priest. But this notable conception is the one that also controls the development of the priestly prayer in John 17! The prayer has an analogous tripartite division: *Christ, the apostles, the Church*. In the prayer Jesus asks that his work of sanctifying men may continue in his Church once he has returned to his Father. The Church must be united in love and thus reflect the very oneness of Father and Son; it must thereby become a permanent stimulus to faith in the world around it. To carry out this task, Jesus relies above all on his apostles who are therefore at the center of his prayer. This is why he asks the Father to consecrate them as he himself had been consecrated.

It is easy to see that we have the same presupposition and the same doctrinal perspective in John 17 and in the letters of the Apocalypse. There is also the fact that we find in both the same pervading atmosphere of liturgy and eucharist. We have already shown this for John 17 (cf. Chapter 1, above). For the letters in the Apocalypse, recall the following themes which remind us of the discourse on the bread of life in John 6: the tree of life (Rv. 2:7), the hidden manna (2:17), the meal shared with Jesus (3:20), and perhaps the morning star (2:28).[141] There is only this important difference between John 17 and the letters that *in the Apocalypse the "angels" of the Churches replace the apostles;* it is upon these "angels" that Christ now relies for the sanctification of the whole people of God. Some pages back we pointed out that the unusual title of "angels" given to the hierarchic leaders turns our attention to the priests and the prophets of the old covenant. We now see more clearly why these leaders must be priests in the same sense as the apostles whom they succeed; that is, why they must be endowed like the apostles with a priesthood which relates them to both the priests and the prophets of the Old Testament.

In order thus to succeed the apostles, the "angels" of the Churches must have received the priesthood and its authority from the apostles themselves, though not those incommunicable privileges that mark the apostle as such.[142] How did this transmission of powers take place? The Apocalypse gives no answer, but we may fill the lacuna by appealing to 2 Timothy 1:6, where St. Paul says to Timothy: "I am reminding you now to fan into a flame the gift that God gave you when I laid my hands on you." We cannot comment at length on this very important text and shall restrict ourselves to a few indispensable clarifications.[143]

In the Old Testament the rite of imposing hands (*semikah, samak*) has numerous meanings. Two passages may be signaled in relation to the ordination of Timothy. In Numbers 8:10 the Levites are consecrated by having all the Israelites lay hands on them; in Numbers 27:18 the same gesture is performed by Moses when he established Joshua as his successor in leadership. But we must take into account the fact that this rite is not a part of the ritual for consecrating priests. It does occur in late Judaism in what is called the ordination of rabbis, but there is question here simply of a juridical transmission of powers. In the gospels Christ does not lay hands on anyone in order to confer powers, but only to heal or bless (Mk. 5:23; 6:5; 7:32; 8:23-25; 10:16), nor does the Jerusalem community when it comes to introduce Matthias into the apostolic group. We are led to conclude, therefore, that the rite of ordination mentioned in 2 Timothy 1:6 (a rite that communicates a divine gift, a grace, and divine powers, and is not a mere symbol[144]) was invented by the early Church when it was confronted with the need to secure apostolic succession. The image in 2 Timothy 1:6 is not of relighting a fire that has gone out; Timothy is always in possession of the gift, but he must continually fan the flame so that it may have its full effect.

At times 2 Timothy 1:6 is contrasted with 1 Timothy 4:14 where Paul seems to imply that he was not the only agent active in Timothy's ordination and that the latter came through the laying on of hands by a group of presbyters, the men responsible for a local community: "You have in you a spiritual gift which was given to you when the prophets spoke and the body of elders laid their hands on you; do not let it lie unused." The difficulty has been resolved in two ways which we think equally plausible. The point has been made that the phrase "laying on of hands" is preceded by the preposition "through" (*dia*) in the case of Paul, but by the preposition "with" (*meta*) in the case of the body of elders. The conclusion has been drawn that only Paul's action conferred God's gift; the action of the elders was only a ceremonial accompaniment.[145] Another solution involves connecting the Greek formula (*epithesis tōn cheirōn tou presbyteriou*) with the Hebrew formula (*semikah zeqenin*), the latter of which means, not the laying on of hands by the elders, but the laying on of hands which confers the dignity of an elder. Accordingly, the laying on of hands in 1 Timothy 4:14 is that which bestows on Timothy the rank of elder. The word *presbyterion* occurs with this meaning (instead of *presbeion*) as a variant in Daniel 13:56 (the story of Susanna). It also occurs twice in Eusebius' *History of the Church:* Origen had not yet been ordained to the presbyterate (VI, 19:16); at Caesarea Origen was ordained presbyter by the Palestinian bishops (VI, 23:4).[146]

There are numerous contacts in thought and expression between the letters in the Apocalypse and the rest of the Johannine writings, and these confirm the unity of authorship. A comparison with the third letter of John is very interesting as far as the hierarchy is concerned. We think it worthwhile to reproduce here the whole of this short letter,[147] which brings out so strikingly a basic aspect of priestly ministry, one that we ourselves highlighted earlier in this book: the service of the truth. In this letter we see the elderly apostle threatening to visit a recalcitrant member of the hierarchy, just as in the

Apocalypse Christ himself threatens to visit the "angels" of the Church who are proving unfaithful.

> The Elder to Gaius, that beloved brother whom I love in truth: Beloved, I hope you are doing well in every way and enjoying health of body and soul. It was a great joy to me to have the brothers come and bear witness to your truth, telling how you walk in the truth. I can have no greater joy than to hear that my children are walking in the truth. Beloved, you act faithfully in what you do for the brothers, even if they be strangers to you. They have borne witness before the Church to your love; you will be doing the right thing if you aid them on their journey[148] in a manner worthy of God, for it is for the Name's sake that they set out without receiving anything from the pagans [the Name is the sacred tetragrammaton, but here it is the name of Jesus; the contact with John 17, as explained earlier in this book, is quite clear]. We ought to welcome such men so that we may be fellow workers for the truth. I wrote something for the Church, but their ambitious leader, Diotrephes, does not accept us. This is why, if I come, I will bring to mind the deeds he has done [cf. the conditional coming of Christ in Rv. 2:5, 16]: he attacks us with malicious words, and, not content with that, he himself does not welcome the brothers and prevents those who would welcome them from doing so, and expels them from the Church. Beloved, imitate good, not evil. He who does good is of God; he who does evil has not seen God. Everyone, including the Truth itself [perhaps personified Truth: Christ or the Holy Spirit; cf. what we said earlier about consecration in the truth], bears witness to Demetrius. We too will bear witness to him, and you know that our witness is true. There were many things I wanted to write to you, but I do not want to write them with pen and ink. I hope to see you soon, and we can talk face to face. Peace be yours. Your friends greet you. Greet our friends by name.

In our brief comments on this movingly simple text, we shall limit ourselves strictly to what relates to our concern in this book. It is easy to see that there is a striking similarity between the hierarchic situation supposed by the letters in the Apocalypse and the one described in John's short letter. In 3 John, the Elder, that is, the apostle John whose voice is unmistakable, addresses two men who are residential Church leaders, similar to the "angels" of the Churches in the Apocalypse. In all likelihood these leaders received their authority from the apostle John, since he calls them "my children" (Verse 3), just as Paul calls Timothy, whom he ordained, "my son" (1 Tm. 1:18; 2 Tm. 1:2; 2:1). A further argument for such dependence is that John passes judgment on these men, just as Christ, through his agent, passes judgment on the "angels" of the Churches in the Apocalypse. The two leaders are Gaius and Diotrephes.

The letter is addressed to Gaius, whom the apostle praises. He congratulates him for having spared no trouble on behalf of brothers who are strangers to the local community. The reference is very probably to itinerant preachers sent out by the Elder himself: "It is for the Name's sake that they set out without receiving anything from the pagans." These men have told the Elder of the kind reception they received from Gaius. The apostle urges Gaius to persevere in this way of acting and, in particular, to help itinerant preachers on their journey in a manner worthy of God.

The other Church leader is Diotrephes. The community he leads cannot be the same one that Gaius leads, although many exegetes seem to think so. For if it were, then, as Dodd points out, why should the Elder feel it necessary to inform Gaius of recent developments in a conflict agitating Diotrephes' community?[149] On the other hand, John can say simply "I wrote something for the Church," because Gaius would know what Church John means. Bishop Diotrephes is the antithesis of Gaius. Despite the instructions the Lord himself had given to his future ministers (cf. what we said in discussing the washing of the feet), Diotrephes is eager for incense, honors, and the first place (*philoprōteuein*);[150] the fault will be a frequent one among ecclesiastics! This is probably why he rebels against the apostolic primacy of John and refuses to accept his directives and welcome his messengers.

The short letter ends with praise of a Demetrius, who may be the head of another Church or possibly an itinerant preacher. Thus, praise and blame alternates here as in the letters of the Apocalypse.

Throughout this lengthy study of the letters of the Apocalypse, we have been stressing a basic characteristic of these letters: the fact that in the "angels" of the Churches we are to see also the communities these men direct, since the latter are held responsible for the spiritual state of the former. This idea occasionally finds its equivalent in the letters of St. Ignatius of Antioch, for whom the bishop is as it were the embodiment of his Church. Thus, Ignatius writes to the Ephesians: "I welcomed all of you in the person of Onesimus" (1:3). And to the Trallians: "In the person of Polybius I see your whole Church" (1:1). In ending this chapter, we would like to dwell for a moment on this lesson which is so relevant today.

In John 17 Christ utters a special prayer for the apostles through whom he intends to reach out to other men. The letters of the Apocalypse, on the other hand, do not have separate sections addressed to the hierarchic leaders and to the Christian people generally. Rather, Christ addresses himself simultaneously to the hierarchic leaders and, through them, to the communities, as if the fervor of the latter were closely dependent on the fervor of the former. Proof of this is the sudden shift from the second person singular to the second person plural (cf. 2:10, 13, 23). A further proof is the very significant fact that has not been sufficiently noticed: A number of terms in the letters are among those used in the New Testament letters to describe the labor, the characteristic traits, and the rewards of apostolic workers.[151]

"To the angel of the Church in Ephesus" Christ says: "I know all about you: how hard you work and how much you put up with" (2:2). The noun used for "work" (*kopos*) is often used by Paul for the apostolic ministry (1 Co. 3:8; 2 Co. 6:5; 10:15; 11:23). "I know . . . how you tested the impostors who called themselves apostles and proved they were liars" (2:2b). In the Pastoral Letters of St. Paul as well as these letters, the unmasking of false teachers is a basic task of apostolic workers.

"To the angel of the Church in Smyrna," Christ says: "Even if you have to die, keep faithful (*pistos*), and I will give you the crown (*stephanon*) of life for your prize" (2:10). Faithfulness and a crown, while not the exclusive privilege of apostolic toil, are frequently mentioned in connection with it (1 Co. 4:2, 17; 7:25; Ep. 6:21; Col. 1:7; 4:7, 9; 1 Tm. 1:12; 3:11; 2 Tm. 2:2–7; 4:8; 1 P. 5:4).

"To the angel of the Church in Thyatira" Christ says: "I know all about you and how charitable you are; I know your faith and devotion (*diakonian*) and how much you put up with" (2:19). The term *diakonia* is one name for the apostolic responsibility.[152] "To the angel of the Church in Sardis" Christ says: "Wake up (*ginou grēgorōn*); revive (*stērison*) what little you have left; it is dying fast" (3:2). The same exhortations to watchfulness and to the strengthening of others in faith, expressed in the same Greek terms, are first addressed by Christ to Peter (Lk. 22:32); Peter in his turn repeats them to Christians generally (1 P. 5:8–9).

"To the angel of the Church in Philadelphia" Christ says: "Now I have opened in front of you a door that nobody will be able to close" (3:8). The image of the "open door" occurs four times in the rest of the New Testament and signifies an opportunity for apostolic ministry (1 Co. 16:9; 2 Co. 2:12; 4:3; Ac. 14:27). "Those who prove victorious I will make into pillars in the sanctuary of my God" (3:12). Despite opinions to the contrary,[153] the image of the pillar seems to apply in 1 Timothy 3:15 to the entire Church "which upholds the truth and keeps it safe." Usually, however, it refers to individuals and finds its most suitable application in the leader who is responsible for defending authentic teaching; thus in Galations 2:9 it is applied to James, Peter, and John. All these points in the letters confirms our view that the "angels" of the Churches are the hierarchic leaders of these Churches.

The clear lesson of the letters in the Apocalypse is that the Christian communities are, to an extent at least, as good as their hierarchic leaders are. In the author's thinking, that lesson holds for the universal Church of all times. Therefore the letters of the Apocalypse should be a preferred text for reading and meditation by everyone engaged in pastoral activity.

It is true, of course, that the Churches to which Christ writes with John as his intermediary are not abstractions but communities fully localized in time and space. We are even told in passing of facts about individual Churches. Thus, the author of the Apocalypse reminds us of the metropolitan role of the Church at Ephesus: "I shall . . . take your lamp stand from its place" (2:5);[154] of the famous altar of Jupiter at Pergamum, which overlooked the surrounding valleys (2:3: the throne of Satan); of the successive names had by Philadelphia (cf. the promise of a new name in 3:3); and of the school of medicine at Laodicea and the trade in eye ointment there (3:13).

Nonetheless we may not limit the lesson of the Apocalypse to the seven Churches of Asia in the time of John. We must remember, to begin with, that in the New Testament view the local Church represents the entire Church; "the church of God in Corinth" (1 Co. 1:2) does not mean that there is a Corinthian Church alongside a Thessalonian, a Roman, and an Ephesian Church, but that the Church in Corinth is the universal Church as represented in Corinth.[155] We must remember also, and above all, that seven is a symbolic number signifying fullness or totality and that the letters to the seven Churches have an oracular character.[156] They are but the first septenary in an essentially prophetic work that looks to the future. This means that the letters are always contemporary and are intended for the Church of all times.

We may note that the Holy Spirit makes Christ's words his own (in accordance with the teaching in John 16:13) and invariably repeats at the end of each letter: "If anyone has ears to hear, let him listen to what the Spirit is saying *to the churches*" ("churches" in the plural). We must also observe that the septenary of letters shows the same pattern as the three prophetic septenaries that follow (the seals, the trumpets, and the cups); namely, the septenary is broken down into a ternary and a quaternary. In the first three letters the invitation to listen to the Spirit precedes the promise, while in the last four the promise precedes the invitation.[157] What are we to conclude but that in the letters that begin the Apocalypse the author is already writing as a prophet and formulating a teaching that is valid for the earthly Church until the second coming of Christ?

General Conclusion

Panoramic View of the Stages of This Study · Some Pointers for the Rediscovery of an Authentic Priestly Spirituality

OUR PURPOSE in this General Conclusion is twofold. We would like, first of all, to offer a broad synthesis of, and at times to shed new light on, the main results of our work. We shall not, therefore, be simply repeating what has been said in the course of the book. For those readers who have been following the thread of thought carefully, the Conclusion will be a means of more clearly grasping its main articulations. For hurried readers, the Conclusion may serve as a first approach that will stimulate them to undertake a more leisurely study of the book when they have the time. Secondly, we think it worthwhile to indicate, in the latter half of the Conclusion, a number of readings from Scripture that are especially suitable for helping in the rediscovery of an authentic priestly spirituality.

The lengthy inquiry we have just completed into the priesthood of Christ and his ministers is different in two ways from all such inquiries hitherto undertaken. First, it pays much greater attention to certain preparations in the Old Testament, especially the prophetic tradition and, within the latter, the Servant songs. Second, the study takes as its starting point, not the New Testament document (the Letter to the Hebrews) that deals explicitly with the priesthood of Christ, but the priestly prayer of Jesus. The latter offers the great advantage, lacking in the Letter to the Hebrews, of linking to the consecration of Christ as priest and victim the idea of a participation of the apostles in this consecration. As the title of the book indicates, we wanted to take John 17 and some complementary texts (derived chiefly, but not exclusively, from the Johannine tradition) and to derive from them as exact as possible an idea of Christ's priesthood and the ministerial priesthood.

THE PRIESTHOOD OF CHRIST

Christ and the Suffering Servant

THE BASIC QUESTION to be answered is: Was Jesus really a priest? Anyone remembering the Letter to the Hebrews would unhesitatingly answer, "Of course," for the Letter proves at length that Christ is the high priest of the Christian dispensation. Yet serious doubts may arise and have, in fact, arisen in recent times. One may well be inclined to relativize the ideas of Hebrews on priesthood, because the concepts and language are clearly apologetic and even polemical in intent; they spring from specific historical circumstances and are found nowhere else. It may be claimed, and has, in fact, been claimed, that the argumentation in the Letter to the Hebrews does not prove Jesus was really a priest, still less that he thought of himself as a priest. Does not an objective examination of the words and behavior of Jesus show that he is to be linked not with the priestly tradition of the Old Testament but with the prophetic? Is it not significant that throughout the gospels Jesus never claims the title of priest and that the title is nowhere given him in the New Testament, except in the Letter to the Hebrews?

These are serious objections, yet commentators have usually been content to meet them by suggesting rather weak indications that Jesus was aware of his own priestly rank: exorcisms, the blessing of the children, the reconciliation of men with God through the forgiveness of sins, etc. These, it is claimed, are priestly actions. The commentators add that Christ showed a great liking for Psalm 110 in which the Messiah is said to be a priest according to the order of Melchizedek and for ever.

In our view we must look elsewhere for a really strong argument that Jesus was indeed a priest and that he thought of himself as a priest. The most decisive argument is that Christ recognized himself above all in the suffering Servant of Deutero-Isaiah; that he first foretold his passion by allusion to the Isaiah 53; and that after him the New Testament writers developed their teaching on the cross as source of salvation for mankind, chiefly on the basis of Isaiah's prophecy.

It is clear, to begin with, that in Isaiah 53 the person of the suffering Servant represents a fusing of the priestly and prophetic traditions and thus paves the way for an immense change in Old Testament religion. Here we have a first transformation: In the Old Testament, "You [Aaron] and your sons, and your whole family shall bear the burden of transgressions against the sanctuary" (Nb. 18:1); Ezekiel, the prophet-priest, had already begun the radicalization of this concept when, in a symbolic action required by Yahweh, he carried all the sins of the chosen people (Ezk. 4:4–8). Isaiah 53 shows us a much more extraordinary priestly act: In his suffering the Servant of Yahweh bears the moral wretchedness of all mankind and thereby wins healing for it: "Ours were the sufferings he bore, ours the sorrows he carried. . . . On him lies a punishment that brings us peace, and through his wounds we are healed" (Is. 53:4, 9).

The second transformation: In the Old Testament priests reconciled men with God by means of expiatory sacrifices of animals. Coming at the culminating point in a long line of prophets who had risked their lives in fulfillment of their mission, the Servant reconciles men with God in a radically new kind of expiatory sacrifice: the generous gift of his own life.

The third transformation: In the Old Testament, along with priestly mediation there was the mediation of the prophets by means of prayer (we may think chiefly of Jeremiah and Moses); these prayers were not predetermined ritual formulas but petitions that sprang spontaneously from the vicissitudinous lives of the these men of God. The Servant, who in many respects is a new Moses and a new Jeremiah, unites intercessory prayer to his sacrifice. Thus he is really a priest, but his priesthood is something new: a living synthesis of the priestly and prophetic mediations.

Jesus fulfills, and goes much beyond, the Servant poems. Consequently, each time Christ's role is described by reference to the Servant's expiatory sacrifice of himself, he is being implicitly presented to us as a priest. In the synoptic gospels we think chiefly of the saying about ransom and the accounts of the Last Supper. The former (Mk. 10:45; Mt. 20:28; cf. Lk. 22:27) confronts us with a paradox: the transcendent Son of Man of whom Daniel says that all nations must one day serve him (Dn. 7:13–14), must first of all serve, after the manner of the suffering Servant, by sacrificing his life as a ransom for the sinful multitude. The accounts of the Last Supper in St. Paul (1 Co. 11:23–25) and the synoptic gospels (Mk. 14:22–25; Mt. 26:26–29; Lk. 22:14–20) allude clearly both to the oracle of Jeremiah on the new covenant (Jr. 31:31–34) and to the Servant of Yahweh who gives his life for the sins of the many.

St. Paul makes use of the same prophetic theme on a number of occasions: "The Lord Jesus Christ, who . . . sacrificed himself for our sins" (Ga. 1:4); "I live in faith: faith in the

Son of God who loved me and who sacrificed himself for my sake" (Ga. 2:20); "What proves that God loves us is that Christ died for us while we were still sinners" (Rm. 5:8); "Since God did not spare his own Son, but gave him up to benefit us all, we may be certain, after such a gift, that he will not refuse anything he can give" (Rm. 8:32); "Follow Christ by loving as he loved you, giving himself up in our place as a fragrant offering and a sacrifice to God" (Ep. 5:2). The connected, eminently liturgical and priestly theme of access to God through Christ occurs three times in the New Testament: Romans 5:1–2; Ephesians 2:14–18; 1 Peter 3:18.

To these passages we might add others from the first letter of St. Peter which is so heavily influenced by the thought of the suffering Servant: "Remember, the ransom that was paid to free you . . . was not paid in anything corruptible, neither is silver nor gold, but in the precious blood of a lamb without spot or stain" (1:18–19; cf. Is. 53:7); "He was bearing our faults in his own body on the cross, so that we might die to our faults and live for holiness; through his wounds you have been healed. You had gone astray like sheep but now you have come back to the shepherd and guardian of your souls" (2:24–25; cf. Is. 53:5, 6, 12); "Christ himself, innocent though he was, had died once for sins, died for the guilty, to lead us to God" (3:18; cf. Is. 53:11).

In a way that is original the fourth gospel also stands within the same tradition. The Lamb of God that takes away the sins of the world (1:29), the Good Shepherd who, as we are repeatedly told, gives his life (literally "lays [down] his soul"—which is a literal translation of Is. 53:10) for the sake of his sheep (10:11, 15, 17, 18; cf. 13:37–38; 15:13), the washing of the feet which symbolizes the redemptive abasement of the passion—all these are echoes of Isaiah 53. The same is true of the words in 17:19 where the verb "sanctify" (*hagiazein*) does not mean moral sanctification or a setting apart for a mission, but a setting apart for sacrifice. The proper translation, therefore, is, "For their sake I consecrate myself," and it is another allusion to Isaiah 53:10 where the Servant offers himself as an expiatory victim.

The Priestly Prayer of John 17 and the Letter to the Hebrews

THE LAST TEXT cited in the preceding paragraph was from the great prayer in John 17, and to the latter we now turn our full attention. The liturgical character of the prayer has sometimes been exaggerated. The truth of the matter is that, on the one hand, it has a clearly eucharistic orientation, as is proved by numerous points of contact with the Didache, and that, on the other, it has for a long time, and with good reason, been known as "the priestly prayer." The functions proper to a priest are to offer sacrifice and to intercede for the faithful. John 17 emphatically assigns Christ this double function. Three points of the prayer show that it eminently deserves the name "priestly prayer."

The first point: Jesus' consecration of himself is certainly a priestly act for it is but his definitive "Yes" to the Father who had made him a priest when sending him into the world to save it. Jesus says about himself in 10:36: He is "someone the Father has consecrated and sent into the world." According to John 3:16 the Father sent him into the world so that he might offer his life for it; the Father was thus sending him as a consecrated priest. This consecration is inseparable from the incarnation. In sending his Son into the world, the Father gives him a human nature that is radically separated by its holiness from the sinful mankind which the Son is to bring back to God. Much more than the Old Testament high priest who wore a diadem with the inscription "Consecrated to Yahweh" (Ex. 28:36), Christ is truly the "Holy One of God," as Peter proclaims him to be in John 6:69. The conception of priesthood already implied in Isaiah 53 is here greatly transcended, since to say that Christ was consecrated a priest at the moment of his being sent into the world amounts to saying that he is a priest by reason of his very being as the incarnate Son of God.

The second point about John 17: not only does Jesus act as a priest in consecrating himself as a victim, but he also prays as a priest. This becomes clear when we recall that the Servant is not satisfied to offer his life as an expiatory sacrifice, but adds to his sacrifice an intercession for sinners, thus uniting in his person the sacrificial mediation of Old Testament priests and the meditation through intercession of the prophets. But there is an important difference between John 17 and Isaiah 53: while the Servant intercedes for sinners generally, Jesus seems to consecrate himself as a victim solely for his apostles and to pray only for his Church. But it would be a mistake to speak here of some Johannine particularism, for the ultimate purpose of Jesus, clearly enough, is that "the world may believe [or realise that] it was you who sent me" (17:21; 23).

In John 17 the seeming limitation placed on a universalist perspective is to be explained in the last analysis by the third point in our proof of the priestly character of the prayer. We refer to the remarkable transposition of the Jewish liturgy of atonement that is to be found in John 17.

Whatever are the different ways in which the structure of John 17 can be analyzed, there is no doubt that the prayer contains a kind of triptych.[1] In the first panel Jesus asks the Father to glorify him and thus enable him to continue that glorification of the Father which he, Jesus, has already begun in his disciples. The third panel is a development of the first. In it we are told that eternal life, as well as that knowledge of Jesus and the Father which will be the fruit of the glorification of Jesus, are to be brought to the world through the unity of future believers, a unity which reflects that of Father and Son.

The central panel is the most important and the most extensive. Here Jesus prays for those whom the Father has

taken from the world and given to him; for those men whom
Jesus himself has preserved so that none of them had been
lost "except the one who chose to be lost" (17:12; cf. Verses
6, 16). Comparison of these texts with earlier texts in the
fourth gospel (especially 6:70; 13:18; and 15:19), as well
as with the synoptic gospels where only the Twelve share
Jesus' last meal, makes it clear that those for whom Christ
offers a special prayer are not all the disciples without exception (as has sometimes been claimed) but only the apostles.
It is through the mediation of these favored disciples who are
closely united with one another (Jn. 17:11) that Jesus intends to communicate to others; that is, to the whole Church,
eternal life and knowledge of Father and Son and to make of
them a community that is truly one.

The similarly tripartite structure of the Jewish liturgy for
the Day of Atonement sheds a vivid light on John 17. During
the festival of atonement the high priest successively makes
atonement for himself, for his family; that is, the Israelite
priesthood, and for the entire chosen people (cf. Lv. 16:6–
11). The threefold prayer of Jesus in John 17 shows us that
he is the high priest of the new covenant.

A further point to be made in this context concerns the
Jewish prohibition against pronouncing the holy name Yahweh: "I Am who I Am." Only the high priest was allowed to
speak "the Name," on one occasion during the year; namely,
during the liturgy of atonement. If we bear this fact in mind,
must we not find it significant that the manifestation of the
Father's name, a theme hitherto not stated in the fourth gospel, should be so prominent in John 17 (Verses 6–8, 26)?
To this theme must also be connected the enigmatic formula
in Verses 11 and 12 (a formula that is not to be emended,
as it is in the Jerusalem Bible): "keep them in your name
which you have given to me." Like the glory that the Father
has from all eternity given to the Son and in which the Son
gives a share to men (17:22), the name that the Father

gives the Son is simply the divine nature itself. "The giving of the name" can be restated as the fact (on which heavy emphasis is laid in the fourth gospel) that the Son, no less than the Father, can say: "I Am who I Am."

Finally, on the Day of Atonement the high priest entered the holy of holies and sprinkled the throne of mercy; atonement for sins was connected with this action. In John 17 Jesus prays as though he had already set foot upon the threshold of eternity. In this connection we must keep in mind that in the fourth gospel Jesus' return to the Father is the climax of the redemptive drama.

In thus transposing the liturgy of expiation the prayer in John 17 also christianizes it. The aim of the festival of atonement was to restore Israel to a state of holiness by expiating the sins of the priests and people of God. In this way the divine injunction laid upon the chosen nation was fulfilled: "You must be holy because I am holy." The demands made by Christ on his Church are much greater, since they flow from the new revelation which the Son of God brings to men. This revelation makes known to them that from all eternity God has a Son and that between Father and Son there exists, in the Holy Spirit, an infinitely perfect unity and communion. Given this revelation, the people of God under the new covenant cannot be satisfied, like the people of the former covenant, simply to reflect in their lives the divine holiness: "You must be holy because I am holy." They must also, through a loving unity which the sanctifying action of the Spirit makes possible, reflect the unity of Father and Son. That is what Jesus prays for in John 17.

These doctrinal perspectives carry over into the first letter of St. John. Here Jesus is twice called an expiatory victim (*hilasmos:* 2:2; 4:10). This term occurs nowhere else in the New Testament but is used in the Greek translation of the Old Testament for the Day of Atonement. Furthermore, Christ, our victim, is also our intercessor with the Father

(2:1); this is a priestly function that calls to mind both the prayer in John 17 and the intercession which the Servant adds to his sacrifice. Finally, not only does the first letter of St. John think of the Christian life as a communion with the Father and the Son; it also uses expressions that remind us of the great Old Testament command that is at the source of the liturgy of atonement: "You must be holy because I am holy." However, the divine model to be imitated has now come near to us in Jesus. This Jesus who fills the writer's every thought is designated by the simple term "That one" or "He." The Christian is to live "the same kind of life as Christ [literally: that one] lived" (2:6); he "must try to be as pure as Christ [that one]" (3:3); he "is to be holy just as he is holy" (3:7); etc.

Once we have examined John's thought on the priesthood of Christ, it is worthwhile—even indispensable—to compare it with the teaching of the Letter to the Hebrews, the only New Testament document in which Christ is called priest and high priest. In this letter the priesthood of Christ, seen in the light of Psalm 110, is said to be everlasting, not in the sense that it had no beginning, but in the sense that it will have no end. The transcendence and uniqueness of Christ's priesthood and sacrifice emerge with great clarity here. These qualities are essentially due to the fact that Christ is the incarnate Son of God who offers himself "through the eternal Spirit" (Heb. 9:14). Such a priest cannot have successors in the proper sense of this latter term; and such a sacrifice is necessarily definitive.

A number of texts in the Letter to the Hebrews may easily lead the reader to think that Christ became a priest only after ascending into heaven; cf. 5:9–10; 6:20; 7:25; 8:4–5; 9:12. Against this interpretation, however, we must note that the Letter also suggests that Christ is already a priest while on earth, and especially on Golgotha. On the other hand, the letter does teach that Christ was perfected in his priesthood through his suffering. Moreover, the letter refers, even more clearly than John 17, to the liturgy of atonement, in which the climactic action was the entry of the high priest into the holy of holies and his sprinkling of the throne of mercy. This being the point of reference, we can understand why Hebrews connects the priestly activity of Christ chiefly with his heavenly exaltation and his glorified life. According to Hebrews, the sacrifice of Calvary was offered "through the eternal Spirit" (9:14); the glorified Christ is constantly offering and interceding. This picture of the risen Jesus corresponds to what is said in 1 John 2:2 and to the heavenly liturgy depicted in the Apocalypse.

Certain conclusions emerge from the comparison of Hebrews and Johannine thought: In both, the Old Testament liturgy is transposed and spiritualized, to the accompaniment of allusions to Isaiah 53; in both, the priesthood of Christ is connected with the mystery of the incarnation; in both, the intercessory prayer of Christ plays an important role, in keeping with Isaiah 53. The Letter to the Hebrews, however, draws its teaching on priesthood and sacrifice not directly from Isaiah 53 but from the gospel tradition and especially, it seems, from the Johannine tradition; the Letter would thus be telling us that according to that tradition Jesus acts as a priest, even if he does not explicitly claim the name of priest.

THE VARIOUS ASPECTS OF MINISTERIAL PRIESTHOOD

SINCE VATICAN II the expression "ministerial priesthood" has come into use for designating the priesthood proper to members of the hierarchy (bishops and priests) and distinguishing it from the priesthood shared by all the baptized. But today there are theologians who formally deny the validity of the distinction, or at least think that it is not an essential part of divine revelation. The latter believe that the distinction arose in specific historical circumstances as the Church adapted itself to the social conditions of a bygone period. As a result of these challenges and of the one-sided stress on the common priesthood of all the faithful, many priests no longer know where they stand within the people of God. Some people have taken an even more serious step and claimed that for consecrating the Eucharist, forgiving sins, etc., only a simple delegation by the community is required. *Suther.*

As we try to come to grips with the problem of ministerial priesthood, which is such a highly topical one today, the Johannine writings provide us with very valuable elements of an answer, although not enough attention has been paid to them. The priestly prayer of Jesus in John 17 speaks to us of the priestly consecration of the apostles. When correctly interpreted, the washing of the feet (Jn. 13:1–20) and the scene that has wrongly been called the Johannine Pentecost (Jn. 20:19–23) show us Christ preparing the apostles for their ordination as priests or completing this ordination. Finally, the letters in the Apocalypse show that the important problem of apostolic succession (which is also the problem of the transmission to others of the priesthood proper to the apostles) has already been resolved in a practical way. Such are the various questions relative to ministerial priesthood that our study has taken up.

The Consecration of the Apostles as Priests in John 17

JOHN 17:17–19 speaks of the consecration of the disciples whom the Father has taken from the world and given to Jesus: "Consecrate them in the truth; your word is truth. As you sent me into the world, I have sent them into the world, and for their sake I consecrate myself so that they too may be consecrated in truth." This consecration is not given to all the disciples of Jesus without distinction but only to the apostles. This fact emerges from several converging pieces of evidence: In the tripartite prayer only the section beginning with Verse 20 looks to the people of God as a whole; the prayer in its structure corresponds to the tripartite liturgy of atonement, and it follows that the apostles, as distinct from the total body of disciples, replace the priests of the old covenant; John 17 is connected with the discourses after the Last Supper which are directly addressed only to the apostles; finally, a comparison with other texts (cf. 6:70; 13:18; 15:19) shows that only the apostles can be meant by the men taken from the world and given to Jesus, of whom "not one is lost except the one who chose to be lost" (17:12).

What is meant by this "consecration" of the apostles? John 17:17–19 is dominated by the idea of complete assimilation to Jesus. Jesus himself had been consecrated a priest by the Father with a view to being sent into the world (10:36); now he asks the Father to bestow a similar consecration on the apostles whom he is sending into the world; that is, to consecrate them as priests. Jesus makes this priestly consecration depend on his own consecration as victim: "For their sake I consecrate myself so that they too may be consecrated in truth." There is nothing unusual about such a dependence, since, like all the other blessings of the new covenant, the priesthood of the apostles is the fruit of Christ's sacrifice on Calvary. By that very fact this priesthood is connected in a special way with the mystery of the eucharist. There is an unexpressed relationship between ministerial priesthood and the "Do this as a memorial of me" of the accounts of the Supper (Lk. 22:19; 1 Co. 11:24–25).

The apostles are consecrated for functions reserved strictly to them. We should not be surprised at this. In the tripartite structure of John 17, which is modeled on the liturgy of atonement, the apostles have the place occupied in that liturgy by the Levitical priests. In the Old Testament the entire people of God is said to be a kingdom of priests, but this does not exclude the existence of priests who are consecrated for functions reserved strictly to them.

As priestly consecration and mission are connected in the life of Christ, so they are in the life of the apostles, as 17:18 indicates: "As you sent me into the world, I have sent them into the world." Here we are reminded of the prophets. The priesthood of the apostles, like that of Christ, is presented to us as the synthesis, at a higher level, of the priestly and prophetic traditions of the Old Testament.

The apostles are appointed or chosen by Jesus. The formula in Mark 3:14, which is translated literally as "he made twelve," uses "make" in the sense of "appoint." Such a use of "make" is not found in classical Greek, but it does occur in the Septuagint for the appointment or installation of priests and of Moses and Aaron (cf. 1 S. 12:6; 1 K. 12:31; 13:33; 2 Ch. 2:18). Because such terminology is applied to them, the apostles remind us of the cultic institutions of the old covenant. They also remind us of these institutions because they are said to be chosen; places of worship, priests, and Levites were chosen in the Old Testament, but not the prophets. On the other hand, the apostles, like the prophets, are called in a direct and personal way; moreover, they are the messengers of Jesus as the prophets had been the messengers of Yahweh (whereas the Old Testament priests had not been messengers). Thus, the apostles in their consecration by the Father resemble both the priests and the prophets of the former covenant.

The Old Testament knows only one divine revealer; Yahweh alone teaches, and Moses and the prophets have no disciples in the narrow sense of the term. But this one revealer does express himself through the agency of numerous prophets who are simply his spokesmen. In the New Testament there is but one priest, the incarnate Son of God; this one priest, however, speaks and acts in the Church through the agency of numerous priests who are simply his instruments;

they may act as priests only in dependence on Christ, since their priesthood and mission are strictly dependent on the priesthood and mission of Christ.

What does "consecration in the truth" (17:17) involve? We must begin by recalling John's idea of truth. Truth, for John, means the revelation that is brought by Christ and summed up in the person of the redeemer; that is, Christ does not simply bring the truth, he is the Truth. Once consecrated in the truth, the apostles will be "penetrated and interiorly changed by the truth."[2] The Spirit Paraclete will lead the apostles into the truth in its entirety (14:13), situate them as it were within the truth and within Jesus who is the Truth, and thus enable them to work for the salvation of mankind in dependence on the one Saviour.

We read in John that the truth brought by the incarnate Son of God (8:32), or the Son himself (8:36), frees men from the spiritual slavery of sin. It is true, of course, that Christ is not indifferent to the bodily afflictions of men and that the inauguration of his kingdom lays the ax at the root of violence and tyranny not only in private life but in public and civic life as well. Yet the essential purpose of Christ is always spiritual liberation, that change of heart that is the indispensable condition of all other liberations. The Servant songs already turn us unmistakably in this direction. So too it is primarily for this work of spiritual liberation that the apostles are consecrated in the truth. This being so, the mingling of politics and religion in a priest's ministry, or a conception of the ministry that gives priority not to the changing of men's hearts but to the changing of economic and social structures by means of class struggle, must inevitably appear to be a betrayal of the gospel.

In the fourth gospel Christ the Truth saves the world both by his word and by the sacraments he institutes; word and sacrament are distinct but inseparable (cf. John 6). Now that they are assimilated to Christ, who had been sent into

the world to save it ("As you sent me into the world, I have
sent them into the world"), the apostles must labor for the
salvation of the world both through preaching and through
the administration of the sacraments.

What does "consecration in truth" (17:19) mean? The
apostles are consecrated for the new worship in spirit and in
truth of which John 4:23–24 speaks, and their consecration
must be explained in the light of that worship. The worship
in question is being contrasted not with a false worship but
with the imperfect worship of the old covenant. Worship in
truth is a worship that conforms to the truth brought by
Jesus, and is inseparable from worship in spirit, inasmuch as
it is made possible only through the rebirth that the Holy
Spirit effects. Connected as it is with worship in truth, the
apostles' consecration in truth is contrasted with the imperfect
priestly consecration of the Old Testament and harmonizes
with the definitive revelation Christ has brought. Their consecration is clearly theocentric in character since the priests
who receive it have as their goal to raise up worshippers in
spirit and in truth.

The theocentric orientation of priestly consecration in John
17:17–19 can be established in another way as well. As a
number of commentators note, the reason Jesus begins the
part of his prayer that looks to the apostles with the invocation
"Holy Father" (17:11) is that he is going to ask the Father
to "sanctify" them so they may manifest the holiness of God
in a far more perfect way than the priests of the old covenant
did.

*Complementary Evidence from the Fourth Gospel and the
Apocalypse*

WE ARE CONVINCED that in the symbolic scene of the *washing
of the feet,* which has been the subject of so much discussion
and varying interpretations (sacramental or moral), Jesus'

primary intention is to prepare the apostles for their consecration as priests. He prepares them, it seems, in two ways.
First of all, he teaches them humility in the exercise of the
authority with which they shall soon be invested. The lesson is
the same as that expressed in the synoptic gospels: "Among
pagans it is the kings who lord it over them. . . . This must
not happen with you. . . . The leader [among you must be-
have] as if he were the one who serves. . . . Here am I
among you as one who serves!" (Lk. 22:24–27; cf. Mk.
10:42–44; Mt. 20:25–28).

Secondly, we have reason to think that the astonishing action of Jesus in washing his apostles' feet is not simply a prefiguration of his abasement as redeemer, inasmuch as the
purifying bath as an image of the passion is more Pauline
than Johannine. Since John 17 represents a transposition of
the liturgy of atonement, we may see in John 13:1–11 a
transposition of the ritual bath that prepared Aaron and his
sons for their consecration as priests; physical cleanness would
then symbolize the purity of soul needed for the liturgical
ministry (Ex. 29:4; cf. also Lv. 8:6; Nb. 8:6–7).

Having once adopted this interpretation, we are much better able to explain Jesus' answer to Peter, which is to be translated literally as, "If I do not wash you, you have no share
with me" (13:8). Jesus here uses a formula that occurs in
the Old Testament *only* in connection with the Levites who
have no share or inheritance with the rest of the Israelites
since Yahweh is their share or inheritance (Dt. 10:9; 12:12;
14:27, 29; 18:1–2; cf. Nb. 18:20). With far deeper truth
than the Levites, Jesus, the sole priest of the new covenant,
can say that he has no share except God the Father. If the
apostles are in principle to "have a share with him" or to have
the same share as he, the meaning may be that they share his
destiny in a special way by sharing his mission and consecration as priest. The apostles will thus be in the same position as
the Levites, since like them and like Christ they have God

alone for their inheritance. If he refused to let Jesus wash him—that is, in the last analysis, if he refused the mystery of the cross which is the source of the sacrament of orders as it is of the other sacraments (Jn. 13:6–8 has the same meaning as Mk. 8:32–33 and the parallel passages)—Peter would be excluded from any share in the priesthood of Christ.

The close connection between John 13 and John 17 (a connection that Bultmann has highlighted but also exaggerated, inasmuch as he locates Chapter 17 immediately after 13:20) is a further argument in favor of the interpretation just given of the washing of the feet. The interpretation has the additional advantage of taking the ground from under the two contradictory interpretations of the scene: the sacramental interpretation based on the words of James to Peter, and the moralizing interpretation expressed in the lesson of humility which Jesus draws.

If the washing of the feet is a prelude to the consecration of the apostles as priests, then John 20:19–23 shows us "the complement of the priesthood."[3] It is the decisive proof that Jesus intended to bestow on his apostles powers that were strictly reserved to them and a ministerial priesthood essentially different from the common priesthood.

We have a very telling illustration of this truth in a paradox (insufficiently noted by the commentators) that obviates any confusion of the event recounted by John with the Pentecostal descent of the Spirit as told in the Acts of the Apostles. At Pentecost the coming of the Spirit effects an astonishing change in its beneficiaries. The situation in John 20:19–23 is quite different. On the one hand, the risen Christ breathes upon his apostles just as Yahweh at the beginning breathed a breath of life into the first man (the same verb, *emphysaō*, occurs both in Gn. 2:7 and Jn. 20:22). In so doing, the risen Lord declares himself to be the source of a new creation that completes and infinitely transcends the first, since the first man received the breath of bodily life whereas the new man receives the Holy Spirit. On the other hand, the new creation is not yet manifested, contrary to what we might expect. This amounts to saying that Jesus, in breathing upon the apostles, is not thinking of them as the beginning of the new creation but rather as coworkers with himself and the Holy Spirit. In the normal course of events it is through their mediation that men will be rescued from the domination of sin and given divine life: "Receive the Holy Spirit. For those whose sins you forgive, they are forgiven; for those whose sins you retain, they are retained."

We are here quite clearly in continuity with the basic idea of John 17, where the apostles are consecrated in order to carry on the work of Christ. In the priestly prayer the Spirit is indeed not named as he is in John 20:23. But his intervention is already presupposed both by consecration in the truth (since it is the Spirit Paraclete who leads men into the truth in its entirety) and by consecration in truth (since this is inseparable from consecration in spirit, as worship in truth is inseparable from worship in spirit).

The Apocalypse was written toward the end of the first century, about fifteen years before the letters of St. Ignatius the martyr. It enables us to discern the transition from the apostles to the hierarchic Church that St. Ignatius of Antioch describes, and which we see today. The inaugural vision (1:9–20) and the letters of the Apocalypse (Chapters 2 and 3) paint a scene in which we can easily see the three basic elements of the Church as shown in the discourses after the Supper and especially in John 17. In the first place, there is the glorified Christ whose action is inseparable from that of the Holy Spirit who is mentioned at the end of each letter (2:7, 11, 17, 29; 3:6, 13, 22). Secondly, there are the seven communities of Asia Minor, which also symbolize the universal Church. Finally, there are the mysterious "angels" of the Churches who link Christ with his Church.

The Christ who appears to John on the island of Patmos is

clothed in the long robe of the high priests (1:13). This is
not surprising, since throughout the book he is the Lamb who
was slain; that is, the Servant, at once priest and victim, of
Isaiah 53. But he is also "the Ruler of the kings of the earth"
(1:5), "the Lord of lords and the King of kings" (17:14)—
the author puts a great deal of stress on this prerogative of
Christ as he resists the proud despots who persecute the
Church. Moreover, since Christ, the king and priest, makes
his disciples like himself, he makes kings and priests of them
all (1:6; 5:10). Better than any other New Testament document, the Apocalypse enables us to grasp the precise meaning of the royal priesthood shared by all the baptized. Christ
became king of the world when he acted as a priest and offered himself as victim. To those whom he has freed from
sin by his death, he gives the power to offer themselves as he
did, by confessing their faith, even to the point of shedding
their blood if need be. By committing themselves with de-
termination to this path, his followers share in his priesthood
and his kingship.

Christ, king and priest, walks as sovereign master amid
the seven lamp stands that are the seven Churches of Asia to
which the seer is to write. These communities are called lamp
stands (or torches), because they are to be a light in a dark-
ened world. But, as Allo pertinently notes,[4] the light they
shed is borrowed from Christ whose "face was like the sun
shining with all its force" (1:16) and who is also called "the
Morning Star" (2:28; 22:26). The communities are clearly
local ones, and the seer knows a number of historical and
geographical details concerning them and is able to diagnose
their spiritual state. Yet it is Christ who in a vision dictates
to John the letters addressed to the communities. In consequence, these letters are quite different from other New Testament letters and much more like prophetic oracles. There are
seven of them, a number which symbolizes fullness or totality,
and they form the first septenary in a book that looks essen-

tially to the future. We are justified, then, in inferring that the seven communities represent the universal Church of all times and that the letters have a permanent value. We may assert, indeed, that in the crisis through which the Church is passing today, the letters are more relevant than ever.

The "angels" of the Churches, who are the immediate addressees of the letters, are certainly not angels in the proper sense of the word, for then Christ would not use a human being in order to communicate with them, especially since everywhere else in the Bible the process is reversed and God uses the angels in order to speak to men. If these "angels" of the Churches are responsible for the spiritual state of the communities, the reason is that they are the hierarchic leaders of these communities. Undoubtedly the title "angel" is an echo of the Old Testament where the expression "angel of Yahweh" as applied to men means sometimes prophets, sometimes priests; the priesthood of the new covenant unites the prophetic and priestly traditions. Undoubtedly, too, the "angels" here represent a transposition of the angels who protect the various nations in the Book of Daniel. For, as the Greek term *episkopos* indicates, the bishops are truly the guardian angels of their communities, being obliged to watch over the faith and moral conduct of these communities; if they do not do this, they fail in their most important duty.

A comparison of the Apocalypse with John 17 and the third letter of John is very informative. In the priestly prayer of Jesus, the latter makes it clear that he intends to govern, sanctify, and unify his Church through the apostles; to this end he gives them a share in his twofold consecration as priest and victim. In the letters in the Apocalypse the "angels" of the Churches—that is, the residential leaders of these Churches—have replaced the apostles as the continuers of Christ's work. In the third letter of John, the aged apostle who calls himself the Elder, addresses two residential leaders of Churches: one of them, Gaius, in order to congratulate him;

the other, Diotrephes, a proud and insubordinate man, in
order to threaten him with a pastoral visitation if he does not
change his ways.

It is clear that these residential leaders received from the
apostles all the authority they needed for their lofty office. It
is because they depended so closely on the apostles whom
they succeeded that John, the last survivor of the apostolic
college, could speak to them in such an authoritative way.
The ordination of Timothy by St. Paul (1 Tm. 4:14, which
must be interpreted in the clearer light of 2 Tm. 1:6) enables
us to understand how the transmission of priesthood and
apostolic powers could be effected.

THE MAIN BIBLICAL SOURCES FOR PRIESTLY SPIRITUALITY

THE PRIESTHOOD of the new covenant is a limitlessly rich and
complex reality which has hitherto been approached in an
overly abstract and insufficiently biblical way. We think it
worthwhile, therefore, to end by calling attention to various
Scriptural texts that we think especially helpful as sources and
guides in exploring this treasure. The Old Testament texts we
have in mind are the Servant songs and Psalms 16 and 73.
The New Testament texts are, first of all, all those passages
in the gospels that clearly relate Christ to Isaiah 53; and secondly, a number of letters: the second letter to the Corinthians,
the pastoral letters, the first letter of St. Peter, the letter to the
Hebrews, and, finally, the letters in the Apocalypse. We wish
to say a few words on the way in which each of these great
texts must be read if it is to help in the discovery or deepening
of an authentic priestly spirituality.

The Old Testament

THE FOUR SERVANT SONGS (Is. 42:1–7; 49:1–6; 50:4–7;
52:13–53:12) form a body of texts that is unparalleled in

the Old Testament. They present us with many problems
which continue to be discussed despite the enormous number
of publications devoted to them.[5]

It is our view, though we cannot justify it here, that the
four poems are independent of their present context and that
the Servant is neither Israel nor some individual in Israelite
history nor a mythological person, but the Messianic Saviour.
The explanation based on the theory of corporate personality
runs into insurmountable difficulties, especially in Isaiah 53
where a completely innocent individual is set over against the
sinful multitude and described by traits taken from Jeremiah.
In addition, we need only read the texts to realize that the
blessings won by the Servant—universal spread of true religion, healing and peace, perfect reconciliation with God—
are the blessings that, according to the prophets, mark the
messianic age. Isaiah is here thinking only of the Messianic
Saviour, and in an entirely new way.

The texts are considered difficult, and indeed they are. But
we may rest assured that we need not know all of the often
extravagant hypotheses that have been constructed to explain
them. If we approach the texts directly and without apriori
views, we will find them quite luminous. In this regard, M.-J.
Lagrange observed: "The history of the exegesis of these
poems . . . does little honor to biblical criticism, for, in order
to eliminate the supernatural, criticism has often abandoned
the natural sense of the texts."[6] Fr. Delitzsch said of the final
song that it might well have been written under the cross on
Golgotha, and E. Renan: "There are touches in the picture
that seem to be anticipations of Jesus himself."[7] We can apply
to these texts G. Martelet's comment on the gospel narratives
concerning miracles or the accounts dealing with Christ's
resurrection: The meaning of these texts is quite clear; if we
reject it, it is because of prejudices that prevent us from ad-
mitting that things could have happened in this way (in this

instance, that Christ's mission could have been foretold so accurately).[8]

An extended study of the four Servant songs, and especially
of the last, enables us better to understand how the priesthood
in the covenant of grace represents an amazing "synthesis"
and "concentration" of the riches slowly elaborated under the
old dispensation. The quoted terms are borrowed from E. Jacob, who also writes:

> The entirely new figure of the Servant is made up of ele-
> ments borrowed from tradition: the *'ebed* is a king and his
> sufferings are not contradictory to his royal aspect. . . . The
> *'ebed* is a prophet, he fulfills to perfection all the functions of
> a prophet: obedience, ministry of the word, intercession.
> . . . He is also the priest and the sacrificial victim offered
> for the forgiveness of sins.

The author might have added that, when looked at from another standpoint, the Servant reminds us of the wise men.
Jacob also notes: "The servant is the elect, the wretched, the
missionary, the glorified one; he summarizes in his person the
whole history of his people, but where Israel failed, the servant
will succeed."[9]

In discussing the washing of the feet, we have assumed that
Jesus' answer to Peter: "If I do not wash you, you can have
nothing in common with me [literally: have no share with
me]" (13:8) transposes and applies to Christ and the apostles the status of the Levitical priests of the old covenant. The
latter possessed no territory because Yahweh alone was their
share and inheritance. But even if we set this hypothesis
aside, Jesus certainly required of the apostles whom he was
to make his priests a detachment from and indifference to the
world which he did not ask of the ordinary disciple. Such an
apartness was, of course, only the reverse side of a special belonging to God and Christ: "Because you do not belong to the
world, because my choice withdrew you from the world,
therefore the world hates you" (15:19); "They do not be-

long to the world any more than I belong to the world. Consecrate them in the truth" (17:16–17).

Given this as their condition, candidates for the priesthood and those already ordained can profit greatly by meditation on Psalms 16 and 73, for these texts express in a splendid way the sentiments of clerics and priests who want to go on intensifying their consecration to God.[10] In Psalm 16 the author, who is probably a Levitical priest, sings of his joy at having been chosen by God. In ancient times people mapped out the sections of an inheritance with a measuring cord, and they used a cup to hold lots to be drawn. Yahweh alone is the psalmist's inheritance and cup; truly, for him "the measuring line marks out delightful places" (16:6)! In return he wants to live for the Lord alone; night and day he has God before his eyes and knows him to be always present.

Priests consecrated to God are not protected from trials, any more than ordinary Christians are, and there are times when their separation from the world can be a heavy burden. Then they will find a model in the author of Psalm 73. The psalmist here tells us of a severe temptation he experienced and how he was freed of his doubts by meditating on the Scriptures or by going to pray in the temple. In this way he found the living God again and, with him, the happiness of having him alone for an inheritance: "Even so, I stayed in your presence, you held my right hand; now guide me with advice and in the end receive me into glory. I look to no one else in heaven, I delight in nothing else on earth. My flesh and my heart are pining with love, my heart's Rock, my own, God for ever! . . . my joy lies in being close to God. I have taken shelter in the Lord" (73:23–28).

The Gospels

EVERYONE KNOWS that the Christian religion is not primarily a book, even an inspired book, but the person of Christ himself. Consequently, the best way for clerics and priests to enter ever more deeply into the mystery of Christian priesthood is to try to understand Christ better with the help of the gospels. To this end they should pay special attention to those passages in which Christ speaks of himself as having to carry out the messianic task of the suffering Servant. Max Thurian has shown very clearly that Christ's priesthood must be connected with his intention to fulfill these prophecies (especially Isaiah 53) and that the attribution of priesthood to Christ is therefore not simply the result of later theological reflection, even when that reflection was inspired.[11] The manifestation of this intention of Christ begins with his baptism and reaches its climax in the drama of his passion; the latter, of course, as a saving mystery, is inseparable from his resurrection, just as in Isaiah 53 the Servant's martyrdom and exaltation are inseparable. We shall restrict ourselves here to a few remarks on how to read in depth the most important texts of the gospels.

Some commentators have mistakenly seen in the baptism of Jesus his ordination as a priest. The baptism is rather to be viewed as an act of solidarity with sinful mankind, in which Christ the priest is already moving toward the expiatory offering of his passion. For if Jesus humbly submitted to the Precursor's ritual act of conversion, the reason could only be that he regarded himself as the messiah. But he did not think of himself as the kind of messiah various groups of his contemporaries expected, and especially not as the political liberator for which many Jews of the day were hoping. From the very beginning Jesus must have had a clear idea of the very special form his messianic activity would take: It would consist first and foremost in fulfilling the ideal of the Servant of Yahweh through a life of humble submission to God and of solidarity with sinful mankind. On the distant horizon he could already glimpse the expiatory offering on Calvary to which this solidarity would lead him.[12]

The account of the temptation in Matthew and Luke is

clearly written in the same perspective. If we look closely at the proposals of the devil, we see that they are far from being simple urgings to gluttony, vanity, or ambition. They are closely connected with the mission of Jesus and constitute a kind of inquiry into his messiahship; the intention is less to make Jesus sin against one or other divine precept than to turn him from the path of humble messiahship proper to the Servant, just as Peter would later try to turn him from it (cf. Mt. 16:23 par., with Mt. 4:10 par.).

It is highly profitable to meditate at length on the four accounts of the passion of Jesus toward which his baptism already directs the reader's attention (Jesus would later call his passion a baptism: Mk. 10:38; Lk. 12:50). John's account is not the only one to have the kind of sacrificial and sacerdotal significance we have been discussing and is given such clear expression in the prayer of John 17. The other three accounts manifest the same meaning, provided we read them in the context of the Supper and Gethsemani. We may note in passing that the explanation usually given of Gethsemani is superficial and quite inaccurate. Commentators forget that the one who suffers and prays in the garden is not just any ordinary man but the transcendent Son of Man who must freely accept the role of expiatory victim foretold in Isaiah 53. That is the cup he fears to drink but nonetheless accepts! Pascal's *Mystery of Jesus* brings this out in a deeply moving way.

If, however, we want to understand the suffering of Jesus in its deepest dimension, we must first carefully examine the words in which he predicts it. In addition to the texts of John, which we have already examined, the most important of these predictions are: the discussion on fasting and the departure of the bridegroom (Mk. 2:18–20); the three major prophecies of the passion and resurrection (Mk. 8:31–32; 9:31; 10:32–34); Jesus' answer to the sons of Zebedee concerning the cup and baptism of suffering (Mk. 10:35–40 par.); the saying on ransom (Mk. 10:45 par.).[13]

In these various predictions of the passion it is possible to discern secondary clarifications that may have been added after the event, but the substance of the predictions is left untouched. The predictions take the form of reminiscences of Isaiah 53, but the reminiscences are for the most part hidden. The reason is that they do not consist of verbal borrowings (which could easily be attributed to the evangelist or to the community). The contact is mainly at the level of ideas, while the vocabulary of Isaiah and the gospels differs. Let us look at a few examples of this important fact which is often overlooked.

Jesus thinks of his suffering as a *cup* that the Father has given him to drink (Mk. 10:38–39 par.; 14:36 par.) The image is not to be found in Isaiah 53, but the idea expressed is the same in both passages. For when seen in the light of the prophets the cup is that of the divine anger that Yahweh reserves for his enemies. Jesus will be drinking it, therefore, in the place of sinners, and because he drinks it we will be able to drink the cup of salvation, the eucharistic cup. Thus, there is a hidden relationship between the two cups of the Supper and Gethsemani.

Jesus calls his death a *baptism* (Mk. 10:38–39; Lk. 12:50); the image is quite new and not to be found in Isaiah 53. Yet it is the fulfillment of that oracle that Jesus has in mind when he speaks of his death as a baptism. By using the image he is connecting his death with the baptism he had received at the beginning of his ministry, and he is showing that in his death he is definitively making his own the cause of sinful mankind. He is thus speaking more clearly of a solidarity at which the baptism in the Jordan had only hinted in an obscure way.

Jesus says that he came in order to give his life as a *ransom* for the many (Mk. 10:45; Mt. 20:28). The word "ransom" (*lutron*) does not occur in Isaiah 53 and probably comes from Psalms 49:8–9, which is not a Messianic psalm. Yet, whatever interest there may be in connecting Christ with Psalm 49, we must look chiefly to Isaiah 53 in order to determine the deeper meaning of the gospel saying on ransom. In the saying we are once again confronted with Christ, the Servant, who is priest and victim of his expiatory sacrifice.

We shall not dwell on the meaning of the priestly prayer of Jesus since the whole of the present study has been devoted to it. It is evident that this sublime prayer, more than any other text, should be the subject of meditation for men who have the high honor of the priesthood. John 17 resembles the prologue of the fourth gospel: Both are written in a very simple style, both are inexhaustibly rich.

If we are to grasp the precise significance of the prayer, as indeed of all the discourses after the Supper, for the priestly ministry, we must bear in mind the point made in Chapter 2 of this book. That is, that the apostles are viewed from two standpoints throughout the discourses: as a group distinct from the other disciples, and as the nucleus of the community of believers. The unity of the Church for which Christ prays in John 17 is impossible without the apostles (and their successors) whom Christ has appointed to guide and sanctify the Church; such an appointment means that their office is instituted from on high and does not arise out of the community itself. On the other hand, the ministry of the apostles is situated within the community of which they are a part, and it exists only for the service of the community.

We cannot leave the gospels without calling attention to some priestly references that are to be noted in the infancy narratives, especially those of Luke. These references can be the subject of fruitful reflection once we have become convinced that Jesus is indeed the high priest of the new covenant. According to Luke 1:5, John the Baptist is the son of an Aaronite priest and of a mother who is "a descendant of Aaron." Nonetheless, instead of exercising priestly functions in the temple at Jerusalem (for in Israel priesthood was hereditary), John devotes himself entirely to the prophetic task of preparing the way for the Messiah whose coming is imminent and who will bring a new priesthood. Furthermore, the Messiah is born at Bethlehem; Jesus is of the family of David, but at the same time, through his mother who is related to Elizabeth (Lk. 1:36) the "descendant of Aaron," he has links with the priestly tribe. Thus, the hint is already given to us that Jesus will be not only a royal Messiah but a priestly Messiah as well. In fact, St. Matthew explicitly tells us that "he is the one who is to save his people from their sins" (Mt. 1:21), and that is at bottom a priestly function.[14]

The verb "to present" (*paristanein*), which is used for the presentation of Jesus in the temple (Lk. 2:22), is used in the Pauline letters in a clearly sacrificial sense (cf. Rm. 6:13–19; 12:1; 1 Co. 8:8; 2 Co. 4:14; 11:2; Ep. 5:27; Col. 1:28). Seen in this light the presentation in the temple is a prelude to the sacrificial offering in the passion. Moreover, Mary, whom John will later show us standing at the foot of the cross (Jn. 19:25–27), is already associated with Jesus as he is offered to God.[15] Mary and Jesus together obey legal prescriptions not really intended for them (cf. the odd statement: "when the day came for *them* to be purified" in Lk. 2:22); together they are offered to the Lord, the outward offering of Jesus being accomplished through the agency of Mary. It is quite true, of course, that Jesus alone is Saviour and mediator. But Mary has received the mission of bringing the incarnate Son of God into the world and of being associated with his entire redemptive work; consequently, she plays a role of exceptional importance which is similar in some respects to priestly mediation.

A further point: Eric Burrows points out that the words of Luke 2:23, (literally) "will be called consecrated to the Lord" (*hagion klēthēsetai*), seem to be a deliberate echo of the words "will be called holy" (*hagion klethesetai*) in the annunciation scene (1:35).[16] Burrows concludes that Luke is distinguishing two consecrations of Jesus: one at his conception, the other at the presentation. As we have seen, according to the fourth gospel, too, Jesus is twice consecrated: He is consecrated priest by the Father at his coming into the world, and he consecrates himself as victim in his passion (Jn. 17:19).

An odd anomaly in the account of the presentation deserves our attention. According to the law, to which Luke explicitly refers (2:22–24), the rite of purification was to be accompanied by a rite in which the first-born male child was to be ransomed for five shekels (Ex. 13:2, 12–15; 34:20; Nb. 8:16 and 3:47; 18:26). Why did the evangelist pass over this rite in silence while mentioning a ceremony of presentation for which the law did not provide? Inasmuch as the law of ransom did not apply to the first-born sons of Levitical families (Nb. 3:12, 46; cf. 8:16), while Levites were in fact presented to the Lord (Nb 8:10), and inasmuch as Elizabeth and Zechariah belonged to the priestly class, while Mary was related to Elizabeth, some commentators have inferred that *Jesus was not subject to the ransom ceremony and that he was presented in the temple because of his priestly blood.* In this way, Luke would be insinuating that Jesus was a Messiah both of Aaron and of Israel, in accordance with ideas we find in the Damascus Document (20:1) and the Testaments of the Twelve Patriarchs (Levi 7:1; Dan 5:10–11; Joseph 19:11). The hypothesis is an attractive one, but it is not the only possible explanation. Luke may simply have thought that because of his transcendent sanctity Jesus had no need of being ransomed.[17]

As we noted above, through the presentation in the temple Mary is already associated with the future sacrifice of Jesus the high priest. The fourth gospel shows her on Calvary sharing intensely in those sufferings of her Son which are, in

John's mind, the birth pangs of the Church. P. Benoit writes in this connection:

> In the birth pangs of the Church, in the agony of the cross, Jesus was not alone. As man, sensitive and suffering, he needed a helper and his mother stood beside the cross. She helped to accept and offer everything to God; like a mother, she shared in the birth of the Church.
>
> In my opinion it is incorrect to speak of Mary as "Virgin Priest"; she is not a priest. Jesus is the one and only Priest and all other priests are his sacramental representatives. But *Mary is the mother of that Priest* and she alone can fill that role. She helped her Son to consummate his sacrifice. Thus all the graces which come to us from Jesus—and they come from him alone since he is the one source of salvation—come through the hands of Mary. Mary, in glory beside her Son, collaborates with him in distributing these graces, just as in her role of mother, a role at once humble and exalted, she had collaborated with him in the winning of grace.
>
> "Woman, this is your son," "Son, this is your mother"— movingly simple as these words are, we see now something of what was concealed in them.[18]

In a little book of our own, *L'Heure de la Mère de Jésus,*[19] we make use of John 16:21, which sheds light on the two scenes involving Mary; namely, Cana and Calvary, to show how the "hour" of Jesus is also the "hour" of Mary, the new mother of all the living. We also indicate there the maternal role that in the divine plan of salvation now belongs to every woman, and especially to consecrated virgins, as they follow in the steps of the Virgin Mary, the greatest woman of the new covenant.

The Letters and the Apocalypse

WE TURN NOW TO ST. PAUL. He is, of course, rightly regarded as the greatest missionary of all time. But this fact should not make us fail to see that he is also an incomparable model for all priests without exception. All priests are to be fathers and shepherds to the souls entrusted to their care; but Paul fulfilled these roles in supreme fashion.[20] Only a misunderstanding could enable interpreters to use 1 Corinthians 1:17: "Christ did not send me to baptize, but to preach the Good News," in order to play down the liturgical functions proper to priests. The point of the text becomes clear when we read it in its context while also bearing in mind the great importance Paul attributes to the sacrament of baptism. Moreover, we find him on several occasions using the language of worship and priesthood to express his understanding of his ministry; we may note especially 1 Corinthians 9:13–14; Romans 15:15–16; Philippians 2:17.[21]

The priest who wants to deepen his understanding and appreciation of his priesthood can find no better guide than some of Paul's letters, especially the second letter to the Corinthians which sheds brilliant light on the importance of the work done by Christ's ministers. One passage may serve as an example:

> For anyone who is in Christ, there is a new creation; the old creation has gone, and now the new one is here. It is all God's work. It was God who reconciled us to himself through Christ and gave us the work of handing on this reconciliation. In other words, God in Christ was reconciling the world to himself, not holding men's faults against them, and he has entrusted to us the news that they are reconciled. So we are ambassadors for Christ; it is as though God were appealing through us, and the appeal that we make in Christ's name is: be reconciled to God. For our sake God made the sinless one into sin, so that in him we might become the goodness of God (2 Co. 5:17–21).

The text is rich in meaning. The "we" is set over against a "you"—namely, the Corinthians—and refers to one or more persons who possess a priesthood that is distinct from the common priesthood. Concretely, the "we" signifies either Paul alone, or, more likely, Paul and his coworkers in the apostolate: Timothy and Silvanus (2 Co. 1:1, 19). These missionaries act as ambassadors of Christ and not in any sense as delegates of the community. The reconciliation of man with God is an eminently priestly task that Christ carried out once and for all on Calvary as the suffering Servant. The statement: "For our sake God made the sinless one into sin," is a clear allusion to Isaiah 53. The equally priestly reconciliation effected by Paul and his associates in the name of Christ is simply a fruit and application of the sacrifice of Calvary, for evidently the apostle and his fellow workers carry out their priestly task in close dependence on Christ the Priest.

When we look at them from the viewpoint we are here adopting, the pastoral letters are unusually valuable.[22] There is, to begin with, the historical value, inasmuch as the hierarchic organization reflected in these letters is still in its embryonic stage, far less developed than the organization that is presupposed by the letters of St. Ignatius of Antioch and to be found equivalently in the Apocalypse. We may note, in passing, that the letter of St. Clement of Rome, which dates from just about the same time as the Apocalypse, shows a hierarchic structure not very different from that seen in the pastoral letters. This is really not surprising for it seems that, perhaps under the influence of converts from Essenism (the Essene sect had a strong hierarchic structure), the development toward the monarchic episcopate was much more rapid in the East than in the West.

But the historic value of the pastoral letters is not our primary concern here since it is from a different angle that they are so instructive for those engaged in pastoral work. In a situation in which false teachers were substituting for revealed doctrine—various dangerous novelties that were often nothing but their own fantasies—the pastoral letters remind the ministers of Christ of their duty to remain faithful to him: "If we disown him, then he will disown us" (2 Tm. 2:12).

The letters give warning that, though the spirit of study and investigation is needed, this cannot mean inventing their priesthood or the doctrine they are to preach. The function of Christ's ministers is to hand on unchanged the "deposit" entrusted to them, as men protect the goods of another that have been put in their charge: "My dear Timothy, take great care of all that has been entrusted to you. Have nothing to do with the pointless philosophical discussion and antagonistic beliefs of the 'knowledge' that is not knowledge at all" (1 Tm. 6:20).

There is another, no less important lesson that the ministers of Christ can derive from meditation on the first letter of St. Peter (whose Petrine authorship we maintain). No other letter is so filled with clear allusions to Isaiah 53. The chief of the apostles now seems almost obsessed by the mystery of the cross that he once had so much difficulty in accepting. And how well he had learned the great lesson of humility that hierarchic leaders must ceaselessly derive from the suffering of Christ!

> Now I have something to tell your elders: I am an elder myself, and a witness to the sufferings of Christ, and with you I have a share in the glory that is to be revealed. Be the shepherds of the flock of God that is entrusted to you: watch over it, not simply as a duty but gladly, because God wants it; not for sordid money, but because you are eager to do it. Never be a dictator over any group that is put in your charge, but be an example that the whole flock can follow (1 P. 5:1–3).

It is quite evident that the Letter to the Hebrews is especially significant for priests. The bibliography we provide at the end of this book shows that down to the present time almost all biblical studies on the priesthood of Christ are studies of the Letter to the Hebrews. The letter is equivalently the first theological treatise on the priesthood of the new covenant; we have already indicated the broad lines of its teaching. The doctrine of the letter is forcefully summed up in a statement that closely connects the priesthood of Christ with the mysteries of the incarnation and of redemption: "It was essential that he should in this way become completely like his brothers so that he could be a compassionate and trustworthy high priest of God's religion, able to atone for human sins" (Heb. 2:17). The text makes it clear that it was as a priest that Christ expiated on Calvary for the sins of the people, in accordance with the ideas expressed in Isaiah 53. Consequently, it cannot be said that he became a priest only in and through his glorification. It is true, however, that the glorified Christ, as an eternal priest, is constantly offering and interceding for us (cf. 7:25; 9:14; cf. 1 Jn. 2:1–2).

The Letter to the Hebrews is not easy reading, but anyone who perseveres in meditation on it will be rewarded for the effort. Moreover, modern exegesis has greatly facilitated the understanding of the letter by bringing to light its structure, its special vocabulary, its exegetical procedures, and its key ideas.

It would be a serious mistake not to advert to the evangelical basis of the teaching of the letter on priesthood. We cannot insist too much on the fact that the letter is not at all a piece of abstract speculation on the priesthood of Christ but is rooted in the gospel tradition, especially in the Johannine tradition.[23] The concrete Jesus of history, merciful to sinners, praying, obedient, and suffering greatly, is before the author's eyes as he tries to describe the ideal priesthood.

Moreover, this essentially liturgical document is attempting to resolve a very concrete problem. How can men who are sinners approach the thrice holy God? (Cf. 4:11; 6:19; 7:25; 9:14; 10:1, 19; 11:6; 12:22; 13:13.) The purpose of a covenant with God is to bring God and men together. Under the old covenant, however, the end was not achieved; this situation found expression in the prohibition against the Hebrews drawing near to Mt. Sinai (Ex. 24:2), for in fact the Law was powerless to sanctify those who wanted to approach God. On the other hand, in the new dispensation that fulfills the prophecy of Jeremiah (31:31–34), Christ, the perfect mediator and perfect priest, enables Christians, even in this life, to draw near the city of the living God. The earthly life of Christians is like the journey of the Hebrews toward the rest of the promised land or to a liturgical procession toward the throne of God.

Numerous commentators have heard, and with good reason, liturgical resonances in the Apocalypse that remind them of the Letter to the Hebrews. We must go a step further and point out how consistently the happiness of the elect in the new Jerusalem is expressed in the Apocalypse in the language of worship and priesthood as well as in the language of kingship (cf. 22:3–5 and 21:22; cf. also 5:9–10 and 7:15). The book seems to be saying that the basic characteristics of the liturgical and priestly life are to have their supreme fulfillment in the eternal blessedness of heaven. Thus, direct contact with God, which is the privilege of priests and especially of the high priest, becomes in heaven, though in an incomparably higher form, the prerogative of all the elect. Only then shall we have the supreme realization of God's dwelling among men (*skēnoun;* cf. 21:3), that had been prefigured in the Old Testament by tabernacle and temple and that was made real in an entirely new way, according to the fourth gospel, in the incarnation and resurrection of Christ (cf. Jn. 1:14; 2:18–22; 7:37–39).[24]

The Apocalypse, then, should not be neglected by anyone who looks in the Bible for the foundations of an authentic priestly spirituality. But we must admit that the proverbial obscurity of this document can well discourage men even of good will. Happily, the letters in Chapters 2 and 3 of the Apocalypse are much more easily understood. We have already shown how relevant they continue to be, since, once we admit that the "angels" of the Churches are the hierarchic leaders of these Churches, the letters tell us quite insistently that Christian communities will be, in large measure, no better than their pastors.

In the letters, P. Ketter has found a picture of the various types of pastors (bishops or priests) to be met with in every age.[25] The "angel" of the Church in Ephesus is the zealous, spirited organizer who mistakes means for ends and forgets the overriding importance of love: "You have less love now than you used to" (2:4). The "angel" of the Church in Smyrna is the humble pastor who is wholly dedicated to a flock that, like him, is unpretentious, humble, and persecuted; both are rich in the spirit and need only to be exhorted: "Even if you have to die, keep faithful" (2:10). The "angel" of the Church in Pergamum is the man who is personally devoted to Christ yet is too conciliatory or timid in face of the evil he must oppose; he compromises with this evil in order not to offend anyone. The "angel" of the Church in Thyatira is also a zealous pastor, but he lacks discernment and fails to see the harm done in the community by false prophets. The "angel" of the Church in Sardis is a pretender who deceives himself with words and thinks he is alive. The "angel" of the Church in Philadelphia is, in the full sense of the words, the good shepherd whom Christ "keeps" because he in turn has faithfully "kept" the word of Christ (3:10); in him the priestly prayer of Christ is answered, and indeed the text of the Apocalypse recalls the very words of that prayer which had been offered for the apostles but was meant for their successors as well: "They have kept your word. . . . I am not asking you to remove them from the world, but to protect them from the evil one" (Jn. 17:6, 15). Finally, the "angel" of the Church in Laodicea is the superficial, pretentious, self-satisfied pastor, whose material wealth blinds him to his own appalling spiritual penury.

The third letter of St. John confirms the interpretation of the "angels" of the Churches as being the hierarchic leaders of these Churches. It tells us once again how St. John understood the duties of the hierarchic leaders of the various local Churches. It tells us, too, of the considerable authority that the elderly apostle still exercised over the Churches of Asia and how the transition from apostolic Church to monarchical episcopate took place.[26]

FINAL SUMMARY

As WE END THIS BOOK, a few lines in summation of our purpose will be appropriate. The problem of the priesthood is one of the most serious confronting the Church today. But it is also one that the progress of scriptural exegesis can help resolve in a much more satisfactory way than hitherto. My intention has been to go back to the biblical source and to draw from it a solution of the problem that will have more than passing interest. Chiefly on the basis of the priestly prayer of Jesus (John 17), I have shown in a new way that Jesus was truly a priest and that he intended to bestow upon his apostles and their successors a priesthood that is quite distinct from the priesthood common to all the baptized.

But what is the priesthood of the new covenant in itself? Instead of using abstract definitions, I have emphasized the lengthy preparation for that priesthood in the experience of the men of God of the old covenant and the anticipation of it in the prophecy of Isaiah concerning the martyrdom of God's Servant. This prophecy represents a remarkable synthesis of the priestly and prophetic traditions that Jesus will bring to perfection in his own person.

I hope that many priests and many Christians generally will be helped by this book to rediscover the magnificent meaning of the consecrated priestly life. They can come to this new insight only if they do not tire of contemplating the person and work of Jesus Christ who is the sole Priest of the new

covenant. The sacrificial and priestly dimension of the life of
Christ must be clearly seen if we are to grasp the unique
greatness of that life, for that dimension is the dimension of
Christ's love for us. On this account, it is not only priests but
Christians generally who will find profit in reading and medi-
tating on these pages.[27]

Notes

Introduction

1. M.-J. Lagrange, *Evangile selon saint Jean* (Paris, 1948⁸), p. 101.

2. *Le ministère sacerdotale. Rapport de la Commission Internationale de Théologie* (Paris, 1971). The report was prepared by a sub-commission the members of which were Fr. Hans Urs von Balthasar, Bishop Carlo Colombo, Fr. González de Cardedal, Fr. M.-J. Le Guillou (chairman), Fr. Lescrauwaet (secretary), and Bishop J. Medina-Estevez.

3. Vatican II, Dogmatic Constitution on the Church, n. 10, in Walter J. Abbott, ed., *The Documents of Vatican II* (New York, 1966), p. 27. (Henceforth cited as Abbott, with page number.)

4. The reference is to the two successive paragraphs of the Constitution on the Church, n. 10 (Abbott, pp. 26–27).

5. D. Olivier, *Les deux visages du prêtre: Les chances d'une crise* (Paris, 1971), pp. 52–53.

6. Cf. A. Robert and A. Feuillet, eds., *Introduction to the New Testament*, trans. by Patrick W. Skehan and others (New York, 1965), pp. 653–56.

7. This position, with variations, is that of numerous critics. Cf., e.g., the study by Käsemann, mentioned in note 10 below. Käsemann's book may have influenced the exegesis proposed by B. Rigaux in his "Les destinataires du IV. Evangile à la lumière de Jn. XVII," *RTL* 1 (1970) 289–319. Rigaux sums up as follows: "This work with its timeless resonances was conceived and written in a definite historical and theological context. Concrete men, the disciples of that day, were

addressed by the risen Jesus who spoke to them of a Church. Even if we must give up trying to apply form-history to the fourth gospel the way we do the synoptic gospels, the formulas themselves are nonetheless vehicles for themes and traditions which must be traced, via the gospel, back to the various strata that lie behind it; we must constantly go back to certain central ideas. The very description of 'the disciple' is subject to this law. The disciple, as we see him, was not at all someone who heard the historical Jesus, but rather a member of a community in which new values were being examined, expounded, and experienced. At a time when a still young Christianity was being ravaged by the world's seductions and by persecution, and the world hated the disciples of Jesus, a master whom tradition calls 'John' gathered a group of men and women who, through meditation on Jesus and through a renewed and deepened sense of his word, his deeds, and his person, would be enabled to resist the evils that lurked in the certitudes proffered by a supposedly enriched and triumphant new revelation" (p. 317).

8. We are thinking especially of 15:1–6 and 15:18–16:4a. In the first of these texts, the allegory of the vine, there is no reference at all to the imminent departure of Jesus; the disciples are thought of as living in union with Jesus, and all the emphasis is on the permanence of the union. The second passage presents numerous parallels both with the apocalyptic discourses in the Synoptics and with the missionary discourse in Matthew 10 (cf., especially, Jn. 15:18 and Mt. 10:22; Jn. 15:20 and Mt. 10:23–24; Jn. 15:26 and Mt. 10:20 or Mk. 13:11; Jm. 15:27 and Mt. 10:18 or Mk. 13:9; Jn. 16:1 and Mt. 24:10; Jn. 16:2 and Mt. 10:17, 24:9, or Mk. 13:9, 12). We can see from the comparison that in the farewell discourses John has made a synthesis of special revelations given to the apostles not only at the Last Supper but on other occasions as well. Cf. Lagrange, op. cit., pp. 397–98.

9. What follows depends chiefly on H. van den Bussche, *Jean: Commentaire de l'évangile spirituel* (Bruges, 1967), pp. 367–71.

10. The following list makes no claim to be exhaustive; titles are given in chronological order. J. Huby, "Un double problème de critique textuelle et d'interprétation: Saint Jean XVII, pp. 11–12," *RSR* 27 (1937), pp. 408–21; J. Bonsirven, "Pour une intelligence plus profonde de Saint Jean," *RSR* 39 (1951), pp. 176–96; A. George, "L'heure de Jean XVII," *RB* 61 (1954), pp. 392–97; J. Giblet, "Sanctifie-les dans la vérité," *BVC* 19 (1957), pp. 58–73; T. E. Pollard, " 'That They All May Be One' (Jn. XVII, 21) and the Unity of the Church," *ExpT* 70 (1958–59), pp. 149–50; E. L. Wenger, " 'That

They All May Be One,' " *ExpT* 70 (1958–59), p. 333; J. L. d'Aragon, "La notion johannique de l'unité," *SE* 11 (1959), pp. 111–19; C. Spicq, *Agapé dans le Nouveau Testament* 3 (Paris, 1959), pp. 204–18; A. Vanhoye, "L'oeuvre du Christ, don du Père (Jn. V, 36 et XVII, 4)," *RSR* 48 (1960), pp. 377–419; J. F. Randall, *The Theme of Unity in John XVII, 20–23* (Louvain University dissertation, 1962; résumé, under same title, in *ETL* 41 [1965], pp. 373–94); B. Schwank, " 'Vater, verherrliche deinen Sohn' (XVII, 1–5)," *Sein und Sendung* 28 (1963), pp. 436–49; idem, " 'Für sie heilige ich mich, die du mir gegeben hast' (XVII, 6–19)," ibid., 28 (1963), pp. 484–97; idem, " 'Damit alle eins seien' (XVII, 20–26)," ibid., 28 (1963), pp. 531–46; A. Laurentin, "We 'attah—Kai nun: Formule caractéristique des textes juridiques et liturgiques," *B* 45 (1964), pp. 168–97, 413–32; J. Perret, "Notes bibliques de prédication sur Jean XVII," *VC* 18 (1964), pp. 119–26; C. D. Morrison, "Mission and Ethnic: An Interpretation of John XVII," *Int* 19 (1965), pp. 259–73; R. Poelman, "The Sacerdotal Prayer: John XVII," *LV* 20 (1965), pp. 43–66; F.-M. Braun, "La seigneurie du Christ dans le monde selon Jean," *RT* 67 (1967), pp. 357–86 (on 17:1–3 cf. pp. 259–66); G. Bornkamm, "Zur Interpretation des Johannesevangeliums," *ET* 28 (1968), pp. 8–25, reprinted in his *Geschichte und Glaube* (Gesammelte Aufsätze 3; Munich, 1968), pp. 104–21; E. Käsemann, *The Testament of Jesus: A Study of the Gospel of John in the Light of Chapter 17* (Philadelphia, 1968); J. Becker, "Aufbau, Schichtung, und theologiegeschichtliche Stellung des Gebetes in Johannes XVII," *ZNTW* 60 (1969), pp. 56–83; S. Agourides, "The High Priestly Prayer of Jesus," *StEv* 4, pp. 137–45; B. Rigaux, "Les destinataires du IV. Evangile à la lumière de Jn. XVII," *RTL* 1 (1970), pp. 289–319; E. Malatesta, "The Literary Structure of John XVII, *B* 52 (1971), pp. 190–214.

11. R. E. Brown, *The Gospel According to John* (Anchor Bible 29, Garden City, N.Y., Vol. 1, 1966; Vol. 2, 1970).

12. W. Thüsing, *Herrlichkeit und Einheit: Eine Auslegung des hohepriesterlichen Gebetes (Johannes 17)* (Düsseldorf, 1963). French translation by Joseph Burckel and François Swessel, *La prière sacerdotale de Jésus* (Paris, 1970).

CHAPTER 1

1. R. Bultmann, *The Gospel of John: A Commentary,* trans. by G. R. Beasley-Murray, R. W. N. Hoare, and J. K. Riches (Philadelphia, 1971), pp. 460–61.

2. Cf. J. Schneider, "Die Himmelsbrotrede," in *In Memoriam Ernst Lohmeyer* (Stuttgart, 1951), pp. 132–42.

3. Cf. R. Poelman, "The Sacerdotal Prayer: John XVII, *LV* 20 (1965), pp. 43–66.

4. *The Fourth Gospel,* ed. by F. N. Davey (London, 1947), p. 495.

5. Cf. Brown, op. cit., p. 746.

6. Ibid., pp. 598 and 744.

7. On the problem of textual transpositions, cf. Robert-Feuillet, op. cit., pp. 628–31; N. Uricchio, "La teoria delle trasposizioni nel Vangelo di S. Giovanni," *B* 31 (1950), pp. 128–63; C. Spicq, *Agapé dans le Nouveau Testament* 3 (Paris, 1959), pp. 126–27. The last-named work contains an extensive bibliography.

8. *L'Apocalypse* (Paris, 1933), p. ccxix.

9. Cf. my study, "Etude structurale de la première épître de saint Jean: Comparaison avec le quatrième évangile," in *Neues Testament und Geschichte: Historisches Geschehen und Deutung im Neuen Testament (O. Cullman zum 70. Geburtstag)* (Zürich, 1972), pp. 307–27.

10. On the eucharistic significance of the allegory of the vine, cf. especially O. Cullmann, "The Gospel According to St. John and Early Christian Worship," in his *Early Christian Worship,* trans. by A. S. Todd and J. B. Torrance (London, 1953), pp. 111–13; H. van den Bussche, *Les discours d'adieu* (Paris-Maredsous, 1959), p. 102; D. M. Stanley, " 'I Am the Genuine Vine' (Jn. XV, 1)," *BT* 8 (1963), pp. 484–91; B. Sandvik, "Johannes XV als Abendmahlstext," *TZ* 23 (1967), pp. 323–28; Brown, op. cit., pp. 672–74.

11. A. Feuillet, "Wisdom's Banquet," in *Johannine Studies,* trans. by Thomas E. Crane (Staten Island, N.Y., 1964), pp. 76–88.

12. It is especially the words of Christ in John 6:35: "I am the bread of life. He who comes to me will never be hungry; he who believes in me will never thirst," that recall Ecclesiasticus 24:17, 19, 21. At first sight, indeed, the two passages seem opposed, but if we examine them more closely we find there is no contradiction. The disciples of Wisdom will always hunger and thirst, because the food is such as does not produce satiety; the disciples of Jesus will not hunger and thirst because the Master who gives himself to them in the eucharistic mystery is able to satisfy all their religious aspirations. We may go a step further and ask why the formula in the fourth gospel differs from that of Ben Sira. The reason is that the former is also recalling the prediction of the new exodus by Second Isaiah; the prophet says that the repatriated exiles will not hunger or thirst, a phenomenon that is also part of the descriptions of the Messianic banquet (Is. 55:1;

65:13). The text of John 6 is thus the synthesis as it were of the two complementary themes of the Messianic banquet and of Wisdom, for the complete satisfaction, which excludes further hunger and thirst, lends a clearly eschatological coloring to the passage. But is is also undeniable that Ecclesiasticus 24:21 is the closer parallel.

13. Cf. our book, *Le mystère de l'amour divin dans la théologie johannique* (Paris, 1972).

14. *La prière sacerdotale de Jésus* (Paris, 1970), p. 139.

15. Lagrange, op. cit., pp. 450–51.

16. Thüsing, op. cit., pp. 114–15, 137.

17. On the Antiochene origin of the Didache, cf. J.-P. Audet, *La Didache: Instructions des apôtres* (Paris, 1958), pp. 208–9; J. Hazelden Walker, "An Argument from the Chinese for the Antiochene Origin of the *Didache,*" *Studia Patristica* (Texte und Untersuchungen 93, Berlin, 1966), pp. 44–45.

18. Cf. H. Hemmer, *Les Pères Apostoliques* I–II: *Doctrine des Apôtres* (Paris, 1907), p. xxxv: "closer to 80 than to 100 A.D."; K. Bihlmeyer, *Die Apostolischen Väter* (Tübingen, 1924), p. xiv: between 90 and 100 A.D.; Audet, op. cit., pp. 208–9: between 50 and 70 A.D.

19. According to St. Cyril of Alexandria, in John 17 Jesus is acting as a priest, since he intercedes in our behalf (*PG* 71:505); Rupert of Deutz says in his *In Ioannem:* "This high priest makes atonement and is the expiatory offering; he who is priest and sacrifice prays for us" (*PL* 169:764). In view of these testimonies, the title "priestly prayer" should not be unconditionally attributed to the Lutheran theologian David Chytraeus (1551–1600). Cf. C. Spicq, *L'Epître aux Hébreux* 1: *Introduction* (Paris, 1952), p. 122, n. 5.

20. Cf. P. Lestringant, *Essai sur l'unité de la révélation biblique* (Paris, 1942); Walther Eichrodt, "Les rapports du Nouveau et de l'Ancien Testament," in *Le problème biblique dans le protestantisme,* by J. Boisset and others (Paris, 1955); Robert-Feuillet, *Introduction to the New Testament,* pp. 917–18.

21. Some studies on this point (the list is not exhaustive): O. Moe, "Das Priestertum Christi im Neuen Testament ausserhalb des Hebräerbriefes," *TLZ* 72 (1947), pp. 335–38; C. Spicq, "L'origine johannique de la conception du Christ-prêtre dans l'Epître aux Hébreux," in *Aux sources de la tradition chrétienne* (*Mélanges Goguel*) (Paris, 1950), pp. 258–89; E. Bammel, "Archiereus prophēteiōn," *TLZ* 79 (1954), pp. 265–311; G. Friedrich, "Beobachtungen zur messianischen Hohepriestererwartung in den Synoptikern," *ZTK* 53 (1956), pp. 265–311;

A. Richardson, *An Introduction to the Theology of the New Testament* (New York, 1958), pp. 200–3; O. Cullmann, *The Christology of the New Testament,* trans. by Shirley C. Guthrie and Charles A. M. Hall (Philadelphia, 1959), pp. 89–107. Cf. also *Letter of the German Bishops on the Priestly Office: Biblical and Dogmatic Considerations,* issued by the Secretariat of the German Conference of Bishops; J. Coppens gives a detailed analysis of this letter in his "Christian Priesthood: Its Origins and Development," in A.-M. Charue and others, *Priesthood and Celibacy* (Milan, n.d.), pp. 67–142.

22. For a critical examination of the various arguments, cf. especially J. Gnilka, "Die Erwartung des messianischen Hohepriestertums in den Schriften von Qumran und im Neuen Testament," *RQ* 2 (1959–60), pp. 395–426; J. Coppens, "Le messianisme sacredotal dans les écrits du Nouveau Testament," in *La venue du Messie,* by E. Massaux et al. (Recherches Bibliques 6; Bruges, 1962), pp. 101–12; F. Hahn, *The Titles of Jesus in Christology: Their History in Early Christianity* (New York, 1969), Excursus 4, pp. 229–39.

23. The interpretation of the Servant poems is one of the most difficult problems in Old Testament study; the bibliography of the subject is large and constantly growing. We ourselves have dealt with the poems on several occasions: "Isaïe," *DBS* 4:709–14; "Richesses du Christ, Serviteur de l'Eternal," *RSR* 35 (1948), pp. 412–41; "Le Messianisme du Livre d'Isaïe: Ses rapports avec l'histoire et les traditions d'Israël," *RSR* 36 (1949), pp. 205–25. We shall mention only three other studies, with which we are in extensive agreement: J. S. van der Ploeg, *Les chants du Serviteur de Yahvé dans la seconde partie du Livre d'Isaïe (Ch. XL–LV)* (Paris, 1936); A. Robert, "Médiation," *DBS* 5:997–1020; J. Schildenberger, "Die Gottesknechtlieder des Isaiasbuches: Ein Höhepunkt messianischer Wissagung," *Erbe und Auftrag* 35 (1959), pp. 92–108. Our own basic conclusions on these poems are: (1) the four songs are a literary unit; (2) they are of later origin than the other oracles in Chapters 40–55. They were inserted later on into their present context and must be read independently of it; (3) they cannot be explained by the theory of "corporate personality" which would make the Servant both a collective and an individual personality; (4) the Servant is an individual, namely, the eschatological saviour; (5) the salvation he brings is purely spiritual and independent of any political stance.

24. A number of exegetes think the word *'asham* should be deleted. Others, however, think the word full of meaning. In the second part of Verse 4, the verb *nagoua* implies that the Servant is like a

leper; the verse should be translated: "We looked on him *as though he were a leper,* struck by God and humbled." The same word and idea recur with greater stress in Verse 8; it should be translated: "Who dreamed that he was cut off from the land of the living because of my people's sins, *being a leper for their sake?"* The translation, "being a leper for their sake," is derived from the Massoretic text which most critics want to emend. The Servant is "a leper for the people," that is, has taken on himself the leprosy of their sins. In light of this reading the choice of the word *'asham* in Verse 10 is perfectly intelligible. At first glance, indeed, the word does not seem very suitable, since in the Mosaic law this sacrifice (unlike the *ḥaṭṭat*) supposes, strictly speaking, only involuntary faults against God (or his priests) or one's neighbor. But the distinction between the two types of sacrifice is, in fact, not that sharp. R. de Vaux, *Ancient Israel: Its Life and Institutions,* trans. by John McHugh (New York, 1961), has observed: "But the fact remains that the last redactors who drew up these confused rulings had no clear idea of what exactly was meant by a *ḥaṭṭa'th* and an *'asham;* either they were trying to draw a distinction between two terms which had originally been synonymous, or they confused terms whose precise meaning they did not understand" (p. 421). The commentators on Isaiah 53 have forgotten that an *'asham* is to be offered by lepers whom the priests determine to have been freed of their illness (Lv. 14:1–32). Moreover, the victim representing the leper is to be a lamb (Lv. 14:12–14, 21–25). These parallels throw all needed light on the final substitution that the writer of the songs so heavily emphasizes: the Servant, carrying the burden of his fellow countrymen's leprosy, is offered as an expiatory victim in their stead; in this way he purifies them, and because of his patience under mistreatment he is compared to a sheep being led to slaughter.

25. Van der Ploeg, op. cit., pp. 199–200.

26. *Le ministère de la nouvelle alliance* (Paris, 1967), p. 44.

27. Cf. W. Eichrodt, *Theology of the Old Testament* 2, trans. by J. A. Baker (Philadelphia, 1967), p. 452.

28. *Theology of the Old Testament,* trans. by A. W. Heathcote and P. J. Allcock (New York, 1958), p. 297.

29. Cf. van der Ploeg, op. cit., pp. 158–59. We have shown in a series of articles how the Servant poems, and especially Isaiah 53, throw light on the way Jesus in the synoptic gospels views his own mission: "Le logion sur la rançon," *RSPT* 51 (1967), pp. 365–402; "Les trois prophéties de la Passion et de la Résurrection," *RT* 67 (1967), pp. 533–60; 68 (1968), pp. 41–74; "La controverse sur le

jeûne," *NRT* 90 (1968), pp. 113–36, 252–77; "La personnalité de Jésus entrevue à partir de sa soumission au rite de repentence du précurseur," *RB* 77 (1970), pp. 30–48.

30. The words "if he offers his life in atonement," which we consider so important, correspond to a Hebrew text that may in fact be preserved in almost its original form, contrary to what a large number of exegetes believe who indulge in arbitrary emendation. The conjunction *im* (if) has here the sense of "when." According to the Massoretic text *naphshô* (his soul) is the subject of the verb. But, as the translator of the Vulgate realized, the context requires that this word be the object of the verb and, therefore, the form of the verb itself must be slightly changed (*iasim* for *tasîm*). The resultant change of meaning is slight but it highlights the Servant's voluntary acceptance of his own sacrifice. Note that the verbs in this verse are in the future tense. The author has spoken of the suffering and death of the Servant as something past, but that was simply a literary fiction; the poems are in fact a prophecy of Messianic salvation. The author in this verse shifts to the future tense as he predicts the final victory.

31. Cf., e.g., C. K. Barrett, *The Gospel According to St. John* (London, 1955).

32. There are numerous studies of the washing of the feet, but this is not the place to discuss them or even to list them; we shall be returning to this scene in our final chapter. We refer the reader the judicious comments of Ph. H. Menoud, *L'Evangile de Jean d'après les recherches récentes* (Neuchâtel-Paris, 1947), pp. 54–56, but above all to F.-M. Braun's study with which we are in entire agreement: "Le lavement des pieds et la réponse de Jésus à saint Pierre (Jn. XIII, 4–10)," *RB* 44 (1935), pp. 22–33. We would add only one reservation: If the action of Jesus reminds us only of his redemptive abasement of himself, the latter is nonetheless symbolized in its aspect of purification, and A. M. Hunter is right in connecting the washing of the feet with 1 John 1:7: "The blood of Jesus, his Son, purifies us from all sin"; cf. his *The Gospel According to St. John* (Cambridge, 1965), p. 135.

33. K. Romaniuk, *L'amour du Père et du Fils dans la théologie de saint Paul* (Rome, 1961), p. 89.

34. Cf., e.g., in favor of such a dependence, F. H. Monse, *Johannes und Paulus: Ein Beitrag zur neutestamentlichen Theologie* (Münster, 1915), pp. 176–200; E. Aleith, *Paulusverständnis in der alten Kirche* (Berlin, 1937), pp. 18–22.

35. Cf. for the same view, Romaniuk, op. cit., pp. 109–10.

36. We offer a detailed study of the origin and doctrinal significance of this important passage in our "Le logion sur la rançon," *RSPT* 51 (1967), pp. 365–402.

37. *The Servant of God* (Studies in Biblical Theology 20; Naperville, Ill., 1957), p. 102.

38. J. H. Bernard, *A Critical and Exegetical Commentary on the Gospel of St. John* (New York, 1929) 2:573–74, rightly observes that *hagiazein* is not equivalent to *katharizein* and that a person who has not been "sanctified" or "consecrated" is not necessarily impure.

39. Cf. O. Procksch, "Hagiazo," *TDNT* 1:111–12.

40. *Jean le théologien: Les grandes traditions d'Israël; L'accord des écritures d'après le quatrième évangile* (Paris, 1964), pp. 81–83.

41. The difficult problems posed by these three passages are well known and we cannot discuss them here. For 1:51 we refer the reader chiefly to J. Fritsch, " 'Videbitis . . . angelos Dei ascendentes et descendentes super Filium hominis' (Jn. I, 51)," *VD* 37 (1959), pp. 3–11; J. Jeremias, "Die Berufung des Nathanael," *Angelos* 36 (1928), pp. 2–5. For 2:18–22, cf. A.-M. Dubarle, "Le signe du Temple," *RB* 48 (1939), pp. 21–44; X. Léon-Dufour, "Le signe du Temple selon saint Jean," *RSR* 39 (1951), pp. 155–75. For 7:37–39, cf. A. Feuillet, "Les fleuves d'eau vive," in *Parole de Dieu et sacerdoce: Homage à Mgr J. Weber* (Tournai-Paris, 1962), pp. 107–20; J. Daniélou, "Jn. VII, 38 et Ez. XLVII, 1–11," *StEv* 2:158–63; P. Grelot, "Jean VII, 38: Eau du rocher ou source du Temple?" *RB* 70 (1963), pp. 43–51.

42. *Die Erhöhung und Verherrlichung Jesu im Johannesevangelium* (Münster, 1960), pp. 186–90; cf. Thüsing, *La prière sacerdotale de Jésus*, pp. 101–4.

43. Cf. Brown, op. cit., p. 134.

44. Thüsing, *La prière sacerdotale de Jésus*, p. 102.

45. We make this qualification in order to leave open a speculative problem on which theologians differ: Did Jesus possess the supreme priesthood because of the hypostatic union or because of the "capital" grace which makes him head of the community of believers? In either case his priesthood is connected with his incarnation.

46. Thüsing, op. cit., p. 102. Lagrange, op. cit., p. 292: "The Father did not have to communicate sanctity to the Son but to the human nature which the Son would take and in which he would be acknowledged as the Holy One of God (6:69)."

47. *Sacerdoce et ministère* (Taizé, 1970), pp. 22–23; we borrow the statements of Theodore and Ephraem from p. 52, n. 8.

48. *Oratio* 3: *In Vigilia Luminum* 5 (*PG* 99:704d).

49. *Commentarium in Diatessaron* 4.

50. The reading "the chosen one of God" of the Codex Sinaiticus is the more difficult reading, but it is more probable than "the Son of God" which is better attested in the manuscripts but looks like a harmonization with the synoptic gospels.

51. Some references: O. Cullmann, *Baptism in the New Testament,* trans. by J. K. S. Reid (Studies in Biblical Theology 1; Chicago, 1950), pp. 16–18; A. M. Hunter, *The Work and Words of Jesus* (London, 1951), pp. 35–36; R. H. Fuller, *The Mission and Achievement of Jesus* (London, 1954), p. 53; W. Grundmann, *Das Evangelium nach Markus* (Berlin, 1959), p. 32; C. E. B. Cranfield, *The Gospel According to St. Mark* (Cambridge, 1959), p. 52.

52. We refer the reader to our two studies: "La coupe et le baptême de la Passion," *RB* 74 (1967), pp. 356–91; "La personnalité de Jésus entrevue à partir de sa soumission au rite de repentance du précurseur," *RB* 77 (1970), pp. 30–49.

53. Cf. J. Maritain, *On the Grace and the Humanity of Jesus,* trans. by Joseph W. Evans (New York, 1969).

54. In favor of the sacrificial exegesis Maldonatus cites Athanasius, Chrysostom, Cyril of Alexandria, Theodore of Mopsuesta, Bede, Theophylact, Euthymius, Rupert, and others.

55. Bultmann gives the Greek text, op. cit., p. 510, note 5. We refer the reader to what we have written on this point in "Le logion sur la rançon," *RSPT* 51 (1967), p. 390. This saying, according to which the Son of Man will give his life as a ransom for many, receives its proper explanation in 1 Timothy 2:5–6: "There is only one mediator between God and mankind, himself a man, Christ Jesus, who sacrificed himself as a ransom for them all."

56. Cf. R. Marcus, *"Mebaqqer* and *Rabbim* in the Manual of Disciple vi. 11–13," *JBL* 75 (1956), pp. 298–302; H. Huppenbauer, "rhym, rwb, rb in der Sektenregel," *TZ* 13 (1957), pp. 136–37; J. Jeremias, "Polloi," *TDNT* 6:536–65.

57. Cf., once again, our *Le mystère de l'amour divin dans la théologie johannique* (Paris, 1972).

58. On this latter, cf. Josephus, *Antiquitatum Judaicarum libri XII,* III, 7:2 Philo, *De fuga,* pp. 110–12.

59. Cf. Cyprian, *De ecclesiae catholicae unitate* 7 (*CSEL* 3:215).

60. Cf. C. Spicq, "L'origine johannique de la conception du Christ Prêtre dans l'Epître aux Hébreux," in *Aux sources de la tradition*

chrétienne (*Mélanges M. Goguel*) (Neuchâtel, 1950), pp. 258–69; F.-M. Braun, "Quatre signes johanniques de l'unité chrétienne," *NTS* 9 L962–63), pp. 150–52.

CHAPTER 2

1. On the festival of atonement, cf. J. Bonsirven, *Le judaïsme palestinien au temps de Jésus-Christ* (Paris, 1925) 2:126–27; L. Ligier, *Péché d'Adam et péché du monde: Bible, Kippur, Eucharistie* 2: *Le Nouveau Testament* (Paris, 1961), pp. 218–18, 225–44 (with abundant bibliography). Our information on Yom Kippur is taken chiefly from these two works, to which we refer the reader.

2. "The Priesthood of Christ in the Epistle to the Hebrews," in *The Sacrament of Holy Orders* (Collegeville, 1962), pp. 39–40.

3. Ligier, op. cit., pp. 290–307. Ligier makes use of six texts from the Seder Abodah for Yom Kippur; he provides a Latin translation of two of them in Appendixes 2–3 (pp. 399–444).

4. E. J. Kissane, *The Book of Isaiah* (Dublin, 1941–43) 2:186, p. 190; A. Gelin, "Messianisme," *DBS* 5:1195 says simply that in the background of the Servant's suffering "the imagery of Yom Kippur is present."

5. Cf. Ligier, *Péché d'Adam et péché du monde: Bible, Kippur, Eucharistie* 1: *L'Ancien Testament* (Paris, 1960), pp. 299–301.

6. On this subject, cf. J. Huby and S. Lyonnet, *Epître aux Romains* (Paris, 1957), pp. 153–54, 575–77. Lyonnet says: "It seems impossible that Paul was not thinking here of the throne of mercy, or mercy seat, as recent commentators believe" (p. 575).

7. Cf. J. F. Randall, "The Theme of Unity in John XVII, 20–23," *ETL* 41 (1965), pp. 373–94.

8. *Super evangelium sancti Joannis lectura* (Rome-Turin, 1952), p. 411.

9. *Commentaire de l'évangile de saint Jean* (reissue, Neuchâtel, 1962), 2:346.

10. "Aufbau, Schichtung, und theologiegeschichtliche Stellung des Gebetes in Johannes XVII," *ZNTW* 60 (1969) 56–83.

11. Brown, op. cit., pp. 748–51.

12. *Le quatrième évangile* (Paris, 1921), p. 441.

13. Cf. 17:6 and 1:1; 17:17 and 1:1–2; 17:22, 24, and 1:14.

14. Lagrange, op. cit., p. 436.

15. *The Interpretation of the Fourth Gospel* (Cambridge, 1953), p. 417.

16. "We 'attah—Kai nun: Formula caractéristique des textes juridiques et liturgiques (à propos de Jn XVII, 5)," *B* 45 (1963), pp. 168–97, 413–32.

17. Becker, art. cit.

18. Brown, op. cit., pp. 750–51.

19. *La prière sacerdotale de Jésus,* p. 71.

20. "The Literary Structure of John XVII," *B* 52 (1971), pp. 190–214.

21. Lagrange, op. cit., p. 440.

22. Ibid., p. 442, on Verse 6.

23. Ibid.

24. Ibid., p. 451.

25. Malatesta counts twenty-four major themes in the Prologue and forty-four in Chapter 17. To show the poverty of the vocabulary, he points to the repetition of several important words: to give (*didonai*), about fifteen times; to send (*apostellein*), six times; the world (*kosmos*), almost twenty times. On the artistry of composition in the fourth gospel, cf. C. H. Talbert, "Artistry and Theology: An Analysis of the Architecture of Jn. I, 19–V, 47," *CBQ* 32 (1970), pp. 341–66.

26. Cf. Bonsirven, op. cit., pp. 119–20.

27. Cf. Ligier, op. cit., 2:218, p. 219, n. 36.

28. *The Gospel According to Saint John* (London, 1955), p. 421.

29. Cf. Thüsing, op. cit., pp. 26–28.

30. Cf. E. Haenchen, "Der Vater, der mich gesandt hat," *NTS* 9 (1962–63), pp. 200–16.

31. Op. cit., p. 132. Thüsing adds: "But why not draw a further conclusion, that the love of which 17:26 speaks is the Holy Spirit in person? Is not the hint given in Verse 26 sufficiently clear? In that verse love is identified with Jesus himself: 'so that the love may be in them, and so that *I may be in them.*' Just as Jesus, the revealer of the Father, must be in believers, so this 'love' must remain in them. We also recall John 17:16 and 19 where the coming of the Paraclete in the disciples is paralleled with the coming of Jesus. We may therefore conclude that the coming of Jesus is effected *by* the coming of the Paraclete. Is not our passage making the same point? Jesus would then be present in us by means of this love-which-is-a-person which unites him to the Father! Exegesis can take us only to the threshold of such a statement, and to deduce it from this text would be asking too much. . . . Therefore, we cannot claim that when he wrote 17:26 the evangelist meant by 'love' the person of the Holy Spirit. . . . Yet when the various statements of the fourth gospel are set side by side (the evidence of a

single verse not being sufficient), they suggest that we should see something deeper in this 'love.' In addition, a personification of love is easy to understand in a theology of the Johannine kind (especially in John's idea that Jesus remains in his disciples through the Paraclete and that the gift of the Spirit is identical with the action of the Paraclete)."

32. Ibid., p. 92.

33. "Un double problème de critique textuelle et d'interprétation: Saint Jean XVII, 11–12," *RSR* 27 (1937), pp. 408–21.

34. "Pour une intelligence plus profonde de saint Jean," *RSR* 39 (1951), pp. 176–96.

35. Lagrange, op. cit., p. 442. The text of St. Thomas: "Et hoc modo nulli erat notus; sed innotuit per Filium, quando apostoli crediderunt eum esse Filium Dei."

36. Ibid., p. 443.

37. Brown, op. cit., pp. 755–56.

38. On the *egō eimi* formulas, cf. E. Schweizer, *Egō eimi* (Göttingen, 1939); D. Daube, "The 'I Am' of the Messianic Presence," in his *The New Testament and Rabbinic Judaism* (London, 1956), pp. 325–29; H. Zimmermann, "Das absolute Egō eimi als die neutestamentliche Offenbarungsformel," *BZ* 5 (1961), pp. 54–69, 266–76; A. Feuillet, "Les Egō eimi christologiques du quatrième évangile," *RSR* 54 (1966), pp. 5–22, 213–40; Brown, op. cit., pp. 533–38.

39. Cf. Barrett, op. cit., p. 421.

40. Cf. Yoma 5:1–4; 7:4; Josephus, *De bello judaico* V, 5:236; Philo, *Legatio ad Gaium* 306; C. Spicq, *L'Epître aux Hébreux* 2: *Commentaire* (Paris, 1953), p. 253.

41. Cf. Jerusalem Bible, p. 151, n.d.

42. Cf. A George, "L'heure de Jn. XVII," *RB* 61 (1964), pp. 392–97.

43. The peculiarities of the prayer in John 17 have been exaggerated. (1) It has been claimed that the prayer is wholly timeless and ignores the real historical situation of the Christ who is depicted as uttering it. In fact, the prayer is connected with the "hour." It is true that several times the language Jesus uses anticipates the future and supposes the passion and even the resurrection to be already past; cf. "I have . . . finished the work" (Verse 4), "I am not in the world any longer" (Verse 11), "while I was with them" (Verse 12), and "I want those you have given me to be with me where I am, so that they may always see the glory you have given me" (Verse 24). But then, at the Last Supper as depicted by the synoptic gospels, does Jesus not anticipate the future by giving as food and drink his body and blood that

will be offered on Calvary? (2) Appeal is also made to the sharp contrast between the tone of the prayer in John 17 where the transcendence of Christ is evident in every line, and the human, anguished prayer in Gethsemani in the synoptic gospels. But, even in the synoptics, there is a sharp contrast between the self-possession of Jesus during the Last Supper and his disturbance of soul a short time later in the Garden of Olives.

44. Lagrange, op. cit., p. 439.

45. Thüsing, op. cit., p. 7.

46. Cf. our study, "Le recherche du Christ dans la nouvelle alliance d'après la christologie de Jn. XX, 11–18," in *L'Homme devant Dieu* (*Mélanges H. de Lubac*) (Paris, 1963), pp. 93–112.

47. Cf. R. Laurentin, *Jésus au Temple: Mystère de Pâques, foi de Marie en Lc. II,* 48–50 (Paris, 1966), pp. 128–32.

48. Ibid., pp. 38–72.

49. In 7:34 we would expect "where I am going" as in 8:21, instead of "where I am." Some exegetes therefore suggest that *eimi* here is a form of *ienai* (to go), not of *einai* (to be). But, as in 17:24, we very likely have in 7:34 a divine "I Am," which is clearly explained by St. Augustine, *In Joannem* 31:9 (*PL* 35:1640): "Christ was always in the place to which he was to return." Cf. Brown, op. cit., p. 314.

50. A number of manuscripts omit the object "me" in "If you ask me for anything," probably because it seemed odd to ask someone for something in his own name. But, once the "me" is omitted, the verse becomes a needless repetition of the preceding verse and leads exegetes to conclude that it is a gloss. In fact, as Lagrange notes (*in loc.*), "the difficult reading is not impossible: we do petition God for his name's sake (Ps. 25:11; 30:4; 79:9; cf. Zahn). The verse thus makes it clearer that prayer addressed to the name of Jesus reaches Jesus himself and that the believer can choose the most direct formula in addressing the glorified Christ. And it is the glorified Christ who will act."

51. Ibid., p. 380.

52. Brown, op. cit., p. 765.

53. Cf. J. Carmignac, *Recherches sur le Notre Père* (Paris, 1969), pp. 369–70.

54. The word *paraklētos,* which is a passive form of *parakalein,* is equivalent to the Latin *advocatus* but does not seem to have acquired the latter's technical sense. In the rare non-biblical texts in which it occurs, *paraklētos* means someone called on to help an accused person; cf. Demosthenes, *De falsa legatione* 1; Bion, in Diogenes Laertius

IV, 50; Dionysius of Halicarnassus XI, 37:1; Dio Cassius XLVI, 20:1. There is no certain Hebrew or Aramaic original of which *paraklētos* would be the translation (*melis,* "interpreter," is not improbable). But in Jewish writings of the second century A.D., *prqlyt* is used as a borrowing; cf. Pirqe Aboth IV, 11. It may be, therefore, that the *paraklētos* of John is simply a retroversion into Greek of a Hebrew word that had earlier been borrowed from Greek. Cf. Lagrange, op. cit., p. 381; Brown, op. cit., pp. 1135–36.

55. This is the chief function of the Spirit Paraclete. But we do not forget that he has other functions as well: to defend the disciples when they are hauled before the judgment seats of the world, to console the disciples for whom he takes Jesus' place, and to bear witness to Christ. This rich complexity of functions means that it is better to transliterate *paraklētos* into English instead of trying to translate it in the discourses after the Last Supper.

56. *An Introduction to the Theology of the New Testament* (New York, 1958), p. 217. Cf. A. Vanhoye, "Le Christ grand prêtre selon Hé. II, 17–18," *NRT* 91 (1969), pp. 466–67.

57. Cf. J. Bonsirven, *Epîtres de saint Jean* (Paris, 1935), p. 105, n. 1. Cf. also F. Zorell, *Lexicon Graecum Novi Testamenti* (2nd ed.; Paris, 1931), col. 610, "Sacrificium expiatorium"; L. Sabourin, *Rédemption sacrificielle: Une enquête exégétique* (Bruges, 1961), p. 323, says that *hilasmos* "should not be understood as a propitiatory offering intended to reconcile God, for it is God who loved us and sent his Son as a *hilasmos* for our sins. *Hilasmos* must therefore mean here an expiation that takes sin away."

58. Cf., e.g., A. Charue, "Les Epîtres Catholiques," in *La Sainte Bible de Pirot* 12 (Paris, 1951), p. 525.

59. On this subject, cf. C. Spicq, "L'origine johannique de la conception du Christ prêtre dans l'Epître aux Hébreux," in *Aux sources la tradition chrétienne* (*Mélanges M. Goguel*) (Neuchâtel-Paris, 1950), pp. 256–69; O. Moe, "Das Priestertum Christi im Neuen Testament ausserhaln des Hebräerbriefes," *TLZ* 72 (1947) 335–38; O. Cullmann, *The Christology of the New Testament,* pp. 104–7.

60. "La tradition synoptique du 'voile déchiré' à la lumière des réalités archéologiques," *RSR* 46 (1958), pp. 161–80.

61. Among the older partisans of Luke's authorship of the Letter to the Hebrews were Origen, Grotius, and Fr. Delitzsch. To these names add: G. Lünemann, *Kritischexegetischer Handbuch über den Hebräerbrief* (Göttingen, 1878); A. R. Eager, "The Hellenic Element

in the Epistle to the Hebrews," *Hermathena* 31 (1901), pp. 263–87. Cf. Spicq, *L'Epître aux Hébreux* 1: *Introduction*, p. 398.

62. A list of these affinities between the third and fourth gospels may be found in W. Grundmann, *Das Evangelium nach Lukas* (Berlin, 1965), pp. 17–22.

63. Pelletier says: "For Mark the tearing of the veil simply signifies the desecration of the rites and places whose secret the veil had hitherto protected. An allusion to the sidereal decoration of the curtain (stressed by Philo *De vita Moysis* II, pp. 17–18, and Josephus, *De bello judaico* V, pp. 212–13) would be in keeping with Matthew's style; he is the only evangelist to have preserved the episode of the Magi in which the astronomical element not only forms a background but plays a role in the story itself. It would also be in accordance with Matthew's large-scale decorative backgrounds such as he provides in his scene for the last judgment. In 27:51 Matthew would be linking the desecration of the Temple, as expressed by the tearing of the veil, with some great divine wrath as expressed in the rending of the astronomical heaven (in its representation on the Temple curtain) and of the earth and the tombs from which the dead arose. This last-named element turns the whole scene into a prelude of the final judgment. The abrogation of past figures and the inauguration of the new reality deserve no less than such a scene" (art. cit., p. 177).

64. Ibid. This interpretation, Pelletier observes, is completely in keeping with Luke's universalism: "no more racial and social distinctions; even thieves can enter the heavenly sanctuary, even if at the last minute."

CHAPTER 3

1. Cf. especially R. Otto, *The Idea of the Holy*, trans. by J. W. Harvey (New York, 1950, 2nd ed.), pp. 8–11.

2. In what follows we draw on P. Grelot, *Le ministère de la nouvelle alliance* (Paris, 1967), pp. 24–25; A. Robert, "Mediation dans l'Ancien Testament," *DBS* 5:997–1020; A. Lefèvre, "Lévitique (organisation)," *DBS* 5:389–97; A. Gelin, "The Priesthood of Christ in the Epistle to the Hebrews," in *The Sacrament of Holy Orders* (Collegeville, 1962), pp. 30–59. We refer the reader above all to *Priesthood and Celibacy*, by A. Charue, et al. (Milan, n.d.), a collection that opens with two very instructive essays: J. Coppens, "Old Testament Priesthood," pp. 3–23, and L. Leloir, "Permanent Values of the

Levitical Priesthood," pp. 31–65; Coppens provides an extensive bibliography on the subject, pp. 24–30.

3. *Ancient Israel: Its Life and Institutions,* translated by J. McHugh (New York, 1961), p. 356.

4. The quoted phrase is from an essay that rightly insists on how forcefully the liturgy of the old covenant brings home the holiness of God and the tragic magnitude of sin: "The Temple at Jerusalem was a huge slaughter house. We find that repugnant. But God intended in this way to make his covenanted people understand the seriousness of sin. The more we study the Old Testament texts, the more impressed we are by the awareness, unparalleled in its intensity, of the infinite gravity of sin that finds expression in texts and rites. The awareness was given to Israel along with the revelation of God's holiness and authentic divinity"; cf. W. Vischer, "Notes sur le culte de l'ancienne alliance," *Foi et vie* 62 (1963), pp. 293, 297.

5. *Old Testament Theology,* Vol. 2: *The Theology of Israel's Prophetic Traditions,* trans. by D. M. G. Stalker (New York, 1965), pp. 250–77. What follows in the text is inspired by these remarkable pages. Our purpose in this chapter dispenses us from discussing the hypothesis of cultic prophetism that has been proposed in varying forms by a number of writers, e.g., G. Hölscher, S. Mowinckel, A. R. Johnson, and A. Haldar. For all the problems raised by the study of the Israelite prophets, cf. L. Ramlot's richly documented study, "Prophétisme," *DBS* 8:909–1222.

6. Robert, art. cit., p. 1008.

7. Von Rad, op. cit., p. 274.

8. "Jeremia und Jeremiabuch," *Religion in Geschichte und Gegenwart,* 2nd ed., 3:75–76.

9. *Ezekiel* (Neukirchen, 1969), p. 117.

10. "Die Eigenart der prophetischen Rede des Ezechiel," *ZATW* 66 (1954), pp. 9–10.

11. O. Procksch, commenting on this passage in his *Iesaja* 1 (Leipzig, 1930), sees in the great parable of the farmer (Is. 28:23–29) a distant preparation for the teaching on the Servant songs in the fruitfulness of suffering. In Isaiah 28 God's plan for salvation is compared to the rules a farmer observes in tilling the earth (Verses 23–26) and gathering the various grains (Verses 27–29); he does not "wound" the earth in order to make it fruitful, and at the harvest he does not thresh all the grains in the same way but reserves the hardest treatment for the noblest grain (the wheat), yet without "crushing" it. The prophet's disciples are to understand that they

should not be scandalized at the severities of the divine plan which reserves the greatest suffering for the devout. May we not indeed say
that Isaiah 28 does give a distant inkling of Isaiah 53?

12. The translation "he shall have multitudes for his share" is that
of the Vulgate and the Septuagint. Such versions take *rabbim* as the
direct object of the verb. Another translation has been defended which
is also very plausible: "Hence I will grant whole hordes for his
tribute; he shall divide the spoil with the mighty" (JB). The "mighty"
here can only refer to kings; cf. 2 Samuel 7:9; Psalms 89:27. To say
that the Servant has a share among them amounts to saying that he
is not inferior to the great conquerors the East had known: Sargon,
Sennacherib, Esarhaddon, Nebuchadnezzar, and, most recently, Cyrus
who is present in Isaiah 40ff, as a saviour sent by God (cf. also Is.
53:2: the root from the dried earth is a clear allusion to Is. 11:1 and
thus to the royal, Davidic origin of the Servant). In the second translation of Isaiah 53:12, the idea would be that by his suffering the
Servant wins in the world of souls a dominion comparable in extent
to that of the great conquerors (from the viewpoint of a Palestinian
of this period these conquerors has taken possession of almost the
entire world).

13. This point is so important that it merits a lengthy note. The
point can be accepted only if one has begun by acknowledging the
complete independence of the Servant songs from their present context. We think this independence is inescapably clear. Nothing, of
course, is easier than to show similarities between the poems and
their context, but such similarities are counterbalanced by doctrinal
changes so radical that the Servant songs give the impression of
having been inserted at a later time into an alien context. Cf. H. Haag,
"Ebed Yahve-Forschung, 1949–1958," *BZ* 3 (1959), pp. 174–204.

The poems must therefore be studied as independent entities. It
is not the fact, though some have maintained it, that the Servant is
regarded in the poems as the leader and guide of the new Exodus nor
that he is to be at the head of the Israelites as they return from their
Babylonian captivity. Where is there any question of this Exodus
in Isaiah 42:1–7, 50:4–9, or 53? The Servant is presented in these
poems as a prophet and wise man, preoccupied solely with the religious salvation of souls, their liberation from sin and death, and
their instruction. There is nothing of the political liberator about him,
and indeed such a function would be incompatible with his role as
teacher of individual souls. Moreover, it seems that he is persecuted by
his fellow countrymen just because his mission is a purely spiritual

one; cf. Isaiah 42:4; 49:4; 50:5–6. He suffers and dies because he is determined to preach only religious truth and thus follows principles which would separate that truth from Jewish nationalism. According to 49:4–5 he has tried without success to bring Jacob and Israel back to God from their excessive concern for a national salvation. He laments his failure: "I have toiled in vain, I have exhausted myself for nothing," but he is comforted by Yahweh "who formed me in the womb to be his servant, to bring Jacob back to him, to gather Israel to him." The divine answer, which is given in Verse 6, means that the political restoration of the chosen people (which is what they were looking for) would be a task unworthy of the Servant, since his vocation was rather to bring religious salvation to all mankind: "It is not enough for you to be my servant, to restore the tribes of Jacob and bring back the survivors of Israel; I will make you the light of the nations so that my salvation may reach to the ends of the earth." It seems clear from the very Hebrew words used that Verse 5 is speaking of that *return* of Jacob and Israel *to God* which it was the Servant's mission to bring about and which he laments that he had not been able to effect. Verse 6, on the contrary, speaks of the captives' *return to the holy land* and of the national resurrection of the "tribes of Jacob." God himself intervenes in a solemn way to exclude this second return from the Servant's mission.

In the lament of the Servant in 50:4–9 we can glimpse the opposition that his preaching arouses in his compatriots, for he is shamefully treated as all the troublesome converters of souls before him, notably Jeremiah, had been. Throughout Chapter 53 any term suggesting a political liberation has been avoided. In Verse 6 the image of the straying flock indeed suggests the scattering of the chosen people in the time of their captivity; cf. especially Ezekiel 34. But in the present context the point is entirely different: It is a matter of the straying of sin and of Yahweh's action through the Servant in bringing the flock back to the straight path. The real dispersion is spiritual, the alienation caused by sin.

We are thus given clearly to understand that the object of God's rule over the world is not the temporal glory of a nation, as some passages of the Old Testament might suggest when taken in isolation. The object is the moral conversion of mankind and the victory of each soul over sin. Thus understood, the divine plan has already been brought to fulfillment in the martyrdom of the Servant which is described in Isaiah 53. His wretched end is apparently a failure. In reality, however, his death guarantees mankind's victory over sin and death, a victory God had promised in the earthly paradise immediately after the fall (Gn. 3:5: the posterity of the woman is to crush the serpent's head); his death is the source of moral conversion for multitudes of men, and the starting point for the spread of authentic religion throughout the world.

In his book *Jesus of Nazareth: His Life, Times, and Teaching,* translated by Herbert Danby (New York, 1926), especially pp. 413–14, J. Klausner, the first Jewish biographer of Jesus, shows that he is attracted by the greatness of Christ whom he considers an incomparable moralist. On the other hand, he criticizes Christ for not having had "the Prophet's political perception and the Prophet's spirit of national consolidation in the political-national sense" (p. 414). This is really to criticize Jesus for having wanted to found, and having in fact founded and sealed with his own blood, a religion that was detached from everything specifically Jewish and open to all mankind. The objection is indeed well founded, but to us it is, of course, the greatest possible praise. We can only repeat here Pascal's famous words: "The Jews rejected him, but not all of them: the saints accepted him, and not the worldly. So far from that detracting from his glory, it was the crowning mark of it. . . . Jesus Christ was killed, they say; he succumbed; he did not subdue the heathen by his strength; he did not give us their spoils; he did not give us riches. Is that all they have to say? It is because of that that I find him lovable. I should have no use for the person whom they expected him to be"; cf. *Pascal's Pensées,* translated by Martin Turnell (New York, 1962), p. 299, frag. no. 655 (Brunschvicg, frag. no. 760).

14. As often in rhetorical passages, the text is a question introduced by *mi* and expects a negative answer: "No one would believe . . ." The thing that is heard comes from God; it is a revelation, at least in the broad sense of the term. In the Hebrew word corresponding to "what we have heard" (*shemuah*), the pronomal suffix expressing the subject is in the plural. Who are the persons who speak? According to some exegetes (Marti, Feldmann, Ceuppens, Kissane, and others), they are the nations and kings to whom 52:15 refers. But with 53:1 there is certainly a change of scene; above all, it is unlikely that the whole divine revelation is addressed to pagans, with Israel playing the role only of the one responsible for the Servant's suffering. On the contrary, we know that divine communications, even concerning the pagans, are addressed only to the people to whom God reveals himself.

Duhm would have it that the "we" of "what we have heard" is not a group but only the poet. However, it is unusual for a biblical writer to refer to himself in the plural. It may also be maintained that the poet is identifying himself with the people; this is the view of J. Fischer who adduces analogous instances (confession of past sins): Isaiah 42:24; 59:12–13; 63:7; 64:12; Daniel 9:4–19; Ezra 9:6–15. In Fischer's view, Isaiah 53:1–6 would be a similar confession. According to M.-J. Lagrange, *Le judaïsme avant Jésus-Christ* (Paris, 1931), p. 372, the words in question are those of a group, a chorus as it were, that is aware of the mystery of God's action and is struck by the strange error of those who have condemned the Servant. His persecutors think they are the instruments of a divine punishment, when in fact the Servant is an expiatory victim.

In an unpublished course of lectures on these poems, A. Robert made an interesting suggestion: The words are those of a group of educated men, scribes, who in the light of current circumstances and with the help of the Holy Spirit, have reflected on the Scriptures generally, the case of Jeremiah, the passages in the Mosaic law on atonement, and so on. They have reached the idea of a suffering Messiah who is persecuted for his universalist doctrine and dies as an expiatory victim. That is the divine revelation (in the broad sense of the term) which they have received and are to pass on, but which no one will believe.

15. Cf. A. Robert, "Médiation dans l'Ancien Testament," *DBS* 5:1001.

16. *The Book of the Prophet Isaiah: XL–LXVI* (Cambridge, 1917), p. 135.

17. In any event, Ezekiel, himself a prophet and priest, is here transposing the priestly lustrations into the eschatological sphere. Cf. S. A. Cooke, *The Book of Ezechiel* (Edinburgh, 1936), p. 391.

18. *L'Ancien Testament,* Vol. 2, in the Bible de la Pléiade (Paris, 1956), p. 187.

19. In Leviticus 4:6, 17, the same Hebrew verb is also used in the accusative case, expressing the object sprinkled; cf. also 1 Q HS 3:8–9.

20. In favor of keeping the reading of the Massoretic text: J. Knabenbauer, *Commentarius in Isaiam Prophetam* (Paris, 1887); W. Vischer, *Betheljahrbuch* 1 (1930), pp. 97–110; M. Hoopers, *Der neue Bund bei den Propheten* (Freiburg, 1933), pp. 65–66; R. Tournay, "Bulletin (Prophètes)," *RB* 56 (1949), p. 458; J. Lindblom, *The Servant Songs in Deutero-Isaiah* (Lund, 1951), pp. 40–41; E. J. Young, *Studies in Isaiah* (Grand Rapids, 1954), pp. 129–206; H. Cazelles, "Les poèmes du Serviteur: Leur place, leur structure, leur théologie,"

RSR 43 (1955), p. 33; L. G. Rignell, *A Study of Isaiah* (Lund, 1956), p. 79; O. Kaiser, *Der königliche Knecht: Eine traditionsgeschichtlich-exegetische Studie über die Ebed-Yahve Lieder bei Deuterojesaja* (Göttingen, 1959); L. Sabourin, *Rédemption sacrificielle* (Paris-Bruges, 1961), pp. 351–52; H. W. Brownlee, *The Meaning of the Qumran Scrolls for the Bible, with Special Attention to the Book of Isaiah* (New York, 1964), pp. 294–95; G. von Rad, *Old Testament Theology* 2 (New York, 1965), pp. 254–55.

21. Recall that Exodus 24 seems to bring together two traditions: the Yahwist (Verses 1–2, 9–12), according to which the covenant is sealed by a meal taken in God's presence, and the Elohist (Verses 3–8), according to which it is sealed by the sharing of the blood in the presence of the people at the foot of the mountain. Cf. the Jerusalem Bible on the passage.

22. Cf. A. Feuillet, *Le discours sur le pain de vie* (Paris, 1967).

23. Here are a few studies of this question: J. Leal, "Exegesis catholica de Agno Dei in ultimis viginti et quinque annis," *VD* 28 (1950), pp. 98–109; C. K. Barrett, "The Lamb of God," *NTS* 1 (1954–55), pp. 210–18; M.-E. Boismard, *Du Baptême à Cana* (Paris, 1956); I. de la Potterie, "Ecco l'Agnello di Dio," *BO* 1 (1959), pp. 161–69; R. E. Brown, "Three Quotations from John the Baptist in the Gospel of John," *Scripture* 13 (1961), pp. 74–80.

24. Since the hyssop stalk is not rigid enough to be used in the way described, exegetes have at times assumed the text to be corrupt (J. Camerarius [1954], Lagrange, Bernard, and others) and have suggested that instead of *hyssōpos* we should read *hyssos* (javelin), the *pilum* of the Roman soldier. But the reading *hyssos* is supported only by an eleventh-century manuscript; furthermore, the plant that John calls *hyssōpos* has not been identified with certainty. It is better, then, to keep the well-attested reading *hyssōpos*. Cf. Brown, *The Gospel According to John*, pp. 909–10; J. Wilkinson, "The Seven Words from the Cross," *SJT* 17 (1964), p. 77.

25. Cf., e.g., Lagrange, *Evangile selon saint Jean*, p. 291.

26. Cf. Brown, op. cit., p. 411.

27. "The Literary Structure of John XVII," *B* 52 (1971), p. 214.

28. We have shown elsewhere that even if the Holy Spirit is not expressly mentioned in John 17, his action is presupposed at every point; cf. our *Le mystère de l'amour divin dans la théologie johannique* (Paris, 1972), pp. 66–68. Cf. also Thüsing, *La prière sacerdotale de Jésus*, pp. 55–67, 103–4.

29. Cf. A. Charue, "Les Epîtres Catholiques," in *La Sainte Bible de Pirot* 12 (Paris, 1951), p. 525.

30. On these false teachers, cf. Robert-Feuillet, *Introduction to the New Testament*, pp. 681–83.

31. J. Bonsirven, *Epîtres de saint Jean*, p. 34. The mysterious "that one" or "he" in the same letter refers at times to the Son, at times to the Father. Are we to take it that Christ is meant by the "one" of John 19:35: "This is the evidence of one who saw it—trustworthy evidence, and he knows that he speaks the truth"? A number of commentators think so: Erasmus, Sanday, Abbott, Lagrange, Strachan, Hoskyns, Braun; cf. the discussion in Brown, op. cit., pp. 936–37. Brown thinks that the *ekeinos* here refers to the eyewitness himself.

32. The *ekeinos* here would refer to God according to what immediately precedes, but the text requires that we refer it to Christ; the ambiguity is highly significant. Cf. Bonsirven, op. cit., p. 115.

33. Cf. A. Charue, op. cit., p. 449: *"Hagnizein* refers to the ritual purification required of Jews before they can be admitted to participation in worship: Ex. 21:10 f.; Nb. 8:21; Jos. 3:5; Jn. 11:55: 'The Jewish Passover drew near, and many of the country people . . . had gone up to Jerusalem to purify themselves.' Christian preaching, which was careful to transpose the obligation of purifying oneself to the moral order (1 Co. 5:7–8) uses the verb *hagnizein* for interior purification: Jm. 4:18; 1 Jn. 3:3; cf. also Heb. 12:14."

34. We are here following Bonsirven, op. cit., pp. 243–44.

35. According to its etymology, *arnion* is a young ram, a fact that has led some exegetes to connect the Lamb of the Apocalypse with the ram of the zodiac or the rams used in Eastern cults. But in the Septuagint (Jr. 11:19; 27:45; Ps. 113:4, 6) the word means simply "lamb." It has the same meaning in Aquila, Josephus, The Psalms of Solomon, and John 21:15. Therefore, we must agree with the majority of commentators who translate *arnion* in the Apocalypse as "lamb." On this point cf. J. Jeremias, "arnion," *TDNT* 1:340–41; E. Lohmeyer, *Die Offenbarung des Johannes* (Leipzig, 1928), pp. 76–78; J. Comblin, *Le Christ dans l'Apocalypse* (Paris, 1965), p. 20, n. 5.

36. We refer the reader to excellent long demonstration given by Comblin, op. cit., Chapter 1: "L'Agneau, Serviteur de Dieu," pp. 11–47.

37. A. Gelin, "L'Apocalypse," in *La Sainte Bible de Pirot* 12:611.

38. *A Commentary on the Revelation of St. John the Divine* (London, 1966), pp. 74–75.

39. We refer the reader to what we wrote on this subject in a review of C. Brütsch, *La clarté de l'Apocalypse* (Geneva, 1966), in *RB* 75 (1968), p. 118.

40. Cf. the commentary on this scene in our article, "La moisson et la vendange de l'Apocalypse (XIV, pp. 14–21): La signification chrétienne de la révélation johannique," *NRT* 94 (1972), pp. 113–32, 225–50.

41. Cf. Hebrews 5:8 chiefly with Philippians 2:6–8, but also with 2 Corinthians 5:21 and 8:9. Here we have a traditional motif which originates in a striking contrast established in the gospels. Without losing any of his dignity, the transcendent Son of Man of Daniel must suffer and be martyred like the Servant of Yahweh. Cf. our study, "L'hymn christologique de l'Epître aux Philippiens (II, 6–11)," *EV* 80 (1970), pp. 737–38.

42. Cf. M. Lepin, *L'Idée du sacrifice de la Mess d'après les théologiens* (Paris, 1926), pp. 691–92, 724–25; C. Spicq, *L'Epître aux Hébreaux 1: Introduction,* p. 306, n. 6; A. Barrois, 'Le sacrifice du Christ au Calvaire," *RSPT* 14 (1925), pp. 145–66; J. Bonsirven, *Saint Paul: Epître aux Hébreux* (Paris, 1943), pp. 50–66. This is the direction taken by those theologians who in explaining the Mass adopt the sacrifice-oblation approach, which excludes the need for an immolation. Cf. A. Michel, "Messe," *DTC* 10:1192–93, 1265–66.

43. Cf. A. Vanhoye, "De aspectu oblationis Christi secundum Epistolam ad Hebraeos," *VD* 37 (1954), pp. 32–38. Some points in the texts we are using: 5:1, 7: "Every high priest . . . is appointed . . . to offer gifts and sacrifices for sins [*prospherein* in the present infinitive]. . . . During his life on earth, he offered up prayer and entreaty, aloud and in silent tears [aorist participle of *prospherein*]"; the tears and entreaties are those of the passion. 7:27: "One [Christ] who would not need to offer sacrifices [aorist tense of *prospherein*]." 9:7, 14: in the second tent the high priest offers [present tense of *prospherein*] the blood; Christ offered himself [aorist of *prospherein*]. 9:25, 28: Christ did not enter heaven to offer himself again and again [*prospherein,* present subjunctive] but he was offered once and for all [aorist passive participle of *prospherein*].

44. As regards the opinion according to which the earthly life of Christ was simply a time of probation and preparation for his priesthood, cf. especially W. G. Holmes, *The Epistle to the Hebrews* (London, 1919), p. 27; S. G. Gayford, *The Epistle to the Hebrews* (New York, 1945), p. 599; A. Vanhoye, *Epistolae ad Hebraeos textus de sacerdotio* (notes for students; Rome, 1969), pp. 120–24; idem,

Lectiones de sacerdotio Christi in He VII (Rome, 1970). On the theological idea of the heavenly sacrifice of Christ, cf. especially M. de la Taille, *The Mystery of Faith* 1: *The Sacrifice of Christ* (New York, 1940), pp. 181–255; J. Grimal, *Le sacerdoce et le sacrifice de Jésus-Christ* (3rd ed.; Paris, 1923).

45. Cf. J. Cambier, *Eschatologie et hellénisme dans l'Epître aux Hébreux: Une étude sur menein et l'exhortation finale de l'Epître* (Paris, 1949); A. Feuillet, "Les points de vue nouveaux dans l'eschatologie de l'Epître aux Hébreux," *StEv* 2:369–87.

46. We must note, in the interests of accuracy and fairness, that even if the defenders of a heavenly sacrifice of Christ use misleading language, they do not mean to imply a new sacrifice which could be set beside that of the cross. Here is how A. Michel, to take but one example, sums up de la Taille's thought on the matter: "The resurrection, ascension, and glorification of Christ at the Father's right hand are an integral part of his one sacrifice. Man offers a gift to God; the giving is completed only when God accepts the gift. Christ offered the sacrifice by which we are saved. The victim was accepted by God, and the public sign of the acceptance was given when the victim offered to God was taken by him. . . . The glory of Christ is proof of the sacrificial value of his offering on the cross." De la Taille indeed speaks of a heavenly sacrifice and of an offering of Christ as heavenly victim, but he explains that this offering consists simply "in the fact that Christ stands before his Father as once immolated and eternally graced by the fact of having been a victim; this state is an act of praise of God and at times a prayer" ("Messe," *DTC* 10:1246). Our own exegesis of the Letter to the Hebrews is consistent with this theological view.

47. I have shown at length that we must avoid making Pauline thought too rigid and that we must use other passages to correct those polemically determined by the response to the Judaizers: "Loi ancienne et morale chrétienne d'après l'Epître aux Romains," *NRT* 92 (1970), pp. 785–805.

48. C. Spicq, *L'Epître aux Hébreux* 1: *Introduction*, p. 411.

49. On this subject cf. Robert-Feuillet, *Introduction to the New Testament*, pp. 612–14.

50. To show the conditional nature of the Mosaic law, St. Paul in Romans goes back beyond the Mosaic institution to Abraham whose faith is a kind of prototype of Christian faith. In a similar way, to prove the conditional and inferior character of the Levitical priesthood, the author of Hebrews goes back to the patriarchal period

where he finds a priest, acknowledged as such by Abraham, who has nothing to do with the Levitical priesthood. This is not the place to go into the approach Hebrews takes to the figure of Melchizedek; the exegesis is disconcerting to us. We may note simply that while the author's thought seems to move from Melchizedek to Christ, in fact it follows the opposite path; once again it is the New Testament that sheds light on the Old.

51. Cf. J. R. Schaefer, "The Relationship between Priestly and Servant Messianism in the Epistle to the Hebrews," *CBQ* 30 (1968), pp. 359–85.

52. *L'Epître aux Hébreux* 2: *Commentaire,* pp. 258–59.

53. This reference is given by Spicq, ibid., p. 198.

54. Cf. U. Luck, "Himmlisches und Irdisches im Hebräerbrief," *NT* 6 (1963), pp. 195–96.

55. J. Bonsirven, *Saint Paul: Epître aux Hébreux,* p. 266.

56. C. Spicq, op. cit., 1:101–2.

57. Cf., in favor of this solution, A. Harnack, "Zwei alte dogmatische Korrekturen im Hebräerbrief," *Sitzungsberichte der Preuss.-Berlin. Akademie der Wissenschaften* (Berlin, 1929), pp. 62–73. Bultmann goes along with this despairing solution in "eulabeia—eliabeisthai," *TDNT* 2:753. Cf. Th. Boman, "Der Gebetskampf Jesu," *NTS* 10 (1964), pp. 267–68.

58. This solution, already suggested by St. Ambrose, has since been adopted by many exegetes: Bengel, Holtzmann, B. Weiss, Zahan, and, closer to us in time, Dibelius, Héring, Strathmann, Bultmann, and Cullmann. Cf. O. Cullmann, *Christology of the New Testament,* p. 96.

59. Cf. H. Kosmala, *Hebräer—Essener—Christen: Studien zur Vorgeschichte der frühchristlichen Verkündigung* (Leiden, 1959), pp. 297–98. And cf. Bauer—Arndt—Gingrich, *A Greek-English Lexicon of the New Testament and Other Early Christian Literature* (Chicago, 1957), p. 322.

60. This paragraph depends primarily on two studies: E. Rasco, "La oración sacerdotal de Cristo en la tierra segun He V, 7," *Greg.* 43 (1962), pp. 723–55; Th. Boman, "Die Gebetskampf Jesu," *NTS* 10 (1964), pp. 268–70.

CHAPTER 4

1. The document was published in *La croix,* Thursday, August 12, 1971, and was presented to the readers in this way: *"The distinc-*

tion between the common priesthood and the ministerial priesthood must be put forward more strongly. A group of eleven priests at Lyons, among them our associate editor Joseph Folliet, submitted to the priests of the dioceses of Lyons and Saint-Etienne a proposed group contribution to the discussion on ministerial priesthood that is now being conducted in the dioceses in preparation for the Synod."

2. The commentaries ask whether *henos* is to be taken as neuter, "of the same race or blood," or as masculine, "of the same father," the latter being identified with God or with Adam. It is difficult to decide. The text seems to be insisting chiefly on the common nature shared by sanctifier and sanctified.

3. The *teleiōsis* (completion or consummation) is one of the most important themes of the Letter to the Hebrews. The perfection is to be understood in relation to Christ: his work was perfect; his one oblation is able to procure for others the fullest perfection; all Christian holiness derives from Calvary.

4. The author chooses two examples of expiatory rites: the blood of goats and bulls that is carried into the holy of holies on the Day of Atonement (Lv. 16:14–15), and the lustral water, mixed with the ashes of a red heifer, which purifies from contact with a corpse (Nb. 19:1–22).

5. We refer the reader here to Chapter 2, where we studied the structure of John 17.

6. *La prière sacerdotale de Jésus,* pp. 101–3.

7. *A Critical and Exegetical Commentary on the Gospel of St. John* (New York, 1929), 2:573.

8. *Sacerdoce et ministère* (Taizé, 1970), p. 256. For a different approach, cf. P. Grelot, *Le ministère de la nouvelle alliance* (Paris, 1967), pp. 117–19.

9. Thüsing, op. cit., p. 140.

10. Cf. the commentaries on 1 Corinthians, especially E. Allo, *Première Epître aux Corinthiens* (Paris, 1934).

11. In Session 23, Canon 1, the Council of Trent defined the sacrament of orders in terms of the power "of consecrating and offering the body and blood of the Lord" and "of remitting and of retaining sins." Cf. *The Church Teaches: Documents of the Church in English Translation,* trans. by John F. Clarkson, S.J., et al. (St. Louis, 1956), p. 531. Cf. H. Jedin, "Did the Council of Trent Create a Prototype of the Priest?" in *Priesthood and Celibacy,* pp. 153–80.

12. Cf. P. Dacquino, "Il sacrificio della nuova alleanza alla luce del sacrificio eucaristico," *RivB* 19 (1971), pp. 137–63.

13. Thurian, op. cit. p. 31.

14. We follow here L. Leloir, "Permanent Values of the Levitical Priesthood," in *Priesthood and Celibacy,* p. 62.

15. Cf. A. Charue, "Les Epîtres Catholiques," in *La Sainte Bible de Pirot* 12:453.

16. Cf. J. de Bovis, "Nature and Mission of the Priesthood," in *Priesthood and Celibacy,* pp. 273–85.

17. The image of embassy (*presbeuein*) is found in 2 Corinthians 5:20 and Ephesians 6:20; that of stewardship (*oikonomos*) in 1 Corinthians 4:1, 2, and especially in the Pastoral Letters, either explicitly as in Titus 1:7 or implicitly as in 1 Timothy 3:4–5, 12; 2 Timothy 2:24. The image of the steward doubtless derives from the gospel parables on stewardship. Cf. C. Spicq, "L'origine évangélique des vertus épiscopales," *RB* 53 (1946), pp. 36–46.

18. Cf. G. Schrenk, "eklogē," *TDNT* 4:176–78.

19. Cf. J. Pfammatter, *Die Kirche als Bau: Eine exegetisch-theologische Studie zur Ekklesiologie der Paulusbriefe* (Rome, 1960), pp. 78–97.

20. Cf. C. Journet, *The Church of the Word Incarnate: An Essay in Speculative Theology* 1: *The Apostolic Hierarchy,* trans. by A. H. C. Downes (New York, 1955), pp. 127–28; idem, "De la collégialité," *Nova et Vetera* 44 (1969), pp. 161–66.

21. Cf. our lttle book, *Le discours sur le pain de vie* (Paris, 1967), pp. 90–91.

22. Cf., e.g., M.-E. Boismard, *St. John's Prologue,* trans. by Carisbrooke Domincans (Westminster, Md., 1957), on this passage; for the opposite interpretation, cf. our book *Le Prologue du Quatrième Evangile* (Paris-Bruges, 1968), pp. 114–15.

23. Cf. his "L'arrière fond du thème johannique de vérité," *StEv* 1:277–94; and "La verità in S. Giovanni," *RivB* 11 (1963), pp. 3–24.

24. A number of texts from Qumran might be added here; translations are from *The Dead Sea Scriptures,* trans. by T. H. Gaster (rev. ed., New York, 1964). For example, the same meaning of the word "truth" is found in the Thanksgiving Psalms (1 QH) 7:26–27: "I give thanks unto Thee, O Lord, for Thou hast given me insight into Thy truth and knowledge of Thy wondrous secrets" (Gaster, p. 165). Cf. also the Manuel of Discipline (1 QS) 1:15: "ordinances of God's truth" (p. 47); 5:10: "majority of their co-covenanters who have volunteered together to adhere to the truth of God" (p. 55); 6:15: "to return to the truth" (p. 58); 9:18: "God's inscrutable wonders and truth" (p. 68). Cf. O. Betz, *Offenbarung und Schriftforschung in der*

Qumransekte (Tübingen, 1960), pp. 53–61; J. Murphy-O'Connor, "La vérité dans saint Paul et à Qumran," *RB* 72 (1965), pp. 23–76.

25. Cf. A. Robert, "Le sens du mot 'loi' dans le Psaume CXIX," *RB* 46 (1937), pp. 182–205.

26. Cf. J. Blank, "Der johanneische Wahrheits-Begriff," *BZ* 7 (1963), pp. 163–73.

27. Cf. Brown, op. cit., p. 745.

28. The author of the fourth gospel does not put on Christ's lips the christological title of Logos; as has often been observed, this is evidence of his honesty and shows that he was able to distinguish between his personal teaching and the teaching of Christ; cf. my *Le Prologue du Quatrième Evangile*, p. 219.

29. *Evangile selon saint Jean*, p. 448.

30. Thüsing, op. cit., p. 103.

31. This is our own translation of this difficult passage, and it allows us to abstract from the dispute over the true reading. The manuscripts leave us unsure of the preposition after *hodagein: eis* with the accusative case according to Codex Vaticanus and Codex Alexandrinus, *en* with the dative case according to the Codex Sinaiticus, the Beza Codex, and the Vetus Latina. Among modern commentators. Westcott, Lagrange, Bernard, Bultmann, Braun, Grundmann, and Michaelis prefer *en*. Against *eis* it is objected that the truth cannot be a goal toward which the Paraclete leads, since he is himself the truth; *en* is preferable and signifies the sphere within which the action of the Paraclete takes place. I. de la Potterie answers that, far from indicating simply a direction, *eis* also means that the movement ends within the place toward which one is moving. Cf. his "Le Paraclet," *Assemblées du Seigneur* 47 (1963), p. 45, n. 1. Cf. Brown, op. cit., p. 707.

32. Cf. our study, "De munere doctrinali a Paraclito in Ecclesia expleto iuxta Evangelium Sancti Iohannis," in *De Sacra Scriptura et Traditione*, published by the Pontificia Academia Marialis Internationalis (Rome, 1963), pp. 130–34.

33. Cf. Brown, op. cit., p. 766; P. Evdokimov, "L'Esprit-Saint et la prière pour l'unité," *VC* 14 (1960), pp. 250–64.

34. Lagrange, op. cit. p. 447

35. Cf. especially O. Cullmann, *Dieu et César* (Neuchâtel-Paris, 1956), pp. 5–53. Cf. the same author's *Jesus and the Revolutionaries*, trans. by Gareth Putnam (New York, 1970); M. Hengel, *Die Zeloten* (Leiden-Cologne, 1961); G. Baumbach, "Zeloten und Sikarien," *TLZ* 90 (1965), pp. 727–40.

36. In Chapter 3, above, we raised the important question: How are we to conceive of the Servant's mission? Was it partly political in character?

37. *Le judaïsme avant Jésus-Christ* (Paris, 1931), p. 469.

38. Cf. my *Johannine Studies,* trans. by Thomas E. Crane (Staten Island, N.Y., 1964), p. 124.

39. For a balanced view that avoids both anti-sacramentalism and pan-sacramentalism, cf. Brown, op. cit., pp. cxi–cxiv.

40. "Le discours de la Cène," *RSR* 2 (1911), p. 538.

41. *Evangile selon saint Jean,* p. 449.

42. Cf. Allo, op. cit., on this passage.

43. We are here following very closely P. Grelot, op. cit., pp. 125–28.

44. The piling up of cultic terms in this text is worthy of note. There is, to begin with, *prosphora* or sacrificial offering. The word *leitourgos* can also be used of civil functionaries (as in Rm. 13:6), but its sacral or cultic meaning is emphasized in Hebrews (*leitourgein* in 10:11; *leitourgia* in 8:6 and 9:21; *leitourgos* in 8:2), as well as in the letter of Clement and in the Didache; cf. H. Strathmann and R. Mayer, "leitourgō," *TDNT* 4:219–31. Finally, while in 4 M 3:20 and 8:8 the terms *hierourgeō* and *hierourgos* signify the holy service of the law, Philo uses *hierourgeō* chiefly of sacrificial rites; cf. G. Schrenk, "hierourgeō," *TDNT* 3:252.

45. Despite the opinion of some commentators, e.g., M. R. Vincent, *Philippians and Philemon* (Edinburgh, 1899), p. 71, the preceding verse, in which St. Paul says that "this would mean that I had not run in the race and exhausted myself for nothing" (Ph. 2:16), shows that the words "sacrifice" and "offering" refer not to the faith shown by the Philippians but to St. Paul's missionary work which gave rise to that faith. For this interpretation, cf. P. Grelot, op. cit., pp. 126–27; at an earlier date, St. Thomas Aquinas, *Super Epistolam ad Philippenses lectura,* n. 85; M. Dibelius, *An die Philipper* (Tübingen, 1937), p. 83; J. Huby, *Les épîtres de la captivité* (Paris, 1935), p. 321.

46. Grelot, op. cit., p. 129.

47. This was the view of several ancient writers: Origen, Athanasius, Ambrose, Bernard, Thomas Aquinas, and of some modern exegetes: Knabenbauer, Fillion, etc. But other writers and exegetes in antiquity realized that "to sanctify" here means "to consecrate" and predestine to the prophetic ministry (Ephraem, Theodoret, Maldonatus, Eslices). Cf. A. Condamin, *Le livre de Jérémie* (Paris, 1920), p. 2.

48. *Méditations sur l'Evangile: La Cène,* 2nd part, 56th day: "Jésus as sanctifie lui-même."

49. Lagrange, op. cit., p. 449.

50. Brown, op. cit., pp. 180–81.

51. Cf. Lagrange, op. cit., p. 113.

52. [The translation in the Jerusalem Bible does not always reflect this verbal distinction; but the author's discussion of the various passages will make it clear which Greek word, or French word (*véritable* and *vrai* respectively), lies behind the "true" of the Jerusalem Bible.—Tr.]

53. Cf. C. Trench, *Synonymes du Nouveau Testament* (Paris, 1869), pp. 29–33; Feuillet, *Le Prologue du Quatrième Evangile,* pp. 64–65.

54. Cf. here the excellent note of the Jerusalem Bible, p. 153, n. h.

55. *The Fourth Gospel* (London, 1940), p. 493.

56. "'Damit alle eins seien' (XVII, 20–26)," *Sein und Sendung* 28 (1963), p. 544.

57. A Jew, addressing God in the liturgy, might have said *abbi* (my Father), but not simply *abba.* Cf. J. Jeremias, "Kennzeichen der ipsissima vox Jesu," in *Synoptische Studien A. Wikenhauser dargebracht* (Munich, 1958), pp. 86–93; J. Kittel, "abba," *TDNT* 1:5–6; A. Richardson, *An Introduction to the Theology of the New Testament* (New York, 1958), p. 149.

58. Brown, op. cit., pp. 772–73.

59. The word *ponēros* can be taken as an abstract for moral evil. But comparison with 1 John 2:13–14; 3:12; 5:18–19 suggests that it refers to the evil one, the devil.

60. Lagrange, op. cit., p. 445.

61. For this view, cf. J. Coppens, "Le messianisme sacerdotal dans le Nouveau Testament," in *La venue du Messie: Messianisme et eschatologie* (Recherches bibliques 6; Bruges, 1962), pp. 106–7.

62. Cf. G. Richter, *Die Fusswaschung im Johannesevangelium* (Regensburg, 1967). The author studies the washing of the feet as interpreted by the Father, the Middle Ages, the Enlightenment (mid-seventeenth century to the first third of the eighteenth), the period of liberalism (first third of the eighteenth century to the end of the First World War), and the modern period (end of the First World War to the present).

63. Cf., e.g., Sts. Jerome, Ambrose, and Bernard (Richter, ibid., pp. 29–31, 79).

64. Cf. F. Spitta, *Das Johannes-Evangelium als Quelle der Ge-*

schichte Jesu (Göttingen, 1910), p. 289; W. Bauer, *Das Johannesevangelium* (Tübingen, 1933), pp. 169–73; R. Bultmann, *The Gospel of John*, pp. 466–73 for the first interpretation and pp. 474–79 for the second; M.-E. Boismard, "Le lavement des pieds (Jn. XIII, 1–17)," *RB* 71 (1964), pp. 5–24.

65. Cf. C. Spicq, *Agapè dans le Nouveau Testament: Analyse des textes* 3 (Paris, 1967), pp. 143–49.

66. Cf. Boismard, art. cit., pp. 10–13. Boismard thinks that even the verb *nipsasthai* (to be washed) was added later and that the original text said simply: "He who has bathed has no need [sc. of washing]."

67. Cf. Brown, op. cit., p. 592.

68. Cf. F.-M. Braun, "Le lavement des pieds et la résponse de Jésus à saint Pierre (Jn. XIII, 4–10)," *RB* 44 (1935), pp. 22–33.

69. Cf. Brown, op. cit., p. 551.

70. Cf. our "Le logion sur la rançon," *RSPT* 51 (1967), pp. 365–402. In this study we suggested the following hypotheses. Since Luke 22:25–26, addressed to those who in fact have authority in the community, does not really answer the question raised in Verse 24: "Who is the greatest?" we thought the verses might be a fragment from the episode about the sons of Zebedee in Matthew and Mark; the third evangelist would then have rewritten the fragment in a better Greek style and put it in a different context. On the other hand, Luke 22:27: "Who is the greater, the one at table or the one who serves?" fits perfectly with Verse 24 and reminds us of the washing of the feet in John 13:1–10, which is inseparable from the Last Supper context.

71. Lagrange, op. cit., p. 358.

72. Bultmann, op. cit., p. 468, n. 6.

73. Cf. F. Dreyfus, "Le thème de l'héritage dans l'Ancien Testament," *RSPT* 42 (1958), pp. 3–49.

74. Boismard, art. cit., pp. 9–10, 15–17.

75. The parable of the steward in Matthew 24:45–51 says that if the steward is conscientious he will share in the full powers of his master (Verse 47), but if he is dishonest his lot, or share (*meros*), will be with the "hypocrites"; that is, the evil spiritual leaders of the Jewish people.

76. This is not the place for a detailed study of this difficult text and the corresponding passage in the first gospel (Mt. 19:28). The participle *krinontes* in Luke signifies the exercise of a permanent power, just as *esthēte* and *pinēte* (eat and drink) signify the enjoyment of a state of permanent happiness. It is clear that the twelve tribes

of Israel are an image of the Church's universality. On the other hand, as P. Joüon observes in connection with Verse 29 ("confer a kingdom on you"), in his *L'Evangile de Notre Seigneur Jésus-Christ* (Paris, 1930), p. 436: "The thrones are those of kings, not of judges, since judgment is wholly reserved to the Son (Jn. 5:22)." As in the Book of Judges, "to judge" here means "to govern"; cf. our essay, "Le triomphe eschatologique de Jésus d'après quelques textes isolés des Evangiles," *NRT* 71 (1949), pp. 715–22.

77. Thurian, op. cit., p. 29.

78. "Die Fusswaschung," *ZNTW* 38 (1939), pp. 74–94; cf. G. Richter, op. cit., p. 238.

79. The reading *lusanti* ("has unbound, or liberated, us") is much better attested than the reading *lousanti* ("has washed us"). It is also preferred by the majority of critics; cf. R. H. Charles, *A Critical and Exegetical Commentary on the Revelation of St. John* (New York, 1920), 1:15. But the reading "has washed" is kept in the Jerusalem Bible.

80. Cf. our essay, "L'Hymne christologique de l'Epître aux Philippiens," *RB* 72 (1965), pp. 352–80, 481–507.

81. Cf. C. Spicq, *Les Epîtres de saint Pierre* (Paris, 1966), p. 171; A. Feuillet, "Quelques réflexions sur le quatrième évangile à propos d'un livre récent," *Bulletin du Comité des Etudes de la Compagnie de Saint Sulpice* 11 (1969), pp. 244–45. It is worth noting that this reminiscence of John is closely connected with numerous other more or less clear allusions to the gospels: humble yourselves so that God may lift you up (5:6; cf. Mt. 23:12; Lk. 14:11; 18:14); cast all your cares upon God (5:7; cf. Mt. 6:25–32; Lk. 12:22–31); be sober and keep watch (5:8a; cf. Lk. 12:22–37); the murderous devil is on the prowl (5:8b; cf. Jn. 8:44; 12:31; 14:30; Lk. 22:31); you must resist him by remaining firm in faith (5:9; cf. Lk. 22:32). This patchwork of gospel echoes supposes lengthy reflection on the words of Jesus by the leader of the apostles.

82. Cf. P. Benoit, *The Passion and Resurrection of Jesus Christ*, translated by Benet Weatherhead (New York, 1969), pp. 284–86, where the narratives of John and Luke are compared. Benoit thinks that Luke makes use of the Johannine tradition as it already existed in its early form and that he adapted it to his own purposes.

83. Cf. R. Bultmann, op. cit., pp. 691–92; Brown, op. cit., p. 1021. Cf. also W. C. van Unnik, "Dominus vobiscum: The Background of a Liturgical Formula," in *New Testament Essays: Studies in Memory of T. W. Manson* (Manchester, 1959), pp. 270–305. The author

reaches two conclusions: When the verb is expressed, the nuance of certainty is more important than that of wishing; when the verb is not expressed, we usually have a declaration, not a wish.

84. In addition to the commentaries, cf. J. Schmitt, "Simples remarques sur le fragment John XX, 22–23," in *Mélanges en honneur de Mgr Michel Andrieu* (Strasbourg, 1956), pp. 415–23.

85. Cf. C. H. Dodd, *The Interpretation of the Fourth Gospel* (Cambridge, (1953), p. 430, who thinks that the evangelist is here giving not his own theology of the Spirit (as found in the farewell discourses) but a tradition of different origin.

86. *The Dead Sea Scriptures,* trans. by T. H. Gaster, p. 53.

87. Schmitt, art. cit., p. 420.

88. Ibid., pp. 420–21.

89. Session 14, Canon 3; cf. *The Church Teaches,* p. 315.

90. Cf. Brown, op. cit., p. 1042.

91. The preceding lines are based on a set of data that we cannot present here; we refer the reader to our essay, "L'*exousia* du Fils de l'homme (d'après Mc II, 10–28 par.)," *RSR* 42 (1954), pp. 161–92.

92. Cf., e.g., Th. Zahn, *Das Evangelium des Johannes* (Leipzig, 1912), p. 679.

93. For the same view, cf. J. R. Mantey, "The Mistranslation of the Perfect Tense in John 20:23, Mt. 16:19, and Mt. 18:18," *JBL* 58 (1939), pp. 243–49; Mantey's interpretation is challenged by H. J. Cadbury, "The Meaning of John 20:23, Matthew 16:19, and Matthew 18:18," ibid., pp. 251–54. Cf. Brown, op. cit., p. 1024.

94. Cf. F. Blass and A. Debrunner, *A Greek Grammar of the New Testament and Other Early Christian Literature,* translated and revised by R. W. Funk (Chicago, 1961), p. 177, n. 344.

95. Cf. C. Spicq, *Théologie morale du Nouveau Testament* (Paris, 1965), p. 176, n. 5.

96. Cf. A Schlatter, *Der Evangelist Matthäus* (Stuttgart, 1948), pp. 509–10.

97. Benoit, op. cit., pp. 325–26.

98. According to J. A. Emerton, "Binding and Loosing—Forgiving and Retaining," *JTS* 13 (1962), pp. 325–31, the words "bind" and "loose," being linked with the power of the keys, are an echo of Isaiah 22:22, where Eliakim is made chief steward of the king: "I place the key of the House of David on his shoulder; should he open, no one shall close; should he close, no one shall open." Consequently, the original words of Jesus may have been: "Every time you close, it will be closed; every time you open, it will be opened." Matthew then

changed the language of Jesus to conform to well-known Jewish formulas. John, for his part, applied the words to sin and used terms that would be more intelligible to Greeks than the language of the first gospel would be. Cf. Brown, op. cit., pp. 1039–40.

99. P. Gaechter, *Das Matthäus-Evangelium* (Innsbruck—Vienna—Munich, 1963), p. 601, draws the same conclusion from the fact that in Matthew 16:16 the power of binding and loosing is conferred only on Peter; if it is given to a group in Matthew 18:18, this group can only be the apostles, not the whole community. And, indeed, the similarity of these three texts—Matthew 16:16; 18:18; 28:18–20—confirms the conclusion. For all three refer to Daniel 7. The vision of the Son of Man in Daniel 7 is very important for understanding the New Testament conception of the Church. Cf. F. Kattenbusch, "Der Quellort der Kirchenidee," in *Festgabe Adolf von Harnack* (Tübingen, 1921), pp. 143–72. In Daniel's vision, the saints of the Most High, who make war on earth, share the privileges of the heavenly Son of Man. In three passages of Matthew and in John 20:19–23, Christ, once he has risen and been glorified, ratifies in heaven what is done on earth by those invested with his mission and authority.

100. Second Council of Constantinople, Canon 12; cf. *The Church Teaches*, pp. 178–79. Against the view that the gift of the Spirit in John 20:23 is simply a symbolic preparation for Pentecost, cf. P. Schanz, *Das Evangelium des heiligen Johannes* (Tübingen, 1885), p. 575; F. Godet, *Commentaire sur l'évangile de saint Jean* (reissue; Neuchâtel, 1962), 3:496.

101. *Résurrection de Jésus et message pascal* (Paris, 1971), p. 239.

102. *La Pentecôte johannique (Jn. XX, 19–23)* (Valence-sur-Rhône, 1939). For a critique of this book, cf. P. Benoit, *RB* 56 (1946), pp. 297–300.

103. R. Bultmann, op. cit., pp. 690–93, believes that for John, Easter and Pentecost are one event; therefore he forces the correspondence between John 20:19–23 and the promises of the Paraclete. According to Brown, op. cit., pp. 1038–39, both Luke and John are speaking of the same gift of the Spirit, which each situates after Christ's return to the Father but conceives in a different way.

104. Lagrange, op. cit., p. 515.

105. Cf. our "La recherche du Christ dans la nouvelle alliance d'après la christophanie de Jn. XX, 11–18," in *L'Homme devant Dieu: Mélanges H. de Lubac* (Paris, 1963), 3:98–99. However, if John 20:17 refers to an invisible ascension of Christ, a difficulty arises: Are we to conclude that only the appearance to Mary Magdalene took

place *before* this ascension, and all the others *after?* B. Schwank does not hesitate to draw this conclusion, in "Das leere Grab (XX, 1–18)," *Sein und Sendung* 29 (1964), pp. 388–400. Brown, op, cit., pp. 1014–15, maintains, however, that in John's own thinking resurrection and ascension are one event and that the words "I am ascending to my Father" in 20:17 should not be taken as determining the time of the ascension but simply as a theological statement connecting ascension and resurrection.

106. Benoit, op. cit., p. 324.

107. "Apostolique et Pneumatique selon saint Jean," *RT* 71 (1971), pp. 459–60.

108. If we stick to the letter of Acts, the beneficiaries of Pentecost are the 120 persons mentioned in 1:15–16. But we may ask whether 1:13–14 is not the original introduction to the account in Chapter 2; in this case, the beneficiaries of Pentecost are the apostles, a few women (among them the Virgin Mary), and the "brothers" of Jesus; cf. *Les Actes des Apôtres* (Bible de Jérusalem) (2nd ed.; Paris, 1958), p. 41, n. b.

109. *The Gospel According to St. John* (London, 1882), p. 294.

110. *Jesus Christ: His Life, His Teaching, and His Work*, trans. by J. J. Heenan (Milwaukee, 1950), p. 433.

111. The Jerusalem Bible translates: "It is as if God were appealing through us." The translation is debatable. E. B. Allo, *Seconde Epître aux Corinthiens* (Paris, 1937), p. 171, writes: "The particle *hōs* here, as frequently when followed by a genitive absolute construction, does not mean 'as' or 'as if' (cf. Toussaint and others) but 'inasmuch as,' 'seeing that' (Plummer and others)."

112. Allo, ibid., p. 172.

113. *Die Offenbarung Johannis* (Göttingen, 1906), p. 239.

114. How was the universe thus represented? Probably by means of the fullness of the robes, their colors and adornment. Cf. E. Tobac, *Les cinq livres de Salomon* (Brussels-Paris, 1926), p. 171; J. Weber, "Le Livre de la Sagesse," in *La Sainte Bible de Pirot* 6 (Paris, 1943), p. 523.

115. *The Revelation of St. John the Divine* (London, 1966), p. 25.

116. *L'Apocalypse de saint Jean* (Paris, 1913), p. 12.

117. Cf. our book, *L'Heure de la Mère de Dieu* (Prouilhe, 1970), pp. 57–59.

118. Cf. our *L'Apocalypse: Etat de la question* (Paris, 1962), pp. 71–73: "Le caractère liturgique de l'Apocalypse."

119. Most commentaries apply Revelation 7:15 to heavenly life in

the world to come. Allo, *L'Apocalypse,* p. 126, thinks otherwise; referring to the eternal life which, according to the fourth gospel, is already begun on earth, he writes: " 'Night and day' is to be taken in a purely figurative sense, as in 4:8, to mean that praise is uninterrupted. But we may note that in Chapters 21–22, which show so many analogies with the present passage, it is expressly said that there is no more temple (21:22) or night (21:25; 22:5)." Cf. also H. B. Swete, *The Apocalypse of St. John* (New York, 1907), p. 104.

120. "L'Apocalypse," in *La Sainte Bible de Pirot* 12:665.

121. A list of the chief defenders of these various positions can be found in C. Brütsch, *La clarté de l'Apocalypse* (Geneva, 1966), pp. 44–45. For Allo's explanation, cf. his *L'Apocalypse,* Excursus 5, pp. 33–35.

122. *Die Offenbarung des Johannes* (Leipzig, 1924) 1:209–10.

123. Some references for the view that identifies the leaders of the Churches with the hierarchic leaders: J. Weiss, *Die Offenbarung des Johannes* (Göttingen, 1904), p. 49, n. 1; Th. Zahn, *Die Offenbarung des Johannes* (Leipzig, 1924) 1:209–25; H. L. Strack and P. Billerbeck, *Kommentar zum Neuen Testament aus Talmud und Midrasch* (Munich, 1922–61) 3:791; W. Hadorn, *Die Offenbarung des Johannes* (Leipzig, 1928), pp. 38–39; J. Colson, *L'Evêque dans les communautés primitives* (Unam Sanctam 21; Paris, 1951), pp. 87–90; P. Ketter, *Die Apokalypse* (Freiburg, 1953), pp. 50–51; W. H. Brownlee, "The Priestly Character of the Church in the Apocalypse," *NTS* 5 (1958–59), pp. 224–25; M. Thurian, "L'organisation du ministère dans l'Eglise primitive selon saint Ignace d'Antioche," *VC* 21 (1967), pp. 28–29; A. Lemaire, *Les ministères aux origines de l'Eglise* (Paris, 1971), pp. 118–22.

124. Not only is the thought of the Book of Daniel different from that of the Apocalypse; it is also peculiar to Daniel, and it is incorrect to liken some other passages of the Old Testament (Jos. 5:14; Dt. 22:8 LXX; Is. 24:21–22; Si. 17:17 v.g.) to Daniel 10:12–13, for none of the former passages speak of angels who protect the various nations. Daniel shows us such angels in conflict with each other; Michael protects the people of God; he and Gabriel are victorious over the guardian angels of Persia and Greece. How is such a strange conflict among the angels possible? Since the prophet learns of it in a vision, it should be taken not as a real event in the heavenly realm and but as a symbolic statement of the rivalry between nations on earth and of the victory of Israel over the pagan nations that threaten her existence. For this interpretation, cf. H. Junker, *Untersuchungen über literarische*

und exegetische Probleme des Buches Daniel (Bonn, 1932), p. 100;
J. Goettesberger, *Das Buch Daniel* (Bonn, 1928), pp. 78–80; L. Denne-
feld, "Les Grands Prophètes," in *La Sainte Bible de Pirot* 7 (Paris,
1946), pp. 695–96. This is a concept that has absolutely no application
to the letters of the Apocalypse. In addition, we must record the valuable observation of J. de Menasce, *Daniel* (Bible de Jérusalem; 2nd
ed.; Paris, 1958), p. 83: "St. Jerome interprets this passage (10:13) to
mean that the Prince of Persia is an evil angel who prevents the liberation of the Israelites. But St. Thomas, following St. Gregory and
adopting a view that is more in conformity with what Scripture tells
us of the angels who protect the nations, explains that a conflict can
exist not between angelic wills—which are all conformed to God's
will—but between the ways in which the angels judge the respective
merits of the nations, since the secret of these merits can be known,
even by the angels, only through a divine revelation."

125. We have stressed this point and supplied examples of it in our
essay, "La moisson et la vendange de l'Apocalypse (XIV, 14–20):
La signification chrétienne de la révélation johannique," *NRT* 94
(1972), pp. 113–32, 225–50.

126. For what follows we refer the reader to C. Spicq, *Les Epîtres
Pastorales* 1 (4th ed.; Paris, 1969), pp. 70–74, for all the necessary remarks and an extensive bibliography.

127. We prescind from Isaiah 42:19 where the *mal'ak* Yahweh is
Israel: "Who . . . so deaf as the messenger I send?"

128. Concerning this passage of Ecclesiastes, the meaning of which
is much disputed, we cannot do better than reproduce the remarks of
E. Podechard, *L'Ecclésiaste* (Paris, 1912), p. 339, with which we are
in full agreement: "Some commentators, following St. Jerome, translate the term by 'angel' (L. Herzfeld, D. Ginsberg, G. Gietmann). Others (E. Renan, V. Zapletal) suppose the existence of a temple messenger whose function is to write down vows and determine what is due on
this score. But most exegetes (G. Zirkel, G. Genesius, A. Knobel,
H. Ewald, E. Elster, P. Kleinert, D. Delitzch, A. Motais, Ch. H. H.
Wright, W. Nowack, R. Ruetschi, C. Siegfried, G. Wildeboer) rightly
maintain that a priest is meant. In Nehemiah 2:7 the same title, in a
fuller form, is given to the priest insofar as he has a teaching function
(cf. ibid., Verses 6 and 8), just as it is given to the prophets who are
charged with communicating a divine message (Haggai 1:13). The
same title here refers to the priest as exercising a ministry of teaching.
This at least is what emerges from Ecclesiastes 5:4–5 as a whole,
since it supposes a discussion between the priest and the author of the

vow as to the validity of the latter or the compensation due for its not being carried out. Ecclesiastes 4:17, no less instructive, shows us the priest-teacher at work in the temple: "Go near [to the priest who is teaching] so that you can hear; the sacrifice is more valuable than the offering of fools." We know from other sources (Lv. 27:8, 12, 14, 18, 23) that priests were to see to the fulfillment of vows. We may recall, furthermore, that the substantive *mel'akah* is used to signify the exercise of priestly functions (Ne. 13:30; 1 Ch. 9:3; 2 Ch. 29:34) or Levitical functions (Ne. 13:10, 30; 1 Ch. 23:4; 2 Ch. 13:10)."

129. Exegetes have looked far afield, even into the pagan world, for the source of the title "morning star" which also occurs in 2 Peter 1:19. Very possibly it is taken from Numbers 24:17: "A star from Jacob takes the leadership." In Revelation 22:16 it is connected with the christological titles "line and root of David" which undoubtedly derive from Isaiah 11:1, as is shown by H. B. Swete, *The Apocalypse of St. John,* p. 309, and R. H. Charles, *A Critical and Exegetical Commentary on the Revelation of St. John* 2:219. Numbers 24:17 and Isaiah 11:1–4 are also linked in the Collection of Benedictions from Qumran, col. 5, ll. 21–28 (cf. *The Dead Sea Scriptures,* trans. by T. H. Gaster, Blessing E, pp. 103–4), although in the latter text the image of the scepter, not the star, is kept. Some exegetes express amazement that Christ should promise the morning star in Revelation 2:28. Allo resolves the difficulty by reminding the reader of John 6 where Christ gives himself in the eucharist; cf. also P. Prigent, *Apocalypse et liturgie* (Neuchâtel, 1964), pp. 25–27.

130. *L'Apocalypse,* p. 45.

131. A very objective and detailed exposition of this question is given by F.-M. Braun, *Jean le théologien et son évangile dans l'ancienne Eglise* (Paris, 1959). Braun rightly maintains that the fourth gospel must have had a very complex prehistory; that a long period must have intervened between the moment when the kerygma of John crystallized into small literary units and the final redaction; that John must have used congenial disciples as secretaries in adapting his gospel to hellenized readers; and that the work was finished only after the apostle's death. We also refer the reader to Robert-Feuillet, *Introduction to the New Testament,* pp. 632–48, on the author of the fourth gospel; pp. 677–80, on the author of the first letter and the similarities and dissimilarities between this letter and the fourth gospel; pp. 687–89, on the authenticity of the last two Johannine letters. Cf. Brown, op. cit., pp. lxxxvii–xcvii; Brown's prudent conclusion (p. xcviii): "There are, then, quite clearly, difficulties to be faced if one

identifies the BD [Beloved Disciple] as John son of Zebedee. However, in our personal opinion, there are even more serious difficulties if he is identified as John Mark, as Lazarus, or as some unknown. When all is said and done, the combination of external and internal evidence associating the Fourth Gospel with John son of Zebedee makes this the strongest hypothesis, if one is prepared to give credence to the Gospel's claim of an eyewitness source." J. Colson, in his *L'enigme du disciple que Jésus aimait* (Paris, 1969), wrongly objects to this view; we think his own position untenable and propose to deal with some aspects of it on another occasion.

132. *Geschichte der altchristlichen Literatur bis Eusebius* II: *Die Chronologie* 1 (Leipzig, 1897), p. 675, n. 1.

133. *L'Antéchrist* (Paris, 1871), p. 25.

134. *Die Offenbarung des Johannes* (Tübingen, 1933), pp. 202–3.

135. On this difficult problem, cf. Robert-Feuillet, op. cit., pp. 637–39.

136. Ph. H. Menoud, *L'Evangile de Jean d'après les recherches récentes* (Neuchâtel-Paris, 1947), p. 76.

137. *L'Apocalypse, le dernier livre de la Bible,* translated from the 5th German ed. by Jean-Luc Pidoux (Paris, 1959), p. 63.

138. Cf. J. Michl, *Die Ältesten in der Apokalypse des Hl Johannes* (Munich, 1938); A. Feuillet, "Les vingt-quatre vieillards de l'Apocalypse," *RB* 65 (1958), pp. 9–11.

139. According to 1 Timothy 1:2, Timothy is head of the Church at Ephesus; a little later, he is to join Paul who is a prisoner at Rome (2 Tm. 4:9, 21). Hebrews 13:23 tells us that Timothy has been freed from an imprisonment concerning which we have no further information: "I want you to know that our brother Timothy has been set free." It is almost certain that this Timothy is the Timothy of the Pastoral Letters, Paul's well-known companion. The rest of Timothy's life must have been spent at Ephesus, but we know little of it; cf. C. Spicq, *Les Epîtres Pastorales* 1:51.

140. The attributes of Christ mentioned at the beginning of each letter seem chosen "to correspond to some characteristic of the Church being addressed" (Allo, *L'Apocalypse,* p. 32). But it is not always easy to see wherein the correspondence lies.

141. The liturgical allusion remains even if one adopts a purely eschatological interpretation of the promises. On the relationship between the tree of life and John 6, cf. our little book *Le discours sur le pain de vie* (Paris, 1967), p. 41. On the probable reference to the eucharist in the morning star image, cf. Allo, op. cit., p. 45; P. Prigent, op. cit., pp. 26–27.

142. Extraordinary and non-transmissible powers were given to the apostles to the extent that Christ wanted them to be, under him, the very foundation on the Church (cf. Ep. 2:20; Rv. 21:18–21). The distinction between two kinds of power—transmissible and non-transmissible—is traditional and solidly based on Scripture. From the distinction it follows immediately that the bishops do not stand in the same relation to the Pope as the apostles did to Peter; as apostles, Peter, James, John, and Paul were in some ways equal, according to St. Thomas Aquinas, Cajetan, and John of St. Thomas. This should be kept in mind when speaking of the famous incident at Antioch; cf. the two references to C. Journet in note 20, above.

143. We follow here chiefly the richly documented study of C. Spicq, op. cit., Vol. 1, Excursus 9: "Imposition des mains et ordination de Timothée."

144. We have here an authentic sacrament, which, as A. Lemonnyer puts it, "gives rise to the ecclesiastical hierarchy" ("Charismes," *DBS* 1:1243). A. Boudou, in his *Les Epîtres Pastorales* (Paris, 1950), p. 150, n. 1, quotes Harnack's judgment in his *The Constitution and Law of the Church in the First Two Centuries,* trans. by F. L. Pogson (London, 1910), p. 26: "That the laying on of hands was regarded as conferring the charisma necessary to the office is obvious from the passages in Timothy, and it is improbable that these express only a later idea."

145. Cf. Spicq., op. cit., 2:728–29.

146. Cf. J. Jeremias, *"Presbyterion* ausserchristlich bezeugt," *ZNTW* 48 (1957), pp. 127–33; idem, "Zur Datierung der Pastoralbriefe," *ZNTW* 52 (1961), pp. 101–4; idem, *Die Briefe an Timotheus und Titus* (8th ed.; Tübingen, 1963), p. 30; C. K. Barrett, *The Pastoral Epistles* (Oxford, 1963), p. 72; A. Lemaire, op. cit., pp. 129–30.

147. We use here, with a few slight changes, the translation of J. Chaine in his *Les Epîtres Catholiques* (Paris, 1939), which is more literal than that of the Jerusalem Bible. The comparison we make has already been suggested by A. Lemaire, op. cit., pp. 118–19. (The English translation has been based directly, and rather literally, on Feuillet's French text.—Tr.)

148. The Greek text has the verb *propempein* (send on ahead; then: escort, accompany on a journey), which expresses the action of a local community on behalf of an itinerant minister: Acts 15:3; 20:38; 21:5; Romans 15:24; 16:6, 11; 2 Corinthians 1:16; Titus 3:13. Cf. A. Lemaire, op. cit., p. 116, n. 1; C. Spicq, op. cit., 1:134, p. 324.

149. *The Johannine Epistles* (London, 1953), p. 161; cf., to the same effect, A. Lemaire, ibid., p. 117.

150. The verb *philoprōteuein,* "to love to be first," is found nowhere else. But profane Greek has the noun *philoprōteia* and the adjective *philoprōtos.* Diotrephes "does not ambition the highest place, since his conduct shows that he is a leader of the community; but he likes to display his authority, and thus exercises an ambitious kind of domination over the faithful of his Church" (J. Chaine, op. cit., p. 256).

151. What follows simply reproduces the valuable notations of Lemaire, op. cit., pp. 118–22. But on one point we disagree. In 2:20 the reading "your wife Jezabel" cannot be retained. Almost all critics reject it and for good reasons: (1) it is poorly attested; (2) like Balaam in 2:24, Jezabel is a symbolic name taken from the Old Testament and is to be interpreted either as a pure symbol or as a reference to an unknown prophetess or group; (3) since the preceding verse already has "your" (*sou*) three times, we may think, with Bousset and Allo, that the *sou* was added here through the distraction of a copyist.

152. Cf. J. Dupont, *Les discours de Milet* (Paris, 1962), pp. 106–7; C. Spicq, op. cit., 1:341.

153. We are thinking here chiefly of two rather interesting studies: A. Jaubert, "L'image de la colonne: 1 Tm. III, 15," *SPCIC* 2:104–8; and J. Murphy-O'Connor, "La vérité chez saint Paul et à Qumrân," *RB* 72 (1965), pp. 67–69. We think that in 1 Timothy 3:15 an application of it to the Church is by far the most plausible. But Jaubert is right in emphasizing the fact that the image of the pillar is usually applied to individuals; thus, male children are the pillars of a household (Euripides, *Iphigenia in Tauris* 57); Jeremiah is an iron pillar (Jr. 1:13); Abraham is a pillar amid the pagan world (Philo, *De migratione* 121); Attala is the pillar and support of the Christians at Lyons (with reference to 1 Tm. 3:15; Eusebius, *Historia Ecclesiastica* V, 1:17, p. 43).

154. Ephesus, now only a village, was the principal city of Asia Minor at the time of the Apocalypse. Its site was shifted several times, and Christ's threat may allude to this fact: "Repent . . . or else, if you will not repent, I shall come to you and take your lamp-stand from its place." But the threat must be interpreted in Christian terms, as with Allo, op. cit., pp. 34–35: "If fervor lessens and enthusiasm fades, as the letters to Timothy seem to indicate has already happened, the influence of Ephesus as mother Church of Asia will disappear; her torch will no longer flame at the heart of this group of Churches. It is much better to interpret the threat in this fashion than to translate, with Grotius and Ramsay, 'I will change your location once again and force your people to go elsewhere,' for, even though such an ingenious allu-

sion to successive changes of site is possible, geographical displacement as such is not a spiritual threat directly affecting the Church."

155. On this point, cf. the excellent remarks of K. L. Schmidt, "ekklēsia," *TDNT* 3:506–7.

156. Cf. L. Poirier, *Les sept lettres, ou le premier septénaire prophétique de l'Apocalypse* (Montreal, 1943). The author rightly points out that, far more than the other New Testament letters, the letters in the Apocalypse remind us of the preaching of the prophets and especially of the seven oracles which begin the Book of Amos. But he exaggerates, and leaves us skeptical, when he maintains that the letters of the Apocalypse reflect the successive stages of the old covenant (paradise and fall, captivity in Egypt, Exodus, reigns of David and Solomon, etc.), while also forecasting, even if only in their broad lines, the seven ages of Church history.

157. In the Apocalypse the septenaries are subdivided into a three plus a four (the letters) or a four plus a three (the seals, the trumpets, the cups). Cf. Allo, op. cit., pp. xcii, 31, 44.

GENERAL CONCLUSION

1. Cf. E. Malatesta, "The Literary Structure of John XVII."

2. Lagrange, *Le quatrième évangile*, p. 448.

3. In the happy phrase of F. Prat, *Jesus Christ: His Life, His Teaching, and His Work*, p. 433.

4. *L'Apocalypse*, p. 55.

5. Two recent monographs will bring the reader up to date on the controversies: P. E. Dion, "Les chants du Serviteur de Yahvé et quelques passages apparentés d'Is XL–LV: Un essai sur leurs limites précises et sur leurs origines respectives," *B* 51 (1970), pp. 17–38; J. Coppens, "Le messianisme israélite: La relève prophétique," *ETL* 47 (1971), pp. 321–39; 48 (1972), pp. 5–36. Coppen's essay supplies an abundant bibliography. The following are some studies to which we are especially indebted. In German: H. Haag, "Ebed Yahve-Forschung, 1949–1958," *BZ* 3 (1959), pp. 174–204; J. Schildenberger, "Die Gottesknecht-Lieder des Isaiasbuches: Ein Höhepunkt messianischer Weissagung," *Erbe und Auftrag* 35 (1959), pp. 92–108. In English: C. R. North, *The Suffering Servant in Deutero-Isaiah: An Historical-Critical Study* (2nd ed.; London, 1956); H. Gross, "Zion's Redeemer," in *How Does the Christian Confront the Old Testament?*, eds., P. Benoit, R. E. Murphy, and B. van Iersel (Concilium 30; New York, 1967), pp. 87–98. In French: M.-J. Lagrange, *Le judaïsme*

avant Jésus-Christ (Paris, 1931), pp. 368–83; J. S. van der Ploeg, *Les Chants du Serviteur de Yahvé dans la seconde partie du Livre d'Isaïe Chapters XL–LV)* (Paris, 1936); A. Robert, "Médiation," *DBS* 5:1011–15; J. Coppens, "Les origines littéraires des poèmes du Serviteur de Yahvé," *B* 40 (1959), pp. 248–58; A. Gelin, "Messianisme," *DBS* 5:1192–95.

6. *Le judaïsme avant Jésus-Christ,* pp. 368–69.

7. Both writers are quoted by A. Condamin, *Le Livre d'Isaïe* (Paris, 1905), p. 544.

8. *Résurrection, Eucharistie, et génèse de l'homme* (Paris, 1972), p. 62.

9. *Theology of the Old Testament,* trans. by A. W. Heathcote and P. J. Allcock (New York, 1958), pp. 340–41, 340, 338.

10. Cf. P. Grelot, *Le ministère de la nouvelle alliance,* pp. 178–84.

11. Cf. *Sacerdoce et ministère* (Taizé, 1970).

12. Cf. A. Feuillet, "La personnalité de Jésus entrevue à partir de sa soumission au rite de repentance du précurseur," *RB* 77 (1970), pp. 30–49.

13. Cf. our articles: "La controverse sur le jeûne," *NRT* 90 (1968), pp. 113–36, 252–77; "Les trois prophéties de la Passion et de la Résurrection," *RT* 67 (1967), pp. 533–60; 68 (1968), pp. 41–74; "La coupe et le baptême de la Passion," *RB* 74 (1967), pp. 356–91; "Le logion sur la rançon," *RSPT* 51 (1967), pp. 365–402.

14. Cf. J. Colson, *Le sacerdoce du pauvre* (Paris, 1971).

15. Cf. M. Schmaus, "De oblatione Jesu in templo (Lc. II, 22–24)," *Acta Congressus Mariologici-Mariani in Republica Dominicana anno 1965 celebrati* (Rome, 1967), 4:287–95.

16. *The Gospel of the Infancy and Other Biblical Essays* (London, 1940), p. 45.

17. Cf. R. Laurentin, *Structure et théologie de Luc I–II* (Paris, 1957), pp. 114–16.

18. *The Passion and Resurrection of Jesus Christ,* p. 193.

19. Prouilhe, 1968.

20. Thus, there was plenty of material for P. Gutierrez' book, *La paternité spirituelle selon saint Paul* (Paris, 1968).

21. Cf. P. Grelot, op. cit., pp. 125–29.

22. C. Spicq has shown us this value in his magisterial commentary, *Les Epîtres Pastorales* (4th ed.; Paris, 1969).

23. As C. Spicq has abundantly shown in his *L'Epître aux Hébreux* 1: *Introduction* (Paris, 1952), pp. 109–38.

24. Cf. E. Schüssler-Fiorenza, *Priester für Gott: Studien zum Herr-schafts- und Priestermotiv in der Apokalypse* (Münster, 1972).
25. *Die Apokalypse* (Freiburg, 1953), pp. 81–84.
26. Cf. J. Dauvillier, *Les temps apostoliques* (*ler siècle*) (Paris, 1970).
27. The present study, which concentrates chiefly on one of the spiritual summits of the fourth gospel, the priestly prayer of Jesus, prolongs and completes our earlier book: *Le mystère de l'Amour Divin dans la théologie johannique* (Paris, 1972).

Bibliography

IN THIS HIGHLY SELECTIVE BIBLIOGRAPHY we list only some of the works referred to in the course of this study, but we add a number of others that will help those who want to go further on their own. Only strictly biblical studies have been included, and these in chronological order under two main headings; moreover, we list only monographs on specific subjects and omit commentaries on the various New Testament writings. The reader will note that among works on the priesthood of Christ those dealing with the Letter to the Hebrews bulk large, while few are devoted to the priestly prayer of Jesus in John. This fact is a further proof both of the novelty and the timeliness of the present book.

I. CHRIST SOLE PRIEST OF THE NEW COVENANT

Otto, W. *Der Apostel und Hohepriester unseres Bekenntnisses.* Leipzig, 1861.

Steuer, J. E. *Die Lehre des Hebräerbriefes vom Hohenpriestertum Christi.* Berlin, 1865.

Luginbuhl, E. *La personne du Christ dans l'Epître aux Hébreux.* Lausanne, 1873.

Maire, Ch. *La personne et l'oeuvre de Jésus-Christ d'après l'auteur de l'Epître aux Hébreux.* Geneva, 1873.

Messervy, T. G. *Essai sur la personne de Jésus-Christ d'après l'Epître aux Hébreux.* Montauban, 1873.

Kluge, O. *Die Idee des Priestertums in Israel-Juda und im Ur-Christentum.* Leipzig, 1906.

Vos, G. "The Priesthood of Christ in Hebrews," *Princeton Theological Review* 5 (1907), pp. 447, 579–604.

Derambure, J. "Melchisédech, type du Messie," *Revue augustinienne* 10 (1908), pp. 36–62.

Porcher du Bose, W. *High Priesthood and Sacrifice.* London, 1908.

van der Heeren, A. "De sacerdotio Christi secundum Epistolam ad Hebraeos," *Collationes Brugenses* 17 (1912), pp. 265–72.

Dimmler, E. *Melchisedek: Gedanken über das Hohepriestertum Christi nach dem Hebräerbrief.* Kempten, 1921.

Harris, R. "The Sinless High Priest," *Expository Times* 33 (1921–22), pp. 217–18.

Rosadini, S. "De Christi sacerdotio in epistola ad Hebraeos," *Gregorianum* 2 (1921), pp. 285–90.

Büchsel, Fr. *Die Christologie des Hebräerbriefes.* Gütersloh, 1922.

Paige Cox, W. L. *The Heavenly Priesthood of Our Lord.* Oxford, 1929.

Charue, A. "Le sacerdoce du Christ Roi dans le Psaume CX," *Collationes Namurcenses* 26 (1932), pp. 217–30.

Padolskis, V. *L'idée du sacrifice de la Croix dans l'Epître aux Hébreux.* Vilkaviskis, 1935.

Bonsirven, J. "Le sacerdoce et le sacrifice de Jésus-Christ d'aprés l'Epître aux Hébreux," *Nouvelle revue théologique* 66 (1939), pp. 641–60, 769–86.

Hydon, P. V. *The Priesthood of Jesus Christ as Presented by the Epistle to the Hebrews.* Boston, 1941.

Rabanos, R. *El sacerdocio de Cristo segun san Pablo.* Madrid, 1942.

Dibelius, M. "Der himmlische Kultus nach dem Hebräerbrief," *Theologische Blätter* 21 (1942), pp. 56–66.

Mackay, C. "The Order of Melchisedek, He V, 6," *Church Quarterly Review* 138 (1944), pp. 175–91.

Soubigou, S. "Le chapitre VII de l'Epître aux Hébreux," *Année théologique* 7 (1946), pp. 69–82.

van der Ploeg, J. "L'exégèse de l'Ancien Testament dans l'Epître aux Hébreux," *Revue biblique* 54 (1947), pp. 187–228.

Moe, O. "Das Priestertum Christi im Neuen Testament ausserhalb des Hebräerbriefes," *Theologische Literaturzeitung* 72 (1947), pp. 335–38.

——— "Der Gedanke des allgemeinen Priestertums im Hebräerbrief," *Theologische Literaturzeitung* 74 (1949), pp. 161–69.

Spicq, C. "L'origine johannique de la conception du Christ Prêtre dans l'Epître aux Hébreux," in *Aux sources de la tradition chrétienne (Mélanges M. Goguel).* Neuchâtel, 1950. Pp. 258–69.

Kennedy, C. K. *St. Paul's Conception of the Priesthood of Melchisedech.* Washington, D.C., 1951.

Descamps, A. "Le sacerdoce du Christ d'après l'Epître aux Hébreux," *Revue diocésaine de Tournai* 9 (1954), pp. 429–34, 529–34.

Bammel, E. "Archiereus prophēteiōn," *Theologische Literaturzeitung* 79 (1954), pp. 351–56.

Rushe, H. "Die Gestalt des Melchisedech," *Münsterische theologische Zeitschrift* 6 (1955), pp. 230–52.

Schille, G. "Erwägungen zur Hohenpriesterlehre des Hebräerbriefes," *Zeitschrift für die neutestamentliche Wissenschaft* 46 (1955), pp. 81–109.

Lécuyer, J. "Jésus, Fils de Josédec, et le sacerdoce du Christ," *Recherches de science religieuse* 43 (1955), pp. 82–103.

Friedrich, G. "Beobachtungen zur messianischen Hohepriestererwartung in den Synoptikern," *Zeitschrift für Theologie und Kirche* 53 (1956), pp. 265–311.

Gelin, A. "Le sacerdoce du Christ d'après l'Epître aux Hébreux," in *Etudes sur le sacrement de l'Ordre.* Lex orandi 22. Paris, 1957. Pp. 43–75. In English: "The Priesthood of Christ in the Epistle to the Hebrews," in *The Sacrament of Holy Orders.* Collegeville, 1962. Pp. 30–59.

Lécuyer, J. *Le sacerdoce dans le mystère du Christ.* Lex orandi 24. Paris, 1957.

Cullmann, O. *Die Christologie des Neuen Testaments.* Tübingen, 1957. In English: *The Christology of the New Testament,* trans. by S. C. Guthrie and C. A. M. Hall. Philadelphia, 1959.

Richardson, A. *An Introduction to the Theology of the New Testament.* New York, 1958. Pp. 200–3, 229–32.

Bourgin, C. "Le Christ Grand Prêtre et la purification des péchés," *Lumière et vie,* No. 36 (1958, No. 1), pp. 67–90.

Teodorico da Castel S. Pietro. "Il sacerdozio celeste di Cristo nella Lettera agli Ebrei," *Gregorianum* 39 (1958), pp. 319–34.

Vallejo, A. *"Melquisedek o el sacerdocio real.* Buenos Aires, 1959.

George, A. "Le sacerdoce de la nouvelle alliance dans la pensée de Jésus," in *La tradition sacerdotale.* Le Puy, 1959. Pp. 61–80.

Best, E. "Spiritual Sacrifice and General Priesthood in the New Testament," *Interpretation* 14 (1960), pp. 273–99.

Gnilka, J. "Die Erwartung des messianischen Hohenpriestertums in den Schriften von Qumran und im Neuen Testament," *Revue de Qumrân* 2 (1960), pp. 395–426.

Coppens, "Le messianisme sacerdotal dans les écrits du Nouveau Testament," in *La venue du Messie*. Recherches bibliques 6. Bruges, 1962. Pp. 101–12.

Bertetto, D. "La natura del sacerdozio secondo He V, i–4, e le sue realizzazioni nel Nuovo Testamento," *Salesianum* 26 (1964), pp. 395–440.

Gaide, G. "Jésus le Prêtre unique (He IV, 14—X, 25)," *Evangiles* 53 (1964), pp. 5–74.

Agourides, S. "The High Priestly Prayer of Jesus," *Studia evangelica* 4: 137–45.

Poelman, R. "The Sacerdotal Prayer: John XVII," *Lumen vitae* 20 (1965), pp. 43–66.

Zerafa, P. "Priestly Messianism in the Old Testament," *Angelicum* 42 (1965), pp. 318–41.

Romaniuk, C. C. *Il sacerdozio nel Nuovo Testamento*. Bologna, 1966.

Grelot, P. *Le ministère de la nouvelle alliance*. Paris, 1967. Pp. 21–59.

Higgins, A. J. B. "The Priestly Messiah," *New Testament Studies* 13 (1967), pp. 211–39.

Nomoto, S. "Herkunft und Struktur der Hohenpriestervorstellung im Hebräerbrief," *Novum Testamentum* 10 (1968), pp. 10–25.

Schaefer, J. R. "The Relationship between Priestly and Servant Messianism in the Epistle to the Hebrews," *Catholic Biblical Quarterly* 30 (1968), pp. 359–85.

Schreiben der deutschen Bischöfe über das priesterliche Amt. Issued by the Secretariat of the German Episcopal Conference. Trier, 1969. Detailed analysis by J. Coppens in his "Christian Priesthood: Its Origins and Development," in A.-M. Charue, et al., *Priesthood and Celibacy* (Milan, n.d.), pp. 67–142.

Vanhoye, A. "Le Christ grand prêtre selon He II, 17–18," *Nouvelle revue théologique* 91 (1969), pp. 449–74.

———— *Epistolae ad Hebraeos textus de sacerdotio Christi* (ad usum auditorum). Rome, 1969.

———— *Lectiones de sacerdotio in He VII* (ad usum auditorum). Rome, 1970.

Thüsing, W. *La prière sacerdotale de Jésus*, trans. by J. Burckel and F. Swessel. Paris, 1970.

Langevin, P. E. "Le sacerdoce du Christ dans le Nouveau Testament, surtout d'après l'Epître aux Hébreux," in *Le prêtre hier, aujourd'hui, demain.* Paris, 1970.

II. THE MINISTERS OF CHRIST

Batiffol, J. "L'Eglise naissante. 3: Les institutions hiérarchiques de l'Eglise," *Revue biblique* 4 (1895), pp. 473–500.

Baltus, R. "L'Eglise primitive et l'épiscopat," *Revue bénédictine* 18 (1901), pp. 26–43.

Batiffol, P. "La hiérarchie primitive," in his *Etudes d'histoire et de théologie positive.* Paris, 1902. Pp. 225–75.

von Dunin-Borkowski, S. "Die Interpretation der wichtigsten Stellen zur Verfassungsgeschichte der alten Kirche," *Zeitschrift für katholische Theologie* 28 (1904), pp. 217–49; 29 (1905), pp. 28–52.

Batiffol, P. "L'apostolat," *Revue biblique* 3 (1906), pp. 520–32.

von Harnack, A. *Entstehung und Entwicklung der Kirchenverfassung und des Kirchenrechts in den zwei ersten Jahrhunderten.* Leipzig, 1910. In English: *The Constitution and Law of the Church in the First Two Centuries,* trans. by F. L. Pogson. London, 1910.

Fabre, A. "L'ange et le chandelier de l'église d'Ephèse," *Revue biblique* 7 (1910), pp. 161–78, 344–67.

von Harnack, A. *Die Mission und Ausbreitung des Christentums in den ersten drei Jahrhunderten,* I. 4th ed. Leipzig, 1924. In English: *The Expansion of Christianity in the First Three Centuries,* trans. by James Moffatt. London, 1904.

Linton, O. *Das Problem der Urkirche in der neueren Forschung: Eine kritische Darstellung.* Uppsala, 1932.

Loisy, A. *La naissance du christianisme.* Paris, 1933.

Beyer, H. W., "Diakoneo, diakonia, diakonos," *Theologisches Wörterbuch zum Neuen Testament* 2 (1935), pp. 81–93. In English: *Theological Dictionary of the New Testament* 2:81–93.

——— "Episkeptomai, episkopeo, episkopē, episkopos, allotriepiskopos," *Theologisches Wörterbuch zum Neuen Testament* 2 (1935), pp. 595–619. In English: *Theological Dictionary of the New Testament* 2:599–622.

Braun, F.-M. *Aspects nouveaux du problème de l'Eglise.* Freiburg, 1942.

Käsemann, E. "Die Legitimität des Apostels," *Zeitschrift für die neutestamentliche Wissenschaft* 41 (1942), pp. 33–71.

Bardy, G. *La théologie de l'Eglise de saint Clément de Rome à saint Irénée.* Paris, 1945.

Muñoz Iglesias, S. "Los profetas del Nuevo Testamento comparados con los del Antiguo," *Estudios bíblicos* 6 (1947), pp. 307–37.

Goguel, M. *Jésus et les origines du christianisme; L'Eglise primitive.* Paris, 1947.

Spicq, C. *Spiritualité sacerdotale d'après saint Paul.* Paris, 1949. In English: *The Mystery of Godliness*, trans. by Jex Martin. Chicago, 1954.

Menoud, P. H. *L'Eglise et les ministères selon le Nouveau Testament.* Neuchâtel, 1949.

Leuba, J. L. *L'institution et l'évenément.* Neuchâtel, 1950.

Aubert, R. "L'institution et l'évenément: A propos de l'ouvrage de M. le Pasteur Leuba," *Ephemerides theologicae lovanienses* 28 (1952), pp. 683–93.

Greeven, H. "Propheten, Lehrer, Vorsteher bei Paulus," *Zeitschrift für die neutestamentliche Wissenschaft* 44 (1952–53), pp. 1–43.

Molland, E. "Le développement de l'idée de succession apoostolique," *Revue d'histoire et de philosophie religieuse* 34 (1954), pp. 1–20.

Daniélou, J. "La communauté de Qumrân et l'organisation de l'Eglise ancienne," *Revue d'Histoire et de Philosophie Religieuse* 35 (1955), pp. 104–15.

Colson, J. *Les fonctions ecclésiales aux deux premiers siècles.* Bruges, 1956.

Nauck, W. "Probleme des frühchristlichen Amtsverständnisses (I Ptr. 5:2f.)," *Zeitschrift für die neutestamentliche Wissenschaft* 48 (1957), pp. 200–20.

Feuillet, A. "Les vingt-quatre vieillards de l'Apocalypse," *Revue biblique* 65 (1958), pp. 1–32.

Futrell, J. C. "The Monarchical Episcopate," *Irish Theological Quarterly* 25 (1958), pp. 305–29.

Schweizer, E. *Gemeinde und Gemeindeordnung im Neuen Testament.* Zürich, 1959. In English: *Church Order in the New Testament*, trans. by F. Clark. Naperville, Ill., 1961.

Paquier, R. "L'épiscopat dans la structure institutionnelle de l'Eglise," *Verbum Caro* 13 (1959), pp. 29–62.

Schmitt, J. "L'organisation de l'Eglise primitive et Qumrân," in *La secte de Qumrân et les origines du christianisme.* Recherches bibliques 4. Bruges, 1959. Pp. 217–31.

Colson, J. *La fonction diaconale aux origines de l'Eglise.* Paris-Bruges, 1960.

Cerfaux, L. "Pour l'histoire du titre Apostolos dans le Nouveau Testament," *Recherches de science religieuse* 48 (1960), pp. 76–92.

Rask, A. "Le ministère néotestamentaire et l'exégèse suédoise," *Istina* 7 (1960), pp. 205–32.

Benoit, P. "L'ordination dans le judaïsme et dans le Nouveau Testament selon E. Lohse," in his *Exégèse et théologie* 2. Paris, 1961. Pp. 247–49.

Bonnard, P. "Le Nouveau Testament connaît-il la transmission d'une fonction apostolique?" *Verbum Caro* 15 (1961), pp. 132–37.

Klein, B. *Die zwölf Apostel: Ursprung und Gestalt einer Idee.* Göttingen, 1961.

Harlé, P. A. "Sacerdoce et ministère dans le Nouveau Testament," *Verbum Caro* 15 (1961), pp. 357–71.

Schmithals, W. *Das kirchliche Apostelamt: Eine historische Untersuchung.* Göttingen, 1961.

Congar, Y. M.-J. "La hiérarchie comme service selon le Nouveau Testament et les documents de la tradition," in *L'épiscopat et l'Eglise universelle,* ed. by Y. M.-J. Congar and B. D. Dupuy. Paris, 1962. Pp. 67–99.

Dupont, J. *Le discours de Milet, testament spirituel de saint Paul (Ac. XX, 18–36).* Paris, 1962.

Guerra y Gomez, M. *Episcopos y presbyteros.* Burgos, 1962.

Gerhardson, B. "Die Boten Gottes und die Apostel Christi," *Svensk Exegetisk Arsbok* 27 (1962), pp. 89–131.

Benoit, P. "Les origines apostoliques de l'épiscopat selon le Nouveau Testament," in *L'évêque dans l'Eglise du Christ: Travaux du Symposium de l'Arbresle (1960),* ed. by H. Bouëssé and A. Mandouze. Bruges, 1963. Pp. 13–57.

Campenhausen, H. F. *Kirchliches Amt und geistliche Vollmacht in den ersten Jahrhunderten.* 2nd ed. Tübingen, 1963. In English: *Ecclesiastical Office and Spiritual Power in the Church of the First Three Centuries,* trans. by J. A. Baker. Stanford, 1969.

Colson, J. *L'épiscopat catholique: Collégialité et primauté dans les trois premiers siècles de l'Eglise.* Paris, 1963.

Bonnard, P. "Ministères et laïcat chez saint Paul," *Verbum Caro* 18 (1964), pp. 56–66.

Konidaris, G. I. "De la prétendue divergence des formes dans le régime du christianisme primitif: Ministres et ministères du temps des apôtres à la mort de saint Polycarpe," *Istina* 11 (1964), pp. 59–92.

Radermakers, J. "Mission et apostolat dans l'évangile johannique," *Studia evangelica* 2:100–21.

Schnackenburg, R. *Die Kirche im Neuen Testament.* Freiburg, 1965. In English: *The Church in the New Testament,* trans. by W. J. O'Hara. New York, 1965.

Grelot, P. "La vocation ministérielle au service du peuple de Dieu," in *Aux origines de l'Eglise.* Recherches bibliques 8. Bruges, 1965. Pp. 159–73.

Chevallier, A. M. *Esprit de Dieu, paroles d'hommes: Le rôle de l'Esprit Saint dans les ministères de la parole selon l'apôtre Paul.* Neuchâtel-Paris, 1965.

Colson, J. *Ministre de Jésus-Christ ou le sacerdoce de l'Evangile.* Paris, 1966.

Buit, F. M. du. "Les fonctions ecclésiales dans l'Eglise primitive," *Evangiles* 64 (1966), pp. 5–73.

d'Ercole, G. "The Prebyteral Colleges in the Early Church," in *Historical Investigations,* ed. by R. Aubert. Concilium 17. New York, 1966. Pp. 20–33.

d'Espine, H. *Les Anciens, conducteurs de l'Eglise.* Neuchâtel, 1966.

Grelot, P. *Le ministère de la nouvelle alliance.* Paris, 1967. Pp. 69–140.

Leenhardt, F. J. "Les fonctions constitutives de l'Eglise et l'épiscopé selon le Nouveau Testament," *Revue d'Histoire et de Philosophie Religieuse* 47 (1967), pp. 111–49.

Bourke, M. M. "Reflections on Church Order in the New Testament," *Catholic Biblical Quarterly* 30 (1968), pp. 493–511.

Moingt, J. "Caractère et ministère sacerdotal," *Recherches de science religieuse* 56 (1968), pp. 569–89.

Ritter, A. M. "Amt und Gemeinde im Neuen Testament und in der Kirchengeschichte," in *Wer ist die Kirche?* Göttingen, 1968. Pp. 21–26.

Colson, J. *Prêtre et peuple sacerdotal.* Paris, 1969.

Spicq, C. "Episcope et episcopat d'après les Epîtres Pastorales," in his *Les Epîtres Pastorales.* 4th ed. Paris, 1969. Pp. 439–55.

Ganoczy, A. "Ministère, épiscopat et primauté," *Istina* 16 (1969), pp. 99–136.

Kasper, W. "A New Dogmatic Outlook on the Priestly Ministry," in *The Identity of the Priest,* ed. by K. Rahner. Concilium 43. New York, 1969. Pp. 20–33.

Dianich, S. "I ministeri della Chiesa nel Nuovo Testamento," *Rivista biblica* 18 (1970), pp. 131–51.

Leonardi, C. "Rapporti tra sacerdozio dei fideli e ministeri nel Nuovo Testamento," *Presbyteri,* Nos. 19–20 (1970), pp. 342–67.

Moingt, J. "Nature du sacerdoce ministériel," *Recherches de science religieuse* 58 (1970), pp. 237–72.

Schlier, H. "Grundelemente des priesterlichen Amtes im Neuen Testament," *Theologie und Philosophie* 45 (1970), pp. 161–80.

Testa, E. "Il clero pellegrino nella Chiesa primitiva," *Rivista biblica* 18 (1970), pp. 241–51.

Penna, A. "Reflessioni sul sacerdozio nel Antico Testamento," *Rivista biblica* 18 (1970), pp. 105–29.

Charue, A.-M, et al. *Priesthood and Celibacy.* Milan, n.d.

Lemaire, A. *Les ministères aux origines de l'Eglise.* Paris, 1971.

Colson, J. *Le sacerdoce du pauvre.* Paris, 1971.

Schüssler-Fiorenza, E. *Priester für Gott: Studien zum Herrschafts- und Priestermotiv in der Apokalypse.* Münster, 1972.

Index of Biblical References

Index of Subjects